Spanish Sociolinguistics in the 21st Century

Issues in Hispanic and Lusophone Linguistics (IHLL)
ISSN 2213-3887

IHLL aims to provide a single home for the highest quality monographs and edited volumes pertaining to Hispanic and Lusophone linguistics. In an effort to be as inclusive as possible, the series includes volumes that represent the many sub-fields and paradigms of linguistics that do high quality research targeting Iberian Romance languages. IHLL considers proposals that focus on formal syntax, semantics, morphology, phonetics/phonology, pragmatics from any established research paradigm, as well as psycholinguistics, language acquisition, historical linguistics, applied linguistics and sociolinguistics. The editorial board is comprised of experts in all of the aforementioned fields.

For an overview of all books published in this series, please see *benjamins.com/catalog/ihll*

Editors

Patrícia Amaral
Indiana University

Megan Solon
Indiana University

Editorial Board

Jennifer Cabrelli
University of Illinois at Chicago

Sonia Colina
University of Arizona

João Costa
Universidade Nova de Lisboa

Inês Duarte
Universidade de Lisboa

Daniel Erker
Boston University

Timothy L. Face
University of Minnesota

Sónia Frota
Universidade de Lisboa

Ángel J. Gallego
Universitat Autònoma de Barcelona

María del Pilar García Mayo
Universidad del País Vasco

Anna Gavarró
Universitat Autònoma de Barcelona

Michael Iverson
Indiana University

Matthew Kanwit
University of Pittsburgh

Juana M. Liceras
University of Ottawa

John M. Lipski
Pennsylvania State University

Gillian Lord
University of Florida

Jairo Nunes
Universidade de São Paulo

Acrisio Pires
University of Michigan, Ann Arbor

Pilar Prieto
Universitat Pompeu Fabra

Jason Rothman
UiT The Arctic University and Universidad Nebrija

Liliana Sánchez
Rutgers University

Ana Lúcia Santos
Universidade de Lisboa

Scott A. Schwenter
Ohio State University

Naomi Lapidus Shin
University of New Mexico

Carmen Silva-Corvalán
University of Southern California

Miquel Simonet
University of Arizona

Juan Uriagereka
University of Maryland

Elena Valenzuela
University of Ottawa

Bill VanPatten
Michigan State University

Volume 42

Spanish Sociolinguistics in the 21st Century. Current trends and methodologies
Edited by Cecilia Montes-Alcalá and Miguel García

Spanish Sociolinguistics in the 21st Century

Current trends and methodologies

Edited by

Cecilia Montes-Alcalá
Georgia Institute of Technology

Miguel García
Georgia Southern University (Statesboro)

John Benjamins Publishing Company
Amsterdam / Philadelphia

The paper used in this publication meets the minimum requirements of the American National Standard for Information Sciences – Permanence of Paper for Printed Library Materials, ANSI z39.48-1984.

DOI 10.1075/ihll.42

Cataloging-in-Publication Data available from Library of Congress:
LCCN 2025005849 (PRINT) / 2025005850 (E-BOOK)

ISBN 978 90 272 2195 7 (HB)
ISBN 978 90 272 4482 6 (E-BOOK)

© 2025 – John Benjamins B.V.
No part of this book may be reproduced in any form, by print, photoprint, microfilm, or any other means, without written permission from the publisher.

John Benjamins Publishing Company · https://benjamins.com

Table of contents

Acknowledgements — VII

Preface — IX
    Lotfi Sayahi

Introduction — 1
    Cecilia Montes-Alcalá & Miguel García

PART I. Spanish in contact and bilingualism in the U.S.

CHAPTER 1. Lexical routinization and productivity of subjunctive use in Spanish — 8
    Isabella Calafate

CHAPTER 2. Sociolinguistic dimensions of flagging behavior: The case of Spanish-English bilinguals in New York City — 33
    Rachel Varra

CHAPTER 3. El code-switching is hitting la aldea: Evidence from Loíza, Puerto Rico — 68
    Piero Visconte

PART II. Sociolinguistic variation in the Spanish-speaking world

CHAPTER 4. Clitic placement in New York City Spanish — 92
    Kevin Martillo Viner

CHAPTER 5. Variation in the use of the interdental fricative in Melilla — 111
    Lotfi Sayahi & Marina Bonilla-Conejo

CHAPTER 6. Does increased grammaticalization yield decreased duration? Testing *vamos a* variants in Spanish — 131
    Javier Rivas & Esther L. Brown

PART III. New approaches to sociolinguistic studies

CHAPTER 7. Subject pronoun expression in Colombian Spanish in Philadelphia: An interdisciplinary analysis of SPE variation and cognitive adaptation — 150
    Camila Franco

CHAPTER 8. Ideologies of linguistic authority and the role
of language choice in *El procés* trial 166
 Marina Cárcamo

CHAPTER 9. A sociolinguistic analysis of a deep learning based
classification model of South American Voseo in X posts 203
 Falcon Restrepo-Ramos

Postface 230
 Chad Howe

Index 235

Acknowledgements

We are deeply grateful to our colleague, Chad Howe, for his invaluable contributions during the early stages of this project. This volume could not have materialized without the critical assistance of the reviewers, whose generous dedication of time, sharp attention to detail, and insightful feedback were essential in ensuring the quality of each chapter. Our sincere thanks go to Jessi E. Aaron, Angélica Amezcua, Bethany Bateman McDonald, Kate Bove, Esther L. Brown, Álvaro Cerrón-Palomino, Ana María Cestero Mancera, Juan Manuel Escalona Torres, Martha Fairclough, Víctor Fernández-Mallat, Nydia Flores-Ferrán, Ager Gondra, Timothy M. Gupton, Joseph Kern, Bryan Kirschen, Dora LaCasse, Scott G. Lamanna, Philip Limerick, Jim Michnowicz, María Irene Moyna, Rafael Orozco, Justin Pinta, Brendan Regan, Pablo Requena, Marta Samper Hernández, Naomi Shin, Robyn Wright, Kathryn A. Woolard, and Eve Zyzik.

We are equally thankful to the authors for their kind patience and active collaboration throughout the process. Our gratitude extends to Patrícia Amaral and Megan Solon, editors of John Benjamins' series *Issues in Hispanic and Lusophone Linguistics,* whose expertise and guidance were vital to bringing this project to fruition, as well as to Ymke Verploegen, part of the John Benjamins team, for her kind support.

Finally, we wish to pay tribute to the late Kimberly Geeslin, whose support and advice were crucial in the initial phases of our book proposal. Her untimely passing in 2023 was a tremendous loss to the Hispanic and Lusophone linguistics community, and we hope this volume honors her memory and legacy.

Preface

Lotfi Sayahi
University at Albany

By the turn of the twenty-first century, motivated among other things by the ease in the use of digital communication to advertise calls for papers and manage abstract submissions, many language and linguistics conferences had grown very large, with, at times, hundreds of participants in attendance. Some conferences extended over several days and holding multiple parallel sessions became the norm. In some cases, it became a challenge for scholars to have meaningful academic interactions and establish connections with others in their same area of focus. In addition to managing the logistics of attending and presenting in such large events, talks were sometimes scheduled by language regardless of field of specialization or by field of specialization without considering the language of interest. There was a need for a leaner and more focused event that would bring together scholars working within a similar framework and focusing on the same language for a different type of academic interaction. At the same time, Spanish, as a world language, was opening a multitude of opportunities for research employing a sociolinguistic methodology and there was a need for participants to be at liberty to present in either English or Spanish knowing that their audience would understand them regardless of their choice. This was the time and the rationale for the organization of the First International Workshop on Spanish Sociolinguistics (WSS1) at the University at Albany, State University of New York. The idea was to have a smaller event where every talk is potentially highly interesting to all attendees and to help promote research on the different varieties of Spanish and their contact with other languages.

    A call for papers requesting presentations that focused on regional and social variation in Spanish and data from contact situations of Spanish with other languages was issued in 2001 and the first workshop was held on March 14th and 15th, 2002. The format was one of a small event with no parallel sessions. Presentations were organized by region with invited session chairs offering brief remarks to introduce the presenters and contextualize the talks. The format allowed participants to interact closely with each other and establish long-lasting relations many of which still endure today. The conference also created a strong esprit de corps among the participants regardless of the point at which they were in their careers and generated enthusiasm for new collaborations. J. Clancy Clements from Indiana University was the keynote speaker. He attended every talk and provided generous feedback throughout the event to the presenters. Other senior faculty who attended that first conference, including Jonathan Carl Holmquist and Gerardo Augusto Lorenzino from Temple University who would later organize the first WSS away from Albany, were equally supportive of the event and of younger colleagues.

The conference (WSS1) proved such a fruitful meeting that we decided to organize a second workshop at the University at Albany. My late colleague, Maurice J. Westmoreland, provided unwavering support from the beginning leading to a very successful event in 2004 (WSS2). A third workshop was organized at Temple University in 2006 (WSS3), before the fourth edition was organized again at UAlbany in 2008 (WSS4). After that, all the editions took place at other campuses where engaged Spanish sociolinguistics colleagues stepped up to the plate: WSS5 (North Carolina State University), WSS6 (University of Arizona), WSS7 (University of Wisconsin-Madison), WSS8 (University of Puerto Rico), WSS9 (Queens College, CUNY), WSS10 (Georgia Tech), and WSS 11 (University at Buffalo).[1]

In each of these conferences a superb selection of papers was presented, together with keynote presentations by some of the most notable scholars in the field of Spanish linguistics and sociolinguistics in general. William Labov was a guest speaker at WSS3 and highlighted how the field of Spanish sociolinguistics "has produced a body of work that contributes directly to the discussion of theoretical issues in both Sociolinguistics and Linguistics in general" (Holmquist et al., 2007). Other keynote speakers over the years included Jorge Guitart, Gregory Guy, Carol Klee, John Lipski, Ricardo Otheguy, Shana Poplack, Carmen Silva-Corvalán, Sali Tagliamonte, Almeida Jacqueline Toribio, Donald Winford, Walt Wolfram, and Ana Celia Zentella, among others.

The 10th edition of the conference was planned for April 2020 at Georgia Tech with Cecilia Montes-Alcalá chairing the organizing committee for what was meant to be a celebration of the first 20 years of WSS. But, just a few weeks away from the start of the conference, the COVID-19 pandemic put a halt to everything. The organizing committee of WSS10 had many difficult decisions to make. At the end, their dedication and admirable hard work resulted in the conference being held virtually on April 7–9, 2022. Despite the many challenges that the COVID-19 pandemic brought upon everyone and the fact that the committee had to organize the conference twice, WSS10 was an outstanding event. It included workshops, keynote addresses, oral presentations, and a poster session all managed through

---

1. An archive with additional information on previous WSS editions is available at: https://www.albany.edu/llc/international-workshop-spanish-sociolinguistics

an online platform that made it possible to have the same high quality WSS experience. I believe no other organizing committee faced as many challenges as the one that organized WSS10, yet they managed to produce an excellent academic event that was very much needed in the middle of a global pandemic.

The proceedings of the First Workshop on Spanish Sociolinguistics were the first volume published in open access by Cascadilla Proceedings Project, long before open access publishing became as common as it is today. The increasing quality of the contributions along the years led to the publication of several volumes of very high quality as is attested in the current volume, *Spanish Sociolinguistics in the 21st Century: Current trends and methodologies*. The variety of studies included in the current selection showcases very well the breadth and depth of sociolinguistic studies that focus on Spanish from a wide range of quantitative and qualitative approaches and covering different aspects of the language in its social context. The editors did as much of a superb job editing the book as they did organizing the conference and for that they deserve to be commended for their rigor and, above all, their tenacity and dedication to the field of Spanish sociolinguistics. It is the hope that the current volume encourages additional studies and continues to solidify the position of the Workshop on Spanish Sociolinguistics as a premier event of encounter for researchers dedicated to the field.

Reference

Holmquist, J., Lorenzino, A., & Sayahi, L. (2007). Introduction. In J. Holmquist, A. Lorenzino, & L. Sayahi (Eds), *Selected Proceedings of the Third Workshop on Spanish Sociolinguistics* (pp. v–viii). Cascadilla Proceedings Project.

Introduction

Cecilia Montes-Alcalá & Miguel García
Georgia Institute of Technology | Georgia Southern University (Statesboro)

In April 2018, at the closing business meeting of the Ninth International Workshop on Spanish Sociolinguistics (WSS9) at Queens College, CUNY, it was decided that the 10th iteration of the conference would take place at Georgia Tech in April 2020. The uninterrupted occurrence of nine Workshops since 2002 stood as a testament to the vitality of this research area in Hispanic Linguistics and a feat worth celebrating. Thus, the 2020 conference was conceived as a special edition to commemorate the remarkable achievements made in the field of Spanish sociolinguistics over the previous two decades in honor of the Workshop's 10th anniversary.

Little did we know at that time how "special" WSS10 would turn out to be. The organizing committee spent the following two years coordinating and preparing for the event with great enthusiasm and built-up momentum. Then, as we all know, COVID-19 happened. In March 2020, just weeks before the conference was set to begin, the entire planet was abruptly brought to a halt. We remained optimistic until the very last moment, when cancelling the event became inevitable, and kept a positive outlook afterwards wishfully thinking we could simply wait until the fall, or perhaps the following spring.

After many months of painstaking considerations and multiple logistical challenges, we decided to hold WSS10 virtually in April 2022, exactly twenty years (and one month) after the inaugural Workshop that took place at the University at Albany, State University of New York, in March 2002 (WSS1). Despite its technological trials and tribulations, WSS10 ultimately resulted in a highly successful event with over 200 registered participants from all over the world, first-class presentations, and topnotch plenary speakers. While it could not be the celebration we had expected, it still symbolized a belated birthday commemoration for the Workshop. In that same spirit, we now present this volume showcasing carefully selected contributors from WSS10. We aim both to further recognize the significant advancements made in the field over the past two decades and to spotlight its most current trends.

Spanish Sociolinguistics has proven to be a vibrant and innovative research area within the field of Hispanic Linguistics. Its scope generally extends beyond

https://doi.org/10.1075/ihll.42.int
© 2025 John Benjamins Publishing Company

the linguistic space. Examining and understanding how Spanish interacts with society, for example, is pivotal when advocating for changes in education, health, and policymaking, to name a few. Although significant progress has been made in the last few years, three areas still require additional attention: a sociolinguistic exploration of under researched Spanish-speaking regions, such as Africa; an in-depth examination of immigrant communities, both in the US and overseas; and the development of an "interdisciplinary mind-set" when analyzing social variation in Spanish (Díaz-Campos, Escalona Torres & Filimonova, 2020, p. 382).

Our main goal in preparing this volume is to highlight recent and exciting studies on sociolinguistic variation in several regions of the Spanish-speaking world (the Americas, Europe, and Africa), in addition to those areas where bilingualism/multilingualism and immigration intertwine. Every scholar included in this volume has garnered that "interdisciplinary mind-set" in their investigations, and at least three of them have directly connected their work to cognitivism, language ideologies, and/or natural language processing methods.

Introducing multidisciplinary approaches and innovative methodologies, the present volume features the most up to date developments in Spanish Sociolinguistics. This collection encompasses studies carried out by seasoned scholars and emerging researchers alike in diverse geographical areas where Spanish is spoken such as Arizona, New York City, Puerto Rico, Galicia, Melilla, Catalonia, Philadelphia, Colombia, and Argentina. Ranging from conventional methodologies like traditional sociolinguistic interviews to cutting-edge computational and natural language processing models, from the use of oral corpora to social media platforms, and from discourse analysis to mix-methods approaches, the volume aptly reflects the evolving landscape of sociolinguistic research and methodologies in the 21st century.

Divided into three main sections, its nine chapters address crucial issues within the Spanish-speaking world and represent current research trends in Spanish Sociolinguistics — Spanish in Contact and Bilingualism in the U.S. (Part I), Sociolinguistic Variation in the Spanish-Speaking World (Part II), and New Approaches to Sociolinguistic Studies (Part III). Part I explores sociolinguistic variation in bilingual communities, specifically in regions where Spanish is in contact with English such as Southern Arizona, New York City, and Loíza, Puerto Rico. In Part II, sociolinguistic variation is examined through morphosyntactic, phonetic, and phonological lenses providing a fresh look on how sociolinguistic methodologies can be used to analyze clitic placement, the interdental fricative, and the structure *vamos a* in Spanish. Finally, Part III presents some of the latest trends in sociolinguistic research, featuring works that employ interdisciplinary methods to study linguistic variation, including computational sociolinguistics.

As described, Part I includes three studies that examine sociolinguistic variation in diverse regions where Spanish is in contact with English and other languages. In Chapter 1, Isabella Calafate delves into subjunctive usage among Spanish-English bilinguals in Southern Arizona marking the first study on the role of lexical identity of the governor (i.e., the main verb) on subordinate complement clauses in the Spanish of these bilingual speakers. Calafate finds that the subjunctive use among bilinguals in Southern Arizona is conditioned by the lexical identity of the governor. Non-frequent governors, for instance, trigger more subjunctive use. Additionally, Calafate finds that governors occurring only once in the data (hapax legomena) account for a large amount of subjunctive use as well. One of the main questions regarding subjunctive use among bilinguals in the literature is whether it is related to contact with English or not. In her study, Calafate finds no evidence to support contact-induced mood selection in the bilingual Spanish of Southern Arizona.

Flagging behavior is typically associated with (un)grammaticality in both monolingual and bilingual speech. Among bilinguals, specifically, flagging behavior often receives negative connotations. The research on flagging behavior among bilinguals from a sociolinguistic perspective, however, remains a relatively uncharted area. In Chapter 2, Rachel Varra aims to fill this gap by exploring flagging behavior among bilinguals and examining how flagging elements might be conditioned by sociolinguistic factors. Varra centers her investigation on the Spanish monolingual speech of bilinguals in New York City, while focusing on the three elements of flagging behavior: extended silent pauses, non-lexical fillers, and lexical false starts. Varra not only finds that these elements do appear in the Spanish of these bilingual speakers, but that ethnonational affiliations may come into play as well. That is, Mexicans appear to flag the most while Ecuadorians appear to flag the least. The amount of Spanish in their daily lives, although marginally significant, is also a factor; the more Spanish a speaker uses daily, the higher rate of flagging behavior a speaker exhibits. These findings are important because, as Varra concludes, flag elements such as the ones analyzed in her study may index ethnolinguistic identity among speakers in a bilingual community.

In Chapter 3, grounding his investigation on Schneider and Barron's (2008) model of Variational Pragmatics, Piero Visconte explores code-switching (CS) in Loíza, an Afro-Hispanic community in Puerto Rico, through sociolinguistic interviews conducted in Spanish. In his analysis, Visconte focuses on bilingual discourse markers (DMs), and reports that *like, so, como que, tú sabes*, and *pues* are the most common DMs used by all informants. Interestingly, only the first four trigger some type of CS. With regards to sociolinguistic variables, Visconte finds that older informants irrespective of gender or education level remain in Spanish, producing less DMs. Conversely, CS is more common among younger speakers.

Visconte's study is important for at least two reasons: it focuses on an understudied bilingual (Spanish-English) region; and second, it sheds light on the rather recent trajectory of English in a bilingual community and its impact in the lives of younger speakers.

Part II of the volume focuses on different types of sociolinguistic variation (morphosyntactic, phonetic, and phonological) across the Spanish-speaking world featuring studies conducted on both sides of the Atlantic. Kevin Martillo Viner in Chapter 4 takes us to New York City while he investigates clitic placement, complementing his extensive work on NYC Spanish. Previous studies on the topic have shown that proclitic position (clitic before the verb), rather than enclitic position (clitic attached to the verb), is the most frequent pattern among monolinguals and bilinguals. It is not yet clear, or sufficiently studied, what social and linguistic factors influence Spanish clitic placement. Regarding social factors, Viner finds that socioeconomic status (SES) is the only significant predictor of clitic placement — those with reportedly lower SES levels exhibit more proclitic placement. In terms of linguistic factors, four variables are strong predictors of clitic placement, and they follow this particular order: pronominality > person > clitic type > clause type. As Viner states, one striking finding in this investigation resides in the fact that generational differences (first- and second- generation Spanish speakers) do not represent a significant factor in clitic placement in NYC Spanish. This finding is interestingly surprising because generational differences have been found in previous investigations with the same group of informants.

In Chapter 5, Lotfi Sayahi and Marina Bonilla-Conejo explore the sociolinguistic landscape of the interdental fricative, [θ], in the autonomous city of Melilla (Northern Africa). The case of Melilla is attractive to investigate because, although Spanish is the official language, the population of Melilla is linguistically diverse, with two main groups: Spanish speakers of Peninsular origin (monolingual in Spanish) and Spanish speakers of Amazigh origin (bilingual in Spanish and Tamazigh). Similar to Viner's approach in the previous chapter, Sayahi and Bonilla-Conejo investigate the role of social and linguistic factors in the presence of the interdental fricative in Melilla. Sayahi and Bonilla-Conejo find that the interdental fricative is the most common sound preferred in Melilla (compared to [s]), but its use is highly variable. Regarding social factors, ethnicity and gender constitute the main predictors of the fricative interdental. Specifically, men of Amazigh origin exhibit the lowest rate of interdental fricative instances, while women of Amazigh origin exhibit the highest rate. Linguistics factors, on the other hand, do not appear as significant predictors of [θ] or [s], although the priming of the interdental fricative triggers additional use of this sound.

Do grammaticalized structures such as [*ir a* + infinitive] undergo phonological reduction in Spanish? If they do, what are some of the linguistic factors that lead to this phonological reduction? These are the research questions Javier Rivas and Esther L. Brown address in Chapter 6. Using corpus data (ESLORA) from Galician Spanish, Rivas and Brown extracted instances of *vamos a* from the corpus to acoustically measure durational differences among four of its meanings: future, hortative, habitual, and movement. The linguistic factors considered were pause adjacency, speaking rate, and word predictability. Rivas and Brown reported that overall phonological reduction of [*vamos a*] is conditioned by three linguistic factors: meaning, predictability, and speaking rate. When [*vamos a*] is used as an auxiliary, its duration is shorter than when it is used as a lexical verb (conveying movement). Second, they found that a faster speaking rate of the context after [*vamos a*] triggers shorter duration of [vamos a]. Lastly, when the word following the [*vamos a*] is highly predictable, [*vamos a*] duration is also shorter. As Rivas and Brown suggest, this phonological reduction may ultimately be due to an auxiliarization process of [*vamos a*] already occurring in Spanish.

The third part of the volume showcases current trends and methodologies in the field, featuring studies that combine cognitive testing and sociolinguistics, explore the relationship between language ideologies and language choice, and employ natural language processing methods to conduct computational sociolinguistics research. In Chapter 7, Camila Franco investigates subject pronoun expression (SPE) variation within the Colombian community in Philadelphia using a mixed-methods approach. Her results unveil an intricate interplay of social, linguistic, and cognitive variables. She concludes that grammatical person, number, and tense-mood-aspect (but not age) are significant predictors of null SPE usage. Her study found that participants who had resided in the US for 5–10 years had the lowest proportion of null SPE usage, while those who had resided for 1–4 years and 10+ years showed higher levels of null SPE usage. However, English contact did not appear to be conclusive for SPE variation. Her findings support previous research on dialectal leveling and shed light on bilingual communities in the US.

In Chapter 8, Marina Cárcamo analyzes the language choices and ideologies behind the *procés* trial in Catalonia, highlighting the political and legal ramifications of bilingualism in Spain's multilingual landscape in general, and within this community in particular. She provides a qualitative thematic analysis of the testimonies and closing arguments of the 12 defendants in the *procés* trial employing a discourse analysis methodology to uncover the implicit ideologies that underlie the themes discussed in connection with the sociopolitical context. One of her main findings is that the defendants chose to speak in Spanish in the trial primarily for communication purposes while Catalan was regarded as the mother tongue and language of expression for them. She concludes that language plays a crucial role in this setting, which partially mirrors the political dynamics between Catalonia and Spain.

More recently, there has been a growing interest in analyzing the social dimensions of language with new computational methods, an emerging field known as computational sociolinguistics. How accurate can a machine learning (ML) model be to classify *voseo* on X posts? What sociolinguistic features are relevant (or not) for the ML model that help in the classification of Colombian and Argentinian *voseo*? These are the research questions posed by Falcon Restrepo-Ramos in the last chapter (9) of the volume. He examines a dataset of 8,334 Tweets from Argentina and 10,217 from Colombia using a transformer-based machine learning classifier. His results suggest the production of a highly accurate, domain-specific dialectal classification model. Additionally, his sociolinguistic analysis of both datasets offers further insights on the accuracy of the classifier, the status of *voseo*, and its discourse function vis a vis other second-person singular forms of address.

Overall, this volume broadens our knowledge of Spanish sociolinguistic research, allows us to further understand sociolinguistic variation in the Spanish-speaking world, and — perhaps more importantly — provides the reader with ideas for research projects as well as opportunities for potential collaborations in the near future. Intended for graduate students, linguists, social scientists, and any other scholars interested in Spanish sociolinguistics, the primary goal of the book is to provide wider accessibility to the field's most recent findings, approaches and methodologies, and to contribute to the intellectual enrichment of a diverse audience.

As editors, we believe that the insightful studies presented here have the potential to shed light not only on linguistic nuances but also on broader social, cultural, and even political issues within the ever-growing Spanish-speaking world. In sum, we hope to make a substantive contribution to the ongoing conversations in the field and foster a deeper understanding of the current dynamics shaping Spanish sociolinguistics.

References

Díaz-Campos, M., Escalona Torres, J. M., & Filimonova, V. (2020). Sociolinguistics of the Spanish-Speaking World. *Annual Review of Linguistics*, 6(1), 363–388.

Schneider, K. P., & Barron, A. (2008). Where Pragmatics and Dialectology Meet: Introducing Variational Pragmatics. In K. P. Schneider & A. Barron (Eds.), *Variational Pragmatics: A focus on regional varieties in pluricentric languages* (pp. 1–32). John Benjamins.

PART I

Spanish in contact and bilingualism in the U.S.

CHAPTER 1

Lexical routinization and productivity of subjunctive use in Spanish

Isabella Calafate
Baylor University

This study explores the role of the lexical identity of the governor in mood variation among Spanish-English bilinguals in Southern Arizona. Based on an analysis of sociolinguistic interviews from the *Corpus del Español en el Sur de Arizona* (Carvalho, 2012-), productivity measures indicate that subjunctive use is lexically routinized to some degree as it is affected by individual governing verbs. The analysis also reveals certain level of subjunctive productivity due to its dispersion across different contexts, evidenced by the high incidence of cases of hapax legomena. Comparisons with previous research (LaCasse, 2018; Poplack et al., 2018; Torres Cacoullos et al., 2017) uncover similar patterns across Southern Arizona and other regions, pointing to clear continuities across monolingual and bilingual Spanish.

Keywords: subjunctive use, lexical routinization, productivity measures, bilingual Spanish

1. Introduction

Mood selection has been traditionally approached from a prescriptive standpoint and a normative effort has been made for dictating when subjunctive should and should not be used. Based on obligatory and variable contexts of subjunctive, several studies claim that US Spanish speakers overextend the use of indicative in contexts where subjunctive is expected. These studies (e.g., Lynch, 1999; Montrul, 2007, 2009; Silva-Corvalán, 1994) often conclude that the overextension of indicative is due to contact with English, claiming that US Spanish speakers' use of subjunctive is the result of simplification or even incomplete acquisition.

Nevertheless, mood selection in Spanish is more variable than is often claimed. Examples in (1) were collected from the *Corpus del Español en el Sur de Arizona* (CESA) (Carvalho, 2012-), and illustrate both variants: indicative (1a) and subjunctive (1b).

(1) a. No tanto como tienes que entrar a detalle, es más como para asegurarte que lo **entiendes**[IND]. (CESA060)
 'Not so much that you have to go into detail, it's more like to make sure that you understand it.'
 b. Estoy haciendo un plan ahora porque yo también quiero que él **agarre**[SBJV] un estudio, un bíblico /ah/ y despacito poco a poquito. (CESA012)
 'I am making a plan now because I also want him to pick up a study, a Bible study, and slowly little by little.'

More recent variationist studies have shown that mood selection in Spanish is inherently variable in both monolingual and bilingual dialects, even in contexts traditionally considered of categorical use of subjunctive (e.g., LaCasse, 2018; Poplack et al., 2018; Schwenter & Hoff, 2020; Torres Cacoullos et al., 2017). Importantly, these studies find that subjunctive is lexically routinized, that is, that what mainly predicts mood variation patterns in Spanish is the lexical identity of the governor, not necessarily the traditional semantic classes to which governors are grouped in grammars, manuals, and theoretical pieces on mood selection. Building on work in monolingual Spanish, LaCasse (2018) finds that bilingual Spanish from New Mexico shares similar patterns of lexical routinization of subjunctive with monolingual Spanish, countering the hypothesis that contact with English leads to accelerated change.

The main purpose of this study is to explore the linguistic conditioning of mood variation among Spanish-English bilinguals in Southern Arizona, more specifically the role of the lexical identity of the governor. To do so, this study presents an analysis based on productivity measures and discusses to what extent subjunctive is lexically routinized in Spanish spoken in Southern Arizona in comparison to other Spanish (monolingual and bilingual) dialects. In addition, the analysis of data from Southern Arizona and its comparison to other Spanish dialects allows us (1) to explore any indications of evidence of contact-induced change (by comparing bilingual Spanish from Southern Arizona to monolingual Spanish, in this case, from Mexico City); and also (2) to investigate potential continuities of US Spanish across the Southwest US (by comparing Spanish spoken in Southern Arizona to New Mexico Spanish).

2. Mood selection in the traditional perspective

As mood selection has been widely approached from a traditional perspective, grammars, manuals, and theoretical pieces on Spanish syntax have focused on listing contexts where one specific mood is categorically used and contexts where there is alternation between indicative and subjunctive.[1] In Spanish, both indicative and subjunctive can occur in matrix and subordinate clauses. While matrix clauses lack a trigger, subordinate clauses feature a different grammatical category as trigger depending on the clause type (i.e., adjective, adverbial, complement clauses). In adjective clauses, mood selection is claimed to depend on the referent of the clause; in adverbial clauses, on the adverb; and in complement clauses, on the semantic meaning of the predicate (Ridruejo, 1999).

This study focuses on subordinate complement clauses. In subordinate complement clauses, the semantic meaning of the predicate, which would be the trigger, has been commonly presented as large semantic classes to which governors belong. According to Bosque (2012), for instance, indicative is used when the complement clause is triggered by governors gathered in semantic classes such as:

(2) a. event (*suceder, ocurrir, acontecer* 'happen')
 b. language, communication (*decir* 'say', *advertir* 'warn', *anunciar* 'announce', *prometer* 'promise')
 c. perception, judgment (*ver* 'see', *creer* 'think, believe', *notar* 'note', *recordar* 'remember', *descubrir* 'discover.')
 d. acquisition, possession or loss of information (*saber* 'know', *enterarse* 'find out', *leer* 'read', *olvidar* 'forget', *indicio* 'sign.')
 e. certainty, objectivity (*probar* 'prove', *demostrar* 'show', *seguro* 'sure', *claro* 'clear') (Bosque, 2012, p.379)

On the other hand, subjunctive is triggered by governors that belong to semantic classes such as:

(3) a. will, intention (*querer* 'want', *aspirar (a)* 'aspire', *decidirse (a)* 'make up one's mind', *esforzarse (por)* 'strive', *luchar (por)* 'fight', *pretender* 'try', *procurar* 'endeavour')
 b. causation, influence (*hacer* 'do', *causar* 'cause', *pedir* 'ask', *recomendar* 'recommend', *favorecer* 'favor')
 c. affection, emotion (*molestar* 'annoy', *alegrarse (de)* 'be glad', *lamentar* 'regret')

---

1. Among the grammars, manuals, and theoretical pieces on Spanish syntax are, for instance, Bosque (1990), Bosque (2012), Bosque and Demonte (1999), Bosque and Gutiérrez-Rexach (2009), Gili Gaya (1964), Real Academia Española (2009), Uriagereka (2015).

d. assessment, evaluation (*convenir* 'suit, be convenient', *bueno* 'good', *desafortunado* 'unfortunate')
e. possibility, necessity, eventuality (*hacer falta* 'to be necessary', *necesitar* 'need', *dar igual* 'be irrelevant', *posible* 'possible')
f. opposition, rejection (*desmentir* 'deny', *negarse (a)* 'refuse', *contrario (a)* 'contrary', *renuente (a)* 'reluctant') (Bosque, 2012, pp. 379–380)

There are also semantic contexts prescribed as cases of mood alternation, which involve meaning differences, such as in the examples in (4). (4a), for instance, illustrates that while there is an interpretation of communication when *insistir* 'insist' triggers indicative (*comportan* 'behave'), there is a sense of influence when the same verb triggers subjunctive (*comporten* 'must behave').

(4) a. communication/influence:
Insisto en que se {comportan/comporten} correctamente.
'I insist that they {behave/must behave} properly.'
b. communication/assessment:
Me reprocha que no le {hago/haga} caso.
'They reproach me for {not paying attention/to not pay attention} to him/her.'
c. thought or belief/intention or will:
He pensado que {es/sea} usted el nuevo embajador.
'I've been thinking that you {are/could be} the new ambassador.'
d. perception / assessment:
Entiendo que lo {has/hayas} perdonado.
'I understand {that you have forgiven him/you forgiving him}.'
e. perception/intention:
Siempre veía que cada cosa {estaba/estuviera} en su sitio.
'I always {used to notice that everything was/saw to it that everything was} in its place.' (Bosque, 2012, pp. 380–381)

Even though these meaning differences occasioned by mood alternation clearly depend on specific governors, there has been an attempt to make generalizations that gather them into broader groups. Considering the examples in (4), Bosque (2012) notes that the predicates with indicative tend to denote communication, perception, or thought, while those with subjunctive have a more intentional or prospective meaning. He states that there have been attempts, or solutions, to deal with these cases. For example, he claims that one of these solutions has been a lexical one, according to which lexical items would be split in two entries. However, he points out that this approach is problematic as it is not generalizable and masks some paradigms such as the ones mentioned above with the examples in (4).

Under the traditional perspective, therefore, mood selection in subordinate complement clauses has been approached through lists of large semantic classes.[2] Such an approach results from an attempt to account for mood selection in a more principled way through generalizations of paradigms. This traditional approach has in a way extended beyond grammars, manuals, and theoretical pieces, and is commonly used as a starting point for many studies on subjunctive use, including those under the Language Variation and Change framework. In delineating their envelope of variation, research done by Silva-Corvalán (1994) in Los Angeles and by Lynch (1999) in Miami, for example, has relied on the notions of obligatory and variable contexts as prescribed in the grammar. Importantly, such work has focused on analyzing mood variation according to large semantic categories, overlooking the relevance of individual lexical governors. More recent variationist research, however, has taken a bottom-up methodological approach in selecting the envelope of variation, not based on prescription but on the data analyzed (LaCasse, 2018; Poplack et al., 2018; and Torres Cacoullos et al., 2017). These studies discuss the relevance of the lexical identity of the governor (i.e., the matrix verb itself), revealing patterns of lexical routinization of subjunctive in Spanish.

3. Lexical routinization of subjunctive and the case of Spanish

Variationist research has highlighted the inherent variability of mood selection in Romance languages. Poplack et al. (2013) show first for French that there is little consensus between prescription and praxis. By carrying out usage-based research with data from the 19th, 20th and 21st centuries, the authors find that subjunctive use in French has been in stable variation for a long time, even though the inherent variability of mood selection has been consistently neglected by prescriptive efforts. Just like in Spanish, Poplack et al. point out that in French:

---

2. Here I use Bosque (2012) as an example of the traditional approach to mood selection with the purpose of briefly showing how obligatory and variable contexts are commonly prescribed based on semantic classes. A more extensive description of semantic classes in which these contexts take place can be found in the descriptive grammar of Spanish edited by Bosque and Demonte (1999) (in Ridruejo's chapter more specifically), and in the grammar of the Real Academia Española (2009). More theoretical references that reflect this description can be found in Bosque (1990), Bosque (2012), Bosque and Gutiérrez-Rexach (2009), and Uriagereka (2015).

> prescriptive discourse has always taken two (seemingly conflicting) directions: the major one deals with identifying the class of lexical governors that require or prohibit the subjunctive in the embedded clause, usually taking the form of list, and the other with the semantic readings that the subjunctive expresses.
>
> (pp. 144–145)

Although whole semantic classes have been prescribed to be the major predictor of subjunctive selection, Poplack et al.'s (2013) investigation of spoken Quebec French shows that, in fact, these classes often correspond to very few governors. Based on an analysis of productivity measures, their results indicate that while approximately 304 verb governors are gathered in semantic classes said to categorically trigger subjunctive, only three matrix verbs account for most of the data. *Falloir* 'be necessary' represents almost ⅔ of all subjunctive governors and is followed by second-tier governors such as *vouloir* 'want' and *aimer* 'like', which are also associated with subjunctive morphology, although to a lesser extent. Therefore, Poplack et al. uncover usage patterns of mood selection that indicate that subjunctive is lexically routinized (and therefore, less productive) in French. This means that subjunctive has been very grammaticalized and is mainly determined by a strong lexical bias (i.e., the lexical identity of the matrix verb), and not necessarily by large semantic classes as prior accounts had suggested. Following this pioneering research, Poplack et al. (2018) investigate the grammaticalization of subjunctive in different Romance languages (French, Italian, Portuguese, and Spanish). While French is considered the most routinized due to such a small number of governors accounting for subjunctive data, subjunctive in Italian, Portuguese and Spanish is also found to be routinized, but less so.

Looking at Spanish data from the *Corpus Sociolingüístico de la Ciudad de México* (CSCM) (Martín Butragueño & Lastra, 2011–2015), Poplack et al. (2018) and also Torres Cacoullos et al. (2017) find two extremes: most governors either highly trigger subjunctive (at rates that go beyond 90%) or rarely do so (less than 20%). For example, they show that *hacer* 'make-cause' categorically triggers subjunctive, while *suponer* 'suppose' triggers subjunctive less than 10% of the time. Thus, they find that variability tends to take place among different governors (such as *hacer* and *suponer*), but not that much within the same governor. This is illustrated in Figure 1 (Torres Cacoullos et al., p. 15).

Torres Cacoullos et al. (2017) reach similar conclusions in their analysis of pre-modern texts (literary texts from the 13th to the 16th centuries). They find evidence of lexical routinization even in pre-modern texts and show that out of 23 frequent verbs, six display a categorical use of subjunctive and three present more than 90% of subjunctive use. In general terms, these verbs are among verbs of volition, influence and cause, and are responsible for the bulk of subjunctive use. However, as the authors emphasize, these semantic classes are not coher-

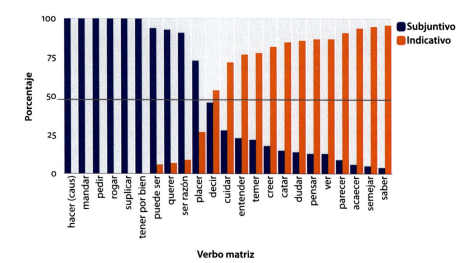

Figure 1. Spanish matrix verbs according to percentage of subjunctive in complement clauses (Torres Cacoullos et al., 2017, p. 15)

ent. In fact, they find that not all verbs classified under the same semantic classes behave in the same way. Different verbs under volitional governors, for example, trigger subjunctive use at different rates: *esperar* 'to hope' has a 66% (5/8) use of subjunctive and *haber esperanza* 'there is hope that' only 11% (1/9). Research on monolingual Spanish, therefore, shows that the subjunctive is mainly triggered by the lexical identity of the governor, instead of semantic and structural considerations that encompass the traditional lists of obligatory and variable contexts of mood choice. Torres Cacoullos et al. point out that while semantic and structural considerations may still condition mood choice, they do so less significantly than often prescribed.

Evidence of lexical routinization has been found in bilingual Spanish as well. Analyzing data from the New Mexico Spanish-English Bilingual (NMSEB) corpus (Torres Cacoullos & Travis, 2018), LaCasse (2018) tests the contact-induced hypothesis (Silva-Corvalán, 1994) and investigates if contact with English leads to an accelerated simplification of the mood system in New Mexico Spanish. In her study, there is not a comparison between different generations as in Silva-Corvalán (1994) given that all participants in the corpus are minimally third-generation speakers. Rather, LaCasse compares bilingual data to a monolingual benchmark — in this case, Spanish from Mexico City (CSCM corpus). Results of her productivity measures analysis show that the bilingual data and the monolingual benchmark have very similar levels of lexical routinization — a small cohort of governors account for most subjunctive use. In addition, she finds that most of the governors that account for subjunctive use do not present variable behavior and co-occur only with subjunctive. Such similar results found for the lexical routinization of subjunctive in monolingual and bilingual Spanish not only reveal an important predictor of mood variation but also provide evidence against claims of acceleration of subjunctive simplification due to contact with English, as pointed out by LaCasse.

These studies on the lexical routinization of subjunctive have relied on the analysis of productivity measures such as the count of governor types, the proportion each governor represents in the entire pool, and the proportion of subjunctive use according to governor frequency and variability. In a large-scale corpus analysis of subjunctive cross-dialectal productivity in Argentine, Mexican and Peninsular Spanish, Schwenter and Hoff (2020) employ similar measures and also find subjunctive use to be mainly lexically-determined by a small set of governors. While there are some differences across dialects regarding how some specific governors pattern, subjunctive productivity within all dialects depends mainly on the governor. An important contribution of their study, which builds from work on the productivity of morphosyntactic constructions (Bybee, 2010), is the use of an additional productivity measure: the ratio of hapax legomena to governor type.

Hapax legomena are the governors that occur only once in the data set. As such, these cases are understood as novelty, as structures that are not common or familiar. Therefore, these low-frequency constructions require more parsing, which activates the different parts of the constructional schema, strengthening their representation more than a very frequent construction (Bybee, 2010). In Schwenter and Hoff's (2020) analysis of mood variation, for instance, they find that while Argentine and Mexican Spanish show no differences in terms of the ratio of hapax legomena to governor type, Peninsular Spanish features a significantly lower ratio, indicative of less productivity and a greater grammaticalization of subjunctive in Spain. This is because they argue that the higher the number of hapax legomena, the higher the subjunctive productivity, given that it represents a greater dispersion of subjunctive forms across different contexts as well as the potential for innovative extension of subjunctive to new constructions.

The studies revisited in this section emphasize the variable character of mood selection in Spanish and pinpoint lexical identity of the governor as a major factor behind variation. It is important to point out that none of these studies claim that subjunctive is being necessarily lost. As Schwenter and Hoff (2020) explain,

> an important take-home point from [these] results should be that the presence of variation in mood choice in a given dialect is not necessarily an indication that the use of the subjunctive is being lost; rather, it can be understood as a sign of its productivity and lesser grammaticalization than in other dialects where freedom of choice between moods is not (or is no longer) possible. (p. 28)

In view of the studies outlined, the following research questions are addressed in this study: (1) What is the role of the lexical identity of the governor in mood selection in Southern Arizona? (2) Do the patterns of mood variation in this region point to the lexical routinization of subjunctive, as seen in other Spanish dialects? and (3) If so, to what extent is mood behavior in Southern Arizona similar to or different from the results of related studies on lexical routinization in monolingual and bilingual Spanish?

4. Methodology

This section briefly describes the corpus used in this study, the delimitation of the envelope of variation and the extraction protocol, as well as the productivity measures used for the analysis.

4.1 The corpus and participants

This study is situated within the Language Variation and Change theoretical framework and offers a quantitative examination that relies on the analysis of naturalistic data. The data was extracted from sociolinguistic interviews available in the *Corpus del Español en el Sur de Arizona* (CESA) (Carvalho, 2012).

CESA is an ongoing corpus aimed at documenting Spanish spoken in Southern Arizona. Currently, it comprises 78 sociolinguistic interviews with Spanish-English bilingual speakers in the Tucson area, a local community with a 43.6% Latinx population (United States Census Bureau, 2019). Under the supervision of the principal investigator, the interviews are conducted by undergraduate and graduate students enrolled in sociolinguistics courses within the Department of Spanish and Portuguese at the University of Arizona. The individual interview sessions aim to elicit spontaneous speech that represents the linguistic practices of the local community. This corpus serves as valuable material for linguistic analyses of local bilingual Spanish, as well as for comparisons with other Spanish dialects.

This study included a total of 48 interviews, which were selected according to the speakers' profile. More specifically, the interviews were selected mainly based on the speakers' immigrant generation, while also having in mind their distribution according to other extralinguistic factors (i.e., language dominance and language use in the family) to be examined in further studies. Among the participants from the interviews analyzed here, there are 13 first-generation speakers (born in Mexico who immigrated to the US after the age of 11), 19 second-generation speakers (born in the US whose parents were born in Mexico), and 16 third-generation speakers (born in the US who have at least one parent born in the US). Based on self-reported data, most speakers (33/48) are considered to be dominant in both languages, and most of them use mainly Spanish (27/48) or both languages (14/48) within their families.

4.2 Envelope of variation and extraction protocol

Before defining the envelope of variation and extraction protocol for this study, it is important to note the methodological differences among previous research on mood variation. Here I refer, on the one hand, to studies that explore the role of clause type (e.g., Silva-Corvalán, 1994) and, on the other, to studies that explore the role of the lexical identity of the governor more specifically (e.g., LaCasse, 2018). The first difference between these studies concerns the nature of clause type. Studies such as Silva-Corvalán (1994) look at different clause types according to their semantic nature (e.g., volitional clauses, purpose clauses, comment clauses), regardless of their classification as adjective, adverbial or complement clauses, for example. Studies such as LaCasse (2018), however, have focused on complement clauses only, therefore, approaching clause type through its subordinate nature. Different subordinate clause types may trigger different rates of subjunctive and may implicate different linguistic conditioners to be investigated. Therefore, including different subordinate clauses within the same envelope of variation can present challenges to the linguistic analysis. Like in LaCasse and related research, this study focuses on complement clauses.

Another point of divergence between the methodologies of previous studies involves the baseline for determining the envelope of variation. As previously mentioned, while studies such as Silva-Corvalán (1994) have mainly defined their envelope of variation based on obligatory and variable contexts as prescribed in the grammar, studies such as LaCasse (2018) have followed a bottom-up approach, selecting the envelope of variation based on their own data. In the current study, the envelope of variation is determined based on usage, following the bottom-up approach used by LaCasse, Poplack et al. (2018), and Torres Cacoullos et al. (2017).

A two-step extraction protocol was followed to specifically decide which complement clauses to include in the envelope of variation of this study. First, all the governors that triggered a complement clause with a subjunctive verb in the interviews were extracted and included in a set of subjunctive-selecting governors. From a total of 318,961 words produced by the participants in the interviews, there are a total of 95 governor types that could trigger subjunctive according to this extraction procedure. With this set of governors, a second search was conducted to extract all the complement clauses triggered by these governors, regardless of mood choice. Example (5) presents a speaking turn in which the speaker uses both variants with the same governor type (*hacerse* 'think'), serving as an illustration of the extraction protocol followed.

(5) Sí sí me gusta (…) y yo le digo (…) o sea (…) sí son muchas llamadas pero UNA me estresa al día si acaso /aham/ y <u>se me hace que</u> es[IND] muy bueno (…) así (…) o sea, <u>se me hace que</u> **fuera** [SBJV] mucho más difícil si dijera "ah de todas mis llamadas, UNA me gusta (CESA062) 'Yes, yes, I like it (…) and I tell him (…) I mean (…) yes, there are many calls but ONE stresses me out per day if anything /aham/ and it seems to me that it is very good (…) like (…) I mean, it seems to me that it would be much more difficult if I were to say *ah out of all my calls, ONE I like*.'

Considering the example in (5), in the first step of the extraction protocol, *hacerse* was identified as a governor type that could trigger subjunctive due to its use with the subjunctive form *fuera* 'would be'. In the second step of the process, all instances in which the lemma *hacerse* introduced a complement clause were extracted, including cases in which this governor triggered indicative forms such as *es* 'is'. In practice, adopting this bottom-up approach leads to a data set that is significantly different from the one used in Silva-Corvalán's (1994) study, for example. Since it is not based on the prescriptive grammar, the data set selected for this study includes not only governors that are commonly expected to trigger subjunctive (e.g., *querer* 'want') but also governors that exhibit a high use of indicative and some degree of variability that allows for subjunctive use as well (e.g., *creer* 'think'). Considering this methodological aspect is crucial for research on mood variation in Spanish given that it has direct implications for the obtained results and determines the feasibility of comparisons to previous research.

4.3 Productivity measures

An analysis of productivity measures allows us to uncover lexical routinization patterns previously found in monolingual and bilingual Spanish. In addition to answering the research questions for this study, which concern the role of the lexical identity of the governor in mood selection and whether patterns found in Southern Arizona resemble the ones found in monolingual and other bilingual dialects of Spanish, the analysis of productivity measures also provides us with a careful exploration of data distribution in the corpus, which can be helpful for further research. Considering LaCasse's (2018) methodology as a starting point, the following three productivity measures are explored: (1) count of governor types; (2) proportion of subjunctive by governor frequency; and (3) proportion of subjunctive by governor variability. An additional measure, the number of hapax legomena to the governor count, is also examined, following Schwenter and Hoff (2020).

To use these productivity measures, two factors must be operationalized: governor frequency and variability. First, regarding governor frequency, as discussed by Erker and Guy (2012), the use of lexical frequency involves different methodological challenges and decisions — what to count (lemmas or surface forms, and in any position or in a specific one), how to count (globally, using large corpora, or locally, focusing on the corpus which the data set comes from), and how to operationalize (as a continuous or as a discrete variable). In this study, lexical frequency is a discrete variable measured based on the 95 governor types identified. Governor frequency is operationalized considering only forms that occur in governor position because some of these verbs may occur very frequently in the corpus, not as governors, but as embedded verbs, for example. Frequency is, therefore, measured according to the proportion each governor accounts for of the entire pool of governors. Governors with a percentage that ranges from 0.05% to 1% are classified as non-frequent and from 1.44% to 28.70% as frequent. These percentages were defined based on the governors' distribution in the data set.

In terms of variability, the operationalization is more straightforward. Governors are first operationalized in two levels: variable (governors that triggered both indicative and subjunctive), and non-variable (governors that triggered subjunctive only). Secondly, governors are classified in three different levels: variable, non-variable, and hapax legomena. This second operationalization includes a specific level for cases of hapax legomena, which are governors that occurred only once in the entire data set. Non-variable governors in such operationalization consist of governors that only triggered subjunctive but occurred more than once.

5. Results

Out of the 48 CESA interviews analyzed, a total of 95 governor types were identified and a total of 2,010 tokens were extracted with this set of governor types. The overall use of subjunctive mood in the data set was 18% (353 tokens) while indicative use reached 82% (1,657 tokens). These rates at first may lead to interpretations such as that subjunctive is rare or simplified in the data set. However, a careful analysis based on productivity measures is needed to reach any conclusions about subjunctive use. In addition, the comparison of these results with other Spanish dialects can better show us where Southern Arizona stands in terms of mood variation.

As one of the research questions of this study refers to whether Spanish spoken in Southern Arizona shows any indications of continuities with other Spanish dialects in terms of lexical routinization of subjunctive, results are compared to a monolingual counterpart (Mexico City) and also to another bilingual dialect (New Mexico). Additionally, a comparison of these results with French, as the Romance language in which subjunctive is most lexically routinized, also allows us to see how mood variation in Spanish may differ from other Romance languages, but not necessarily across dialects. The comparison of subjunctive behavior in Southern Arizona with other Spanish dialects and French replicates and adds to the analysis provided by LaCasse (2018). Table 1 lists each study revisited as well as the corpora from which these studies collected their data.

Table 1. Corpora used in the comparative analysis and rates of subjunctive use per data set

Language/dialect	Corpus	% of subjunctive
Bilingual Spanish (Southern Arizona) (current study)	*Corpus del Español en el Sur de Arizona* (CESA) (Carvalho, 2012-)	18% (353/2,010)
Bilingual Spanish (New Mexico) (LaCasse, 2018)	New Mexico Spanish-English Bilingual (NMSEB) corpus (Torres Cacoullos & Travis, 2018)	27% (149/550)
Monolingual Spanish (Mexico City) (Poplack et al., 2018; Torres Cacoullos et al., 2017)	*Corpus Sociolingüístico de la Ciudad de México* (CSCM) (Martín Butragueño & Lastra, 2011–2015)	37% (430/1,153)
French (Poplack et al., 2013; Poplack et al., 2018)	*Corpus du français parlé à Ottawa-Hull* (Poplack, 1989)	76% (1,953/2,569)

Table 1 also shows the rates for subjunctive use in each of the corpora considered in the analysis. As previously mentioned, Spanish spoken in Southern Arizona shows a subjunctive rate of 18%. This is the lowest rate of subjunctive, followed by bilingual Spanish from New Mexico (27%), and then by monolingual Spanish from Mexico City (37%). French is the language with the highest rate of subjunctive use (76%). As discussed in previous studies, raw frequencies and global percentages are still commonly used to advocate for the simplification of subjunctive in US Spanish (LaCasse, 2018). Comparing monolingual and bilingual Spanish, for example, one could easily interpret the difference in subjunctive rates as evidence of simplification of mood distinction in bilingual Spanish. However, these rates can be misleading.

Beginning with the analysis of governor type count, it is essential to understand the data set that these governors come from as well as the corpus size. Table 2 presents the word count, number of governor types and the type:word count ratio for each corpus.

Table 2. Word count, number of governor types, and ratio of governor to word count for each data set

Corpus	Word count	Governor type count	Type:word count ratio
Bilingual Spanish (CESA)	318,961[*]	95	.00029
Bilingual Spanish (NMSEB)	150,000[**]	42	.00028
Monolingual Spanish (CSCM)	410,000	111	.00027
French	3,500,000	37	.00001

[*] The word count provided for the *Corpus del Español en el Sur de Arizona* (CESA) includes only the participants' speaking turns in the 48 interviews analyzed in this study.
[**] According to LaCasse (2018), although the New Mexico Spanish-English Bilingual (NMSEB) corpus consists of 300,000 words, it has an equivalent amount of Spanish and English clauses, leading to an approximate of 150,000 words in Spanish.

The interviews analyzed from the CESA corpus (Southern Arizona) consist of 318,961 words and contain a total of 95 governor types. At first, one could assume that in Southern Arizona subjunctive is less productive, given that in monolingual Spanish (CSCM corpus) a higher amount of governor types is found (111). In the same vein, subjunctive use in bilingual Spanish from New Mexico could be interpreted to be even less productive since the data analysis of the NMSEB corpus yields only 42 governor types, less than half the number of subjunctive governor types found in monolingual Spanish. Nevertheless, as LaCasse (2018) points out, looking at the governor type count only is not sufficient, and we must take the corpus size into consideration.

Considering that the CSCM corpus is almost three times larger than the NMSEB corpus, more environments in which subjunctive could be produced are expected in the corpus of monolingual Spanish. By the same token, the CESA data set is expected to have a higher number of governors than the NMSEB data set, given that it is more than twice its size. Similarities between the monolingual and bilingual Spanish corpora become even more evident when French is considered. Only 37 governors are found in the 3,500,000-word Ottawa-Hull corpus, which aligns with the high routinization of subjunctive in French discussed in previous studies (Poplack et al., 2013; Poplack et al., 2018). The type:word count ratio for French (.00001) stands out due to the very small number of governor types for such a large corpus. On the other hand, the three Spanish corpora, regardless of being monolingual or bilingual, have a similar proportion of governors per word count (ranging from .00027 to .00029).

Another productivity measure that needs to be considered is the proportion of subjunctive by governor frequency, which allows us to explore the dispersion of subjunctive across frequent and non-frequent governors. Table 3 shows the number of frequent and non-frequent governors, the percentage of all data they account for, and the percentage of subjunctive tokens they account for in each data set.

Table 3. Proportion of all data and all subjunctive data by governor frequency in each data set (adapted from LaCasse, 2018, p. 71)

	Number of governors	% of all data	% of all subjunctives
Bilingual Spanish (CESA)			
Frequent governors	12	86% (1,728/2,010)	54% (190/353)
Non-frequent governors	83	14% (282/2,010)	46% (163/353)
Bilingual Spanish (NMSEB)			
Frequent governors	9	87% (481/550)	62% (92/149)
Non-frequent governors	33	13% (72/550)	38% (53/149)
Monolingual Spanish (CSCM)			
Frequent governors	15	78% (903/1,153)	60% (259/430)
Non-frequent governors	96	22% (250/1,153)	40% (171/430)
French			
Frequent governors	14	97% (2,500/2,569)	98% (1,907/1,953)
Non-frequent governors	23	3% (69/2,569)	2% (46/1,953)

In CESA, from 95 governor types, 12 are categorized as frequent and 83 as non-frequent. Frequent governors account for 86% of all data (regardless of mood choice), while non-frequent governors account for only 14%, indicating that frequent governors account for most of the data. In terms of subjunctive use, although frequent governors account for a higher percentage of subjunctive (54%) than non-frequent governors (46%), the difference between these percentages is not as pronounced. Having in mind the percentage of all data that frequent and non-frequent governors account for, we observe that non-frequent governors account for proportionally more subjunctive use in Southern Arizona.

This pattern resembles what was found for Spanish spoken in New Mexico and in Mexico City as well. In the NMSEB data set, nine frequent governors account for 87% of all data and 62% of subjunctive use. In the CSCM data set, 15 frequent governors account for 78% of all data and 60% of subjunctive use. Altogether, these results indicate that in all three Spanish dialects frequent governors account for most of the total data, but for proportionally fewer subjunctive tokens. In other words, non-frequent governors, despite accounting for a small percentage of all data, account for proportionally more subjunctive tokens. In French, however, as the language in which subjunctive is most routinized, frequent governors account for most of the data (97%) and for almost all subjunctive tokens (98%) as well. All the subjunctive data is primarily accounted for by a few very frequent governors. This comparison confirms results found in Poplack et al. (2018) that although subjunctive use is lexically routinized in both languages, in Spanish it is to a lesser extent.

These results can be even better visualized in Figure 2, which clearly shows a difference in patterns between Spanish and French but not across monolingual and bilingual Spanish dialects as commonly assumed. In summary, while subjunctive tokens in French are distributed across a small set of frequent governors, which also account for most of the data, in Spanish, subjunctive tokens are distributed among a larger set of less frequent governors.

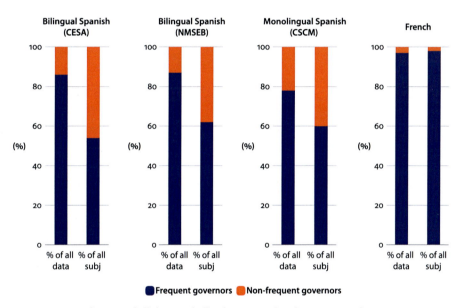

Figure 2. Distribution of all data and all subjunctive data by governor frequency (adapted from LaCasse, 2018, pp. 72–73)

Another way of seeing the patterns of dispersion of subjunctive in terms of governor frequency is by looking at the percentage of subjunctive use in complement clauses introduced by these different governors. Table 4 shows the proportion of subjunctive usage among complement clauses introduced by frequent and non-frequent governors.

In CESA, out of 2,010 tokens, there are a total of 1,728 complement clauses introduced by frequent verbs and 282 introduced by non-frequent verbs. From the 1,728 clauses introduced by frequent governors, only 11% represent subjunc-

Table 4. Subjunctive rates across clauses introduced by frequent and non-frequent governors in each data set (adapted from LaCasse, 2018, pp. 74–75)

Governor type	Subjunctive rate
Bilingual Spanish (CESA)	
Frequent governors	11% (190/1,728)
Non-frequent governors	58% (163/282)
Bilingual Spanish (NMSEB)	
Frequent governors	20% (95/485)
Non-frequent governors	82% (53/65)
Monolingual Spanish (CSCM)	
Frequent governors	29% (259/903)
Non-frequent governors	68% (171/250)
French	
Frequent governors	76% (1,907/2,500)
Non-frequent governors	67% (46/69)

tive use. On the other hand, out of a total of 282 complement clauses introduced by non-frequent verbs (more than six times less), 58% account for subjunctive use. This pattern reflects the results previously discussed: subjunctive use is mainly accounted for by non-frequent governors, as can also be observed in New Mexico and Mexico City. In NMSEB, out of a total of 550 tokens, 485 were introduced by frequent governors and 65 by non-frequent governors. Among the 485 clauses introduced by frequent governors, 20% are accounted for by subjunctive, while 82% of the 65 clauses introduced by non-frequent governors display subjunctive use. In CSCM, out of 1,153 tokens, 903 occurrences are clauses introduced by frequent governors, while 250 are introduced by non-frequent governors. Subjunctive is used in 29% of the 903 clauses introduced by frequent governors, and in 68% of the 250 clauses introduced by non-frequent governors.

In French, on the other hand, out of 2,500 complement clauses introduced by frequent governors, 76% account for subjunctive use. In the 69 complement clauses introduced by non-frequent governors, subjunctive is triggered at 67%. Different from Spanish, in French we see that, despite the high percentage of subjunctive use in clauses introduced by non-frequent governors, subjunctive use is still mostly triggered by clauses introduced by frequent governors. These results reinforce the findings presented in Table 3 and Figure 2. While frequent governors have a higher subjunctive rate in French, in all three dialects of Spanish the higher subjunctive rate is found in non-frequent governors. In other words, subjunctive use is accounted for by a large set of non-frequent governors in Spanish, and by a smaller set of frequent governors in French.

Finally, a third productivity measure explored in LaCasse's (2018) work and replicated here with some adjustments is the proportion of subjunctive by governor variability, presented in Table 5. The classification of governors as variable or non-variable is based on their behavior in the data set, not necessarily as traditionally prescribed. Variable governors are the ones that triggered both indicative and subjunctive in the data sets, while non-variable governors triggered subjunctive only.

Table 5. Proportion of subjunctive by governor variability in monolingual and bilingual Spanish (adapted from LaCasse, 2018, p. 76–78)

Governor type	Number of governors	% of all subjunctives
Bilingual Spanish (CESA)		
Variable	38% (36/95)	70% (248/353)
Non-variable	62% (59/95)	30% (105/353)
Bilingual Spanish (NMSEB)		
Variable	36% (15/42)	64% (95/149)
Non-variable	64% (27/42)	37% (55/149)
Monolingual Spanish (CSCM)		
Variable	30% (33/111)	39% (166/430)
Non-variable	70% (77/111)	61% (264/430)

In CESA, 38% of the governor types are found to be variable while 62% are classified as non-variable. Despite the lower percentage of variable governor types, these governors account for most of subjunctive use (70%). A similar trend is observed in NMSEB, with 36% of governors classified as variable accounting for 64% of subjunctive use. Comparing bilingual and monolingual data, we can observe that in all three data sets the majority of governors show a categorical use of subjunctive, as most of the governor types are classified as non-variable. However, data from monolingual Spanish shows different results for the percentage of subjunctive tokens accounted for by these governors.

Even though there is a lower percentage of variable governors in monolingual Spanish (30%) like in bilingual Spanish, they do not account for most subjunctive use. Instead, variable governors account for only 39% of subjunctive data while 61% of subjunctive tokens are accounted for by non-variable governors. Since these non-variable governors account for most subjunctive tokens, LaCasse (2018) points out that there is no room for linguistic factors other than the lexical identity of the governor to predict mood behavior in the data set. Comparing this to results in New Mexico, she asks whether the lower percentage of subjunctive use accounted for by non-variable governors in NMSEB (37%) could be interpreted as indicative of subjunctive being more simplified in bilingual Spanish given that formerly non-variable governors would be allowing for variability. Nevertheless, the author finds that this is not the case since non-variable governors in monolingual Spanish are also non-variable in bilingual Spanish, as illustrated in Figure 3 (LaCasse, 2018, p. 78).

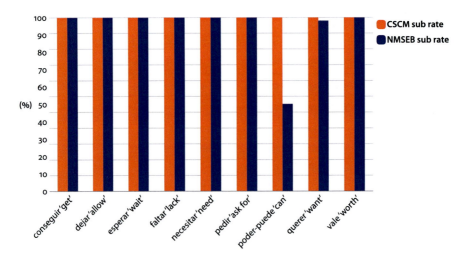

Figure 3. Subjunctive rates with non-variable CSCM governors (LaCasse, 2018, p. 78)

Figure 3 shows that rates of subjunctive use for governors found in bilingual Spanish from New Mexico are very similar to their rates in monolingual Spanish, reaching categorical or near categorical subjunctive use in all cases except for *poder* 'can'. It is hard to know, however, what this similarity in subjunctive rates tells us since these percentages do not provide a full picture of data distribution. For instance, governors such as *conseguir* 'get' and *faltar* 'lack' occurred only once in the NSMEB data set, so how can we determine whether they are truly non-variable or not? Other governors are also non-frequent, such as *necesitar* 'need' (*n* = 2), *pedir* 'ask for' (*n* = 3), and *esperar* 'wait' and *valer* 'worth' (*n* = 4), meaning that their chances to show variability are reduced.

Returning to Table 5, as previously discussed, non-variable governors account for more subjunctive tokens in monolingual Spanish, while in bilingual Spanish (both in CESA and NMSEB) most subjunctive data is accounted for by variable governors. In other words, in the bilingual data sets most of the governors are non-variable, but these account for proportionally fewer subjunctive tokens.

These different patterns could be interpreted as indicative of acceleration of subjunctive simplification in Southern Arizona and New Mexico in light of subjunctive being more accounted for by variable governors in bilingual Spanish while in monolingual Spanish subjunctive is more accounted for by non-variable governors. Nevertheless, such conclusions would be premature. To understand what is behind these results for variability, Table 6 presents a cross-tabulation between variability and frequency of governors in the CESA data set.

Table 6. Distribution of governors by variability and frequency in the data set of Spanish spoken in Southern Arizona

	Frequent governors	Non-frequent governors
Variable governors	12	24
Non-variable governors	NA	59

As shown in Table 6, there is some level of collinearity between how variable and how frequent governor types are. Variable governors can be either frequent or non-frequent, but all the non-variable governors are non-frequent in this data set. Such data distribution clearly shows that a discussion of variability must also take frequency into account. Thus, any conclusions based on the measure of variability needs to be considered with caution due to this collinearity.

While it is true that all non-variable governors are also non-frequent, it is crucial to examine how many times these governors occur in the data set. The process of data coding the process of data coding allowed for the identification of a large quantity of governors that occurred only once. If this is the case, to what extent can we categorize these governors as non-variable? Table 7 presents a different operationalization of governor variability, discriminating between non-variable governors and cases of hapax legomena.

Although rates for variable governors remain the same, the non-variable category presented in Table 5 is here redefined in two groups: non-variable governors and hapax legomena. Non-variable governors are the ones that happened more than once and present a categorical use of subjunctive. In contrast, hapax legomena refers to governors that happened only once in the data set. Table 7 brings to our attention the high incidence of cases of hapax legomena in all three dialects, especially in Southern Arizona. In CESA, we see the highest proportion as 45% of the governor pool is represented by these cases. As shown in Table 7 and also discussed in a more recent publication by LaCasse and Torres Cacoullos (2023), the proportion of hapax legomena in the governor pool of the NMSEB and the CSCM data sets is basically the same, 36% and 35% respectively.

Table 7. Proportion of subjunctive across variable governors, non-variable governors, and cases of hapax legomena in monolingual and bilingual Spanish

Governor type	Number of governors	% of all subjunctives
Bilingual Spanish (CESA)		
Variable	38% (36/95)	70% (248/353)
Non-variable	17% (16/95)	18% (62/353)
Hapax legomena	45% (43/95)	12% (43/353)
Bilingual Spanish (NMSEB)		
Variable	36% (15/42)	64% (95/149)
Non-variable	28% (12/42)	26% (39/149)
Hapax legomena	36% (15/42)	10% (15/149)
Monolingual Spanish (CSCM)		
Variable	30% (33/111)	39% (166/430)
Non-variable	34% (38/111)	52% (225/430)
Hapax legomena	35% (39/111)	9% (39/430)

These rates can be interpreted considering Schwenter and Hoff's (2020) work. As previously mentioned, considering research done on morphosyntactic productivity, these authors understand the number of hapax legomena as an indicator of productivity. Given that these less common structures strengthen the subjunctive representation more than a very frequent structure due to parsing and activation of different parts of the construction, the higher the number of hapax legomena, the greater the dispersion of subjunctive across different contexts. In all three corpora, although most of the governors are non-hapax and happen more than once, the proportion of hapax legomena is fairly high. In CSCM and NMSEB, the number of hapax legomena represents a little more than one third of the entire governor pool. In CESA, this number is higher and reaches almost half of the governor pool, featuring an even greater dispersion of subjunctive across different contexts. This is indicative of a less grammaticalized and more productive use of subjunctive, as well as of a potential for innovative extensions of subjunctive to new structures.

In summary, the results discussed here indicate that Spanish subjunctive in Southern Arizona is lexically routinized due to the role of the lexical identity of the governor in mood variation, but to a certain extent, as there is still productivity accounted for by cases of hapax legomena. It must also be noted that the productivity of subjunctive in Spanish is also evident when comparing the degree of lexical routinization in Spanish to French, for example, in which subjunctive is extremely routinized. Additionally, the comparison of different data sets reveals that similar patterns are shared not only by monolingual Spanish from Mexico City and bilingual Spanish from New Mexico, but also by bilingual Spanish spoken in Southern Arizona.

6. Final considerations

Although bilingual Spanish spoken in Southern Arizona shows a low percentage of subjunctive use — and the lowest compared to monolingual Spanish from Mexico City and bilingual Spanish from New Mexico —, the analysis of productivity measures presented in the current study evidences the need to consider more than overall rates in the study of mood variation. This study explores, for the first time, the role of the lexical identity of the governor in mood variation among Spanish-English bilinguals in Southern Arizona. Despite focusing on offering an understanding of where Southern Arizona stands in terms of mood variation in US Southwest Spanish and Spanish overall, this study also establishes a brief comparison of Spanish data to French, the Romance language in which subjunctive is most lexically routinized. While French, as expected, displays very high levels of lexical routinization, results show that Spanish features lexical routinization of subjunctive as well, but to a lesser extent. In addition, findings point to similarities in this variable behavior across both monolingual and bilingual Spanish.

Results indicate that in Spanish spoken in Southern Arizona subjunctive use is affected by the lexical identity of the governor and its frequency. Productivity measures analyzed indicate that although frequent governors account for most of the data, non-frequent governors account for proportionally more subjunctive tokens, similar to patterns observed in New Mexico and Mexico City. While results point to the lexical routinization of subjunctive in Spanish, by looking at not only governor frequency but also variability, the high number of hapax legomena reveals productivity of subjunctive in all three Spanish dialects examined, especially in bilingual Spanish from Southern Arizona. This study is a first step into the exploration of the lexical identity of the governor as a linguistic conditioning of mood variation in Southern Arizona. A natural progression of this work is a statistical analysis that examines other linguistic conditioners that may affect mood variation, without disregarding, of course, the role of the lexical identity of the governor, as discussed here.

Similarities found between Southern Arizona and Mexico City, the monolingual benchmark in this study, indicate no evidence of contact-induced change in the mood system of Spanish in Southern Arizona. This study adds to the research conducted by LaCasse (2018) by incorporating an additional bilingual dialect into the discussion, thereby together providing a stronger indication to counter the hypothesis of contact-induced change in subjunctive behavior in US Spanish. It is important to mention, however, that testing this hypothesis in different ways is essential to confirming such an indication. In the current study, Spanish from Mexico City was considered as the monolingual benchmark for replication and comparison purposes. Further work should be carried out to replicate the analysis using a different monolingual benchmark, one more related and geographically proximate, such as Spanish spoken in Sonora. Additionally, the contact-induced change hypothesis should be further investigated by operationalizing language contact through extralinguistic predictors in a statistical analysis of mood variation conditioning.

In addition to the parallels with monolingual Spanish, it is also worth noting the striking similarities between Southern Arizona and New Mexico. The comparison of data from CESA and NMSEB clearly points to continuities across US Southwest Spanish in terms of subjunctive behavior. Although these regions in the Southwest US share clear continuities and do not show evidence of simplification, previous research such as Silva-Corvalán (1994) claimed for a simplified mood behavior in Los Angeles Spanish. An important question that remains is whether the divergence in findings for these regions are due to community differences, methodological differences, or a combination of both. While this discussion exceeds the scope of the current study, it is crucial for future research to continue conducting replicable investigations on different communities where Spanish is spoken in the US. This will contribute to a more comprehensive understanding not only of mood variation, but also, more broadly, of grammatical simplification and the impact of language contact on US Spanish.

To conclude, this study adds to the growing body of research that highlights the relevance of the lexical identity of the governor to the investigation of mood variation in Spanish. Taken together, the results of the analysis of productivity measures show that subjunctive in Spanish spoken in Southern Arizona is lexically routinized to some degree while also productive as indicated by the high incidence of hapax legomena. By investigating where Southern Arizona stands in terms of mood variation in comparison to monolingual and bilingual Spanish dialects, this study also contributes to the field by offering a replicable study that can serve a larger discussion on continuities across Spanish dialects, especially throughout the US Southwest.

References

Bosque, I. (1990). *Indicativo y subjuntivo*. Taurus.

Bosque, I. (2012). Mood: Indicative vs. Subjunctive. In J.I. Hualde, A. Olarrea, & E. O'Rourke (Eds.), *The handbook of Hispanic linguistics* (pp. 373–395). Wiley-Blackwell.

Bosque, I., & Demonte, V. (1999). *Gramática descriptiva de la lengua española* (Colección Nebrija y Bello). Espasa.

Bosque, I., & Gutiérrez-Rexach, J. (2009). *Fundamentos de sintaxis formal*. Madrid: Akal.

Bybee, J. (2010). *Language, usage and cognition*. Cambridge University Press.

Carvalho, A.M. (2012–). *Corpus del español en el sur de Arizona (CESA)*. University of Arizona. cesa.arizona.edu

Erker, D., & Guy, G. (2012). The role of lexical frequency in syntactic variability: Variable subject personal pronoun expression in Spanish. *Language, 88*(3), 526–557.

Gili Gaya, S. (1964). *Curso superior de sintaxis española*. Vox.

LaCasse, D. (2018). The subjunctive in New Mexican Spanish: Maintenance in the face of language contact. [Doctoral dissertation, The Pennsylvania State University].

LaCasse, D., & Torres Cacoullos, R. (2023). Simplification in bilinguals' parallel structures? Spanish and English main-and-complement clauses. In M. Waltermire & K. Bove (Eds.), *Mutual influence in situations of Spanish language contact in the Americas* (pp. 7–28). Taylor and Francis.

Lynch, A. (1999). The subjunctive in Miami Cuban Spanish: Bilingualism, contact, and language variability [Doctoral dissertation]. University of Minnesota.

Martín Butragueño, P., & Lastra, Y. (2011'2015). *Corpus sociolingüístico de la Ciudad de México (CSCM)*. Colegio de México.

Montrul, S. (2007). Interpreting mood distinctions in Spanish as a heritage language. In K. Potowski & R. Cameron (Eds.), *Spanish in contact: Policy, social and linguistic inquiries* (pp. 23–40). John Benjamins Publishing Company.

Montrul, S. (2009). Knowledge of tense-aspect and mood in Spanish heritage speakers. *The International Journal of Bilingualism: Cross-Disciplinary, Cross-Linguistic Studies of Language Behavior, 13*(2), 239–269.

Poplack, S. (1989). The care and handling of a mega-corpus. In R. Fasold & D. Schiffrin (Eds.), *Language change and variation* (pp. 411–451). John Benjamins.

Poplack, S., Lealess, A., & Dion, N. (2013). The evolving grammar of the French subjunctive. *Probus, 25*(1), 139–195.

Poplack, S., Torres Cacoullos, R., Dion, N., Berlinck, R., Digesto, S., Lacasse, D., & Steuck, J. (2018). Variation and grammaticalization in Romance: A cross-linguistic study of the subjunctive. In W. Ayres-Bennett and J. Carruthers (Eds.), *Manuals in linguistics: Romance sociolinguistics* (pp. 213–246). de Gruyter.

Real Academia Española. (2009). *Nueva gramática de la lengua española*. Espasa Libros.

Ridruejo, E. (1999). Modo y modalidad. El modo en las subordinadas sustantivas. In I. Bosque and V. Demonte (Eds.), *Gramática descriptiva de la lengua española V. II.* (pp. 3209–3251). Espasa.

Schwenter, S., & Hoff, M. (2020). Cross-dialectal productivity of the Spanish subjunctive in nominal clause complements. In S. Sessarego, J.J. Colomina-Almiñana, & A. Rodríguez-Riccelli (Eds.), *Variation and evolution: Aspects of language contact and contrast across the Spanish-speaking world* (pp. 11–31). John Benjamins Publishing Company.

Silva-Corvalán, C. (1994). The gradual loss of mood distinctions in Los Angeles Spanish. *Language Variation and Change, 6*, 255–272.

Torres Cacoullos, R., LaCasse, D., Johns, M., & De la Rosa Yacomelo, J. (2017). El subjuntivo: hacia la rutinización. *Moenia, 23*, 73–94.

Torres Cacoullos, R., & Travis, C. (2018). *Bilingualism in the community: Code-switching and grammars in contact.* Cambridge University Press.

United States Census Bureau. (2019). *2019 Census.* Retrieved from https://www.census.gov/quickfacts/tucsoncityarizona

Uriagereka, J. (2015). Subordinación: indicativos y subjuntivos. In Á. J. Gallego (Ed.), *Perspectivas de sintaxis formal* (pp. 273–301). Akal.

CHAPTER 2

Sociolinguistic dimensions of flagging behavior
The case of Spanish-English bilinguals in New York City

Rachel Varra
College of William & Mary

Pauses, fillers (*eh, um*) and false starts (e.g. *recu — recuperación*) are often interpreted as 'disfluency' in monolingual and bilingual speech. Recent research on these elements (here called 'flags') increasingly recognizes their communicative functions, but few studies examine how sociolinguistic factors contribute to their use. This study investigates how social factors interact with flagging among Spanish-English bilinguals. Silent pauses, fillers and false starts in the monolingual discourse of 115 bilinguals are examined and results indicate that ethnonational affiliation is the main predictor of flagging. Results suggest that flagging elements may function as sociolinguistic indices for bilinguals and that bilinguals use flagging elements differently than in bilingual mixed speech and differently than monolinguals. Methodological implications and limitations of the study are discussed.

Keywords: Spanish in the U.S., sociolinguistic index, disfluency, flagging, filler, pause, false start

1. Introduction

This study investigates intra-group variation in the use of extended silent pauses, non-lexicalized fillers (e.g. *uh, eh, ah*) and lexical false starts (e.g. *la recep — la recepcionista*) by Spanish-English bilinguals during monolingual stretches of Spanish discourse. These phenomena are three of the most common phenomena investigated as interrupting the production of fluent speech (Fox Tree, 2003). In the investigation of speech produced by bilinguals, these phenomena have been referred as 'flags' and 'flagging behavior' (e.g. Gardner-Chloros & Edwards, 2004;

Muysken, 2000; Rosignoli, 2011; Poplack, Wheeler & Westwood, 1987). Such elements when produced by bilinguals, and in particular in mixed speech, have also generally been associated with something problematic in the discourse, no doubt owing to early psychological and psycholinguistic studies which took discourse phenomena like pauses or fillers to be evidence of 'disfluency' (e.g. Kasl & Mahl, 1965). For bilinguals, for example, pausing, fillers (*eh, uh*), false starts and repetitions have typically been interpreted (a) as signals of disfluency in one or the other language or (b) in the case of mixed-speech, as signals that the inclusion of 'other language' discourse is or is not a 'true' or 'authentic' instantiation of a group's typical speech behavior (see §3 "Literature on flagging in speech production"). Although these discourse elements have been linked to disfluency on the one hand (e.g. Poulisse, 1997) and to the presence of 'other' language strings on the other (e.g. Hlavac, 2011), literature on the use of these elements reveals that, far from being markers of disfluency, pauses, fillers, false starts and the like not only provide information about linguistic processing and message planning (e.g. Levelt, 1989), but also play a functional role in communication. They organize conversation (Levinson, 2002), demarcate discourse/narratives (Chafe, 1980), betray affective states (like anxiety) (Kasl & Mahl, 1965) and facilitate an interlocutor's comprehension (e.g. Clark & Fox Tree, 2002).

Despite recognition of the multiple functions of flagging elements, few studies explicitly examine how flagging elements may be conditioned by sociolinguistic factors (but see the review of work by Tottie, 2011 and others in §3), how they are used by bilinguals (but see Hlavac, 2011) or use large corpora which can be probed for intra-group variation. This study attempts to redress the situation with an exploratory investigation of three speech phenomena that, across the literature, are often implicitly interpreted as indications of disfluency when encountered in the speech of bilinguals: the use of extended silent pauses, non-lexical fillers and lexical false starts. These elements are part of what I conceptualize as a vaster category of phenomena, which I shall refer to as 'flags' or 'flagging behavior' (see §2, "Note on terminology"). The question to be answered is whether these so-called 'disfluency' elements may function in sociolinguistically indexical ways — that is, whether flagging may mark speakers as belonging to different social groups, beyond those characterized by a speaker's linguistic proficiency in a language. Thus, the purpose of this investigation is to examine the use of flags when produced by bilinguals in monolingual speech (i) to obtain a more comprehensive understanding of flagging behavior in a particular group of bilinguals as well as more generally and (ii) to determine whether flags, often associated with linguistic processing and (lack of) linguistic proficiency, index social meaning for a large corpus ($n = 115$) of conversational Spanish produced by bilinguals.

2. Note on terminology

It is important at this juncture – prior to the review of relevant literature – to note the complexity of terminology and variation in typologies of the phenomena investigated. In accordance with the theoretical framework of the researcher, one will find the use of different hypernyms to classify the speech elements that are of interest here (silent pauses, fillers and false starts). Further, diverse sorts of speech elements are included (or not) within any given typology. For example, Stenström (2011) uses the term 'pausology' for the area of investigation that explores the use of pauses, fillers and false starts. Pausology also variably includes verbal fillers (e.g. *well, pues* 'well, so', *como* 'like'; elsewhere referred to as discourse markers), lengthening (e.g. English *aaaand, theee*), repairs (what here would be called 'lexical false starts'), reformulations (e.g. *y tiene que ir a recla... a a llegar...* 025C), restarts (e.g. *No*[interjection] *era un era un colegio de de de... un padre, con un padre tú ves pero no de monjas* 113D) and repetitions (e.g. *entonces yo yo tenía la tarjeta que le llené ante...*367E). Chafe (1980) uses 'hesitation phenomena' to refer to pauses, false starts, afterthoughts and repetitions. Crible (2018, pp. 22–23) uses the term 'fluenceme' to refer to unfilled pauses, filled pauses (what is here simply called 'fillers'), truncation (like a lexical 'lexical false start' in this study), false starts (*Porque hay una cosa. Los niños... la educación en este país, desde un punto de vista, cuando uno llega, es muy floja.* 201U), propositional substitution (*no importa que, que pudiera estar haciendo.. buscando trabajo...* 308M), morphological substitution (*El HBO* [eishbió] *así que yo lo veo. Es... son películas, claro que de antes pero yo las veo.* 024C), lexical insertion (*y a mí me agarraron con pongamos una onza y con plata, mil pesos, y me dicen "deme la plata"...* 311C), parenthetical insertion (*un año de literatura de Shakespeare, el... el escritor inglés, tú sabes, que es el más viejo en literatura americana, y tengo... deja ver qué más tengo: español* 005U), deletion (*Mary didn't want to come Mary didn't come*), misarticulation (*Aquí era una zona dominada por los irlandeses, que en su lucha ganguera trata... trataron de sacar...* 002U), identical repetition (*Y yo creo y yo creo, ¿no?...* 183U), modified repetitions (*a lot of time a lot of money*), embedded fluencemes (*she and she*) and change of order (*normally would take you would normally take you*). The expression 'temporal variables of discourse' (in spontaneous oral language) is used by Deschamps (1980, p. 256) with a focus on the use of silent pauses and filled pauses, while also taking note in transcriptions of "drawls, repetitions and false starts" (also see Grosjean & Deschamps, 1975). Other contributions to the book in which Deschamps' (1980) publication is included refer to the field of 'pausology' and mention silent pauses, filled pauses, false starts, repeats, (e.g. O'Connell & Kowal, 1980) as well as intonation (e.g. Cook, 1980) and other suprasegmental elements of speech (e.g. Ballmer, 1980). Hlavac (2011, p. 3798), investigating Croatian-English speakers using bilingual mixed speech, uses the term 'hesitation and monitoring phenomena' (HMP) and includes: unfilled pauses, (non-lexical) filled pauses (e.g. *eh, um*), lexicalized filled pauses (e.g. *like, you know,* Cr. *ovaj* 'this', *kao* 'like', *znas*ˇ 'you know'), false starts, backtracking, repairs, explicit pre-empting (metalinguistic commentary or drawing attention to the language being used), explicit justification (post-positioned), paralinguistic markers (laughter, nervous coughing) and "equivalents from Croatian accompanying English code-switches" (that is, something akin to translation or 'other-language' paraphrase). Finally, in some bilingual speech studies the terms 'flag' or 'flagging behavior' have been used to refer loosely to the presence of silent pauses, fillers and false starts (Muysken, 2000; Poplack, Wheeler & Westwood, 1987) and might include translations, repetitions or metalinguistic commentary (e.g. Pfaff, 1979; Poplack, 1985, also see §3 "Literature on flagging in speech production").

The selection of a hypernym from the extant literature is difficult both because of connotations of the terms[1] and because adopting a particular term might imply acceptance of or limiting oneself to a particular typology of phenomena. Inventing one's own term, which is both broad enough to include a range of speech elements (even previously unanticipated ones) and maintains an openness to exploration, is not only difficult in this area of investigation,[2] but also risks com-

---

1. For example, I have considered using the terms mentioned above – 'pausology', 'fluencemes' and 'temporal (speech) variables' and 'HMP' – but find them unsatisfactory. The term 'pausology' is too narrow in that it makes pauses the central element of investigation – also see Baars (1980) who finds this term problematic. 'Temporal variables' presumes to focus on elements that affect things like speech rate and it is unclear whether discourse markers/lexicalized filled pauses (*well, pues, so, tú sabes*) could count as 'temporal' elements of speech in the same way that silent pauses or (non-lexicalized) fillers (*eh, em*) would. Further, discourse markers, which are also of interest to me, may perform functions similar to silent/unfilled pauses or fillers, making it helpful at some time to be able to include them in a study alongside silent pauses and fillers. 'Hesitation and monitoring phenomena' already suggests the function of the phenomena under investigation, on which I would for the moment like to remain neutral. 'Fluencemes' reinforces the link between such phenomena and fluency or linguistic proficiency. This term does not allow space for the idea that these speech elements may convey information apart from one's proficiency in a language. Further, 'fluenceme' used with respect to bilinguals will likely bring to mind more negative connotations (i.e. the lack of proficiency) than positive, despite the fact that the term was coined as an alternative to 'disfluency' phenomena (Crible, 2018, pp. 22–23) and, in that sense, is a terminological and theoretical improvement.

2. In approaching this, and planned future studies, I have wanted to maintain the ability to address a large majority of the phenomena included in the typologies mentioned above. I have considered the phrase 'non-propositional speech elements', but that excludes metalinguistic commentaries and translations (which are propositional) and are important to bilingual mixed speech. I have considered 'message peripheral elements of speech' in an attempt to isolate them

plicating the terminological landscape, especially if a term already in circulation might do the job well enough. On the other hand, simply employing the relevant and precise terms used by investigators themselves complicates the consolidation of previous work and reinforces a fragmented approach to the phenomena. It also makes a literature review somewhat more challenging to assimilate.

Thus, to not proliferate terminology unnecessarily, to facilitate the task of the reader and to maintain as neutral a position with respect to the function of the speech elements examined, I will employ the term 'flag' or 'flagging element' as the hypernymic expression that includes the phenomena under study here (silent pauses, non-lexicalized fillers and lexical false starts), but which is not limited to those phenomena. The term 'flag' perhaps is not ideal in that it may, like 'hesitation and monitoring phenomena', imply that the function of such elements has been determined already (i.e. 'bringing attention to'). However, the reader may keep in mind that the actual functions of these elements, or to what *precisely* attention is being drawn, is a matter of investigation. 'Flags' may draw attention to a speaker's cognitive processing, message planning, focal elements of discourse or any other intentional or non-intentional message conveyed by a speaker or inferred by a hearer. Furthermore, while I am employing the term 'flag' as a cover term for any or all of these phenomena, I will review mainly those findings relevant to the types of flags investigated here (though studies invariably include other phenomena), namely: silent pauses, non-lexicalized fillers and lexical false starts. These are the three phenomena most commonly included in studies of 'pausology', 'fluencemes', 'HMP', 'temporal variables' and the like (e.g. see Fox Tree, 2003). The reader should keep in mind that the general terminology I employ is not being attributed to authors themselves, but rather represents an attempt to facilitate comprehension of the literature.

3. Literature on flagging in speech production

The examination of verbal flagging elements has an established investigative history in psychology and linguistics in relation to affect and language processing, including message planning, encoding units, language fluency and organization of the mental lexicon (see Stenström, 2011). In psychology, for example, flagging elements (referred to as 'disfluencies' in this line of investigation) have been correlated with affective states and cognitive states, particularly anxiety and uncer-

---

from what one might consider the main narrative thread of a bit of discourse. That, however, implies that these elements do not themselves send messages that may be just as important as any perceived central narrative thread in a person's speech.

tainty. Kasl and Mahl (1965) examined false starts, repetitions and slips of the tongue (but did not look at *ah*) of 40+ individuals during two psychological interviews, which were manipulated to include anxiety-provoking elements. Goldman-Eisler (1972), examining nine samples of spontaneous speech (e.g. from radio talk and conversations) and five samples of reading speech, found that the quantity of hesitation pauses (vs. breathing pauses, from which they are distinguished) was higher when and where there was uncertainty in the linguistic message being produced. In psycholinguistics, Maclay and Osgood (1959) examined pauses, fillers, false starts and repetitions in monolingual English speech at an academic conference in order to make inferences about psycholinguistic encoding units. An important result of their work was the recognition that the extent of use of flagging elements can vary greatly from speaker to speaker. Goldman-Eisler (1967, pp. 126–127), using ten samples of spontaneous speech, 12 reading texts and 38 translations (3–6 minutes of speech each) found evidence to confirm that the flags they investigated were related to cognitive planning as well as 'fluency' (defined as the percent of time spent in pausing).

In the psycholinguistics of second language (L2) acquisition and bilingualism, experimental research often measures participants' reaction time to stimuli. These reaction times, which could be construed as silent pauses, are used to make inferences about the level of activation of one language or another (Grosjean, 1997) and about the relative organization and mapping of languages in the mind (Chapnik Smith, 1997; Kroll & de Groot, 1997). Flags in spontaneous L2 production are also frequently used to make inferences about the encoding of linguistic units in speech production (Boomer, 1965; Maclay & Osgood, 1959; Levelt, 1989). Further, in language acquisition studies, flagging elements are generally taken as an indication of fluency or proficiency, such that a lack of flags, particularly pauses, for example, is generally associated with greater proficiency or fluency in language (see Lennon, 1990; Olynik, D'Anglejan & Sankoff, 1987; Temple, 1992; Wiese, 1984; Wray, 2002, pp. 35–36). Indeed, it is well-established that in comparative studies of L1 and L2 speech, pauses and other flags generally seem to be more frequent in L2 speech, such that their occurrence tends to be associated with lesser proficiency in a language (Poulisse, 1997, p. 206).

The relationship between certain sorts of flagging elements (particularly, pauses, non-lexical fillers and false starts) and proficiency is so well-attested that it is perhaps unsurprising that the relationship is taken as "given" in many studies of bilingual discourse. In such studies, flagging elements are used to help distinguish 'good', 'accepted' or 'fluent' strings of bilingual mixed speech from 'not-so-good', 'not true' or 'unauthentic' ones; and in this capacity, they are sometimes explicitly or implicitly used to determine the status of other-language strings in the bilingual discourse (e.g. as a codeswitch or a borrowing) (e.g. Clyne, 1997;

Clyne, 2003; Muysken, 2000, pp. 31, 94–95; Poplack, Sankoff & Miller, 1988; also see Poplack, 1987; Teschner, 1972, pp. 1140–1142). For instance, in several studies, it has implicitly been assumed that the presence of pauses, fillers and false starts indicate that the discourse produced is not an authentic or 'natural' example of fluent performance, especially as concerns language mixing. For example, Pfaff (1979) used the presence of hesitations, translations and metalinguistic commentary in her informants' speech to classify other-language strings as either borrowing or codeswitching, because she takes the presence of flagging as "evidence that the speaker is aware of switching to a special term, code, or register" (p. 297). Pfaff (1979) interprets some flags (particularly 'hesitation' and metalinguistic commentary) near a foreign-origin string as a sign that the string is not part of the Spanish lexical repertoire of the speaker.[3] Also, in a study of English lexical borrowing in French, Poplack, Sankoff and Miller (1988) note that they only examined borrowings that were "used *naturally* in the contexts of French discourse" (p. 54, *my emphasis*) and that did not occur in the immediate context of "perceptible hesitations or false starts". Poplack (1985) has also contrasted 'fluent' or 'skilled' codeswitching with unskilled or 'inauthentic' switching, implicating flagging elements in this distinction. For instance, she states that a feature of "skilled" or "fluent codeswitching" is a "smooth transition between L1 and L2 elements", as opposed to non-fluent codeswitching which would be "flagged" (1985, p. 54). She later states "true" codeswitching, as among Spanish-speaking bilinguals in New York, "minimized the salience of the switch points" (1985, p. 65), but that in Ottawa, Canada, speakers "draw attention to their code-switches by repetition, hesitation, intonational highlighting, explicit metalinguistic commentary, etc." (1985, p. 65). Likewise, Toribio (2001, p. 419), in examining the codeswitching competence of Spanish-English bilinguals, says some participants' editing of "potential[ly] ill-formed intrasentential switches, gave rise to disfluencies," which she indicates are instantiated in pauses and reiterations.

Notably, though, some investigations of bilinguals have indicated that the use of some of these elements may be functional, particularly with respect to mixed speech. Poplack, Wheeler and Westwood (1987), for instance, note that the presence of "perceptible pauses and repetitions or explanations" may be a means by which 'ungrammatical' codeswitching structures are avoided (p. 391). Muysken (2000, pp. 101–102, 230–231) regards the use of what he calls 'flagged' or 'specially marked' mixing as a characteristic of code-mixing of the 'alternation' type (as opposed to other types he identifies, such as 'insertion' or 'congruent

---

3. On the other hand, Pfaff (1979, pp. 297–298) indicates that Spanish translation or paraphrase of an English string may indicate that the English phrase is in fact integrated into the speaker's lexical repertoire in Spanish.

lexicalization'). In exemplifying flagging behavior in a French-Dutch corpus, he cites the use of extended pauses and use of *eh* and *huh* (called 'fillers' in, for example, Fox Tree, 1995; Fox Tree, 2003; Maclay & Osgood, 1959). Similar to Poplack, Wheeler and Westwood (1987), Muysken notes that in some cases, "flagging helps to overcome conflicts in linearization patterns [i.e. in Finnish and English bilingual mixed discourses]" (Muysken, 2000, p. 106). Likewise, Gardner-Chloros and Edwards (2004, p. 108) note that "in monolingual conversation, such interruptions, reformulations, etc [sic] are often functional in terms of the meaning produced/the message conveyed. In CS [codeswitching] they are all the more functional..." and that "speakers use pauses, interruptions, 'left/right-dislocation' and other devices to neutralize any grammatical awkwardness resulting from [code-]switching at a particular point in the sentence". Despite the acknowledgements of their functionality by these researchers, it should not escape the reader's attention that, still, these flagging elements tend to be associated with notions of (un)grammaticality.

Recognition of their functionality in bilingual mixed speech notwithstanding, flags in the aforementioned studies, further, tend to be overtly linked to notions of 'impurity', 'inauthenticity' or as indicating that something in the discourse is or might be problematic. Poplack, Wheeler and Westwood (1987), for example, state: "In keeping with the distinction drawn above between flagged and smooth codeswitching we also noted the presence of various discourse phenomena in the environment of the English-origin items which might indicate *poor integration* into host-language discourse. Included here were perceptible pauses, [...] and false starts, [...] preceding or following the noun in question and the presence of material repeating, translating or explaining the English origin form [...]" (p. 393, *my emphasis*). Muysken (2000, p. 106) endorses this perspective as well, saying "*true cases of flagging* can be seen as revealing the *hesitation* of speakers to mix intrasententially, as in French/English or French/Dutch mixing (perhaps due to strong pressures to produce monolingual, pure sentences, or to use Grosjean's terms, stay in the monolingual mode)" [*my emphasis*].

While the employment of flagging elements as methodological tools to delimit data sets or find the best example of some phenomena (e.g. codeswitching) is typically justified in the contexts of investigation, it is clear that, in studies of bilingual speech, such elements have acquired negative associations. These notions typically relate to ideas of ungrammaticality, lack of fluent speech production or linguistic processing difficulties. In so doing, research with bilingual speakers has missed opportunities to examine how flagging behavior may be functionally and communicatively contributive to their speech.

Indeed, a growing body of research approaches flagging elements in monolingual speech from functional perspectives, including not only their implications for linguistic processing and message planning, but also their communicative functions, their discursive functions and socio-cultural differences in their deployment. Stenström's (2011) comprehensive overview of flags explicitly notes that hesitation phenomena (including pausing, fillers, reformulations and repetitions) have functional benefits for both for speakers and listeners. For instance, Stenström (2011, pp. 542–547) notes that silent pauses, fillers and verbal fillers have been implicated in the cognitive planning of constituents of speech as well as to organize discourse into larger units, similar to 'paragraphs'. Likewise, she notes that filled pauses and silent pauses, along with reformulations and repetitions, have been found to give a speaker time to stop and think, give a listener time to comprehend the message and to fulfill discourse functions, like turn-holding and turn-yielding. Clark and Fox Tree (2002) examine the use of *uh* and *um* in English. They find that, contrary to previous ideas about these items, *uh* and *um* function like words and that speakers in fact plan for and select, as they would other words. They conclude that *uh* and *um* are listener-oriented devices that are used "for comments on the on-going performance" (p. 107) and alert the listener to expect upcoming shorter or longer delays in message transmission (*uh* signals minor delays; *um* signals major delays). Other studies also make mention of their listener-oriented functions (e.g. Shriberg, 2001; Van Der Wege & Ragatz, 2004). Chafe (1980) examines flags with a corpus of 20 female American speakers recounting a 7-minute film. He proposes that the presence of hesitation (a cover term for various phenomena) is not necessarily problematic – as indicating ungrammaticality or disfluency. Rather, he says that "pauses, false starts, afterthoughts, and repetitions do not hinder" a speaker's goal of achieving "the adequate verbalization of his [sic] thoughts, but are steps on the way to achieving it" (p. 170). He links flags to pivotal moments in establishing or changing the focus of a narrative (e.g. introducing an image, such as a character, or recounting events, such as a character's fulfillment of their intentions) (1980, pp. 173–174).

Several studies have also highlighted the differential deployment of flags for social and cultural groups. For instance, Jaworski (1993, pp. 46, 51), in an exploration of silence, notes that in Western cultures, shorter pauses (as well as shorter turns and faster speech) seem to be evaluated more positively than more frequent or longer pausing. Tannen (1984), examining English language conversations among friends at a Thanksgiving dinner, noted that individuals speaking the same language, but belonging to different communities, may have more or less tolerance for silence (as well as for turn overlap and faster speech rates). Candea, Vasilescu and Adda-Decker (2005) examined eight different languages (Arabic, Mandarin Chinese, French, German, Italian, Portuguese, English and Spanish) in an attempt to uncover cross-linguistic universals in the phonetic realization of the vowels of fillers (as in *uhh, um, eh*). Using a multilingual broadcast corpus of news or news-related shows, they examined the duration, the F1/F2 characteristics and the pitch (F0) of the vowel in the filler item. They found that filler vowels showed language-specific characteristics and some cross-linguistic similarities. Each language, they found, prefers vowels of a certain timbre. Different languages also have preferences for different types of 'vocalic supports' (e.g. the fact that English optionally includes a following nasal, as in *um*). On the other hand, these elements cross-linguistically show similarities in their pitch (all having a flat F0 contour) and temporal duration, which tend to be longer than lengthened intralexical vowels.

However, few studies indeed have examined intra-group variation in the use of flagging phenomena or how these elements might be sociolinguistic markers. Fruehwald (2016) examines *uh* and *um* by English speakers, finding that they act like typical sociolinguistic variables in the process of change (there was increased use of *um* over *uh* in younger generations and by women). Tottie (2011) finds that *er/uh* and *erm/uhm* are sociolinguistic markers for gender, age and social class in a large corpora of British English. In fact, several studies on monolingual speakers have noted that age and gender seem to influence the use of flags. It has been found in several studies that men use more of a particular type of flag than women (e.g. Bortfeld Leon, Boom, Schober & Brennan, 2001, p. 139 and Shriberg, 2001 for fillers in English; Bilous & Krauss, 1988 for pauses in English). These studies also usually find that older people use some types of flags more than younger folks (e.g. Bortfeld *et al.*, 2001 for 'disfluencies' (combining repetitions, restarts and fillers) used by English speakers; Tottie, 2011 for *er/uh* and *erm/uhm* among British English speakers).

Even fewer studies, if any, examine intra-group variation with respect to bilinguals.[4] This study, then, aims to determine whether flagging may act as sociolin-

---

[4] Although they do not examine intra-group variation for speakers in a similar context, Rosignoli (2011) and Gardner-Chloros, McEntee-Atalianis & Paraskeva (2013) are novel in that their investigations of flagging elements used by bilinguals are comparative. They, however, examine how flagging may be different for the same group of bilinguals in different contexts or types of discourse (rather than how bilinguals differ from each other in the same/similar context of talk). Gardner-Chloros *et al.*, (2013) compares pauses and fillers used by English-Cypriot Greek speakers ($n=4$) in monolingual and bilingual discourse. Rosignoli (2011) compares flagging elements used by Italian-English bilinguals ($n=20$) in two different settings: Manchester and Milan. Gardner-Chloros *et al.* (2013) found no difference in the use of pauses in monolingual versus code-switched discourse, but insist that "sociolinguistic and discourse variables should form an essential element in attempts to model bilingual speech production" (p.1). Rosignoli (2011) found that the frequency of an other-language segment was inversely related to the use of flags, i.e. that "higher frequency [items or categories, such as nouns] generally is related to less flagging" and that "through flagging, participants reveal to one another their orientation to single instances of language alternation as belonging or not to the medium" (p. iii).

guistic index when used by bilinguals in monolingual segments of discourse.[5] In particular, the purpose of this investigation is to examine flagging behaviors by bilinguals in *monolingual speech* (i) to determine whether such elements, often associated with 'disfluency' for bilinguals, communicate or index social meaning and (ii) to obtain a more comprehensive understanding of these speech elements. It does so with a large corpus of spoken Spanish produced in sociolinguistic interviews with 115 Spanish-English bilinguals, all residing in New York City at the time of their interview. This study is different than other studies in that (a) the speakers are bilingual (as opposed to monolinguals in the vast majority of studies of flagging not in the field of language acquisition), (b) the corpus is larger than others that have been examined for flagging elements used by bilinguals (e.g. see note 4), (c) the flag types examined are those most frequently linked to 'disfluency' (as opposed to other elements like lexicalized fillers / discourse markers, which are not necessarily seen as problematic and have been more widely explored for sociolinguistic variation among Spanish speakers (e.g. Repede, 2002))[6] and (d) flag types are examined in monolingual stretches of speech. The first and last points are important in that research in sociolinguistics on bilingual speech has emphasized that bilinguals avail themselves of the same or similar linguistic resources as monolinguals, but do so differently (e.g. Gardner-Chloros & Edwards, 2004).

Given that the purposes of this study were exploratory — aiming to get a sense of the phenomena for a particular group of bilinguals and to understand them more generally — no specific hypotheses about flagging behavior among these bilinguals was posited. However, recurrent findings with respect to flagging by bilinguals lend themselves to the adoption of three hypotheses. First, the fact that flagging elements tend to be universally (cross-linguistically) correlated with cognitive/linguistic processing and psycho-emotional states (see §3), the researcher imagined that differences might be found with respect to speakers' proficiency in Spanish. Particularly, since lower proficiency in a language tends to correlate with greater amounts of flagging, and given that it is not possible to definitively determine the cause or motivation for the use of a flag (as is the case with most linguistic behaviors), it could be expected that those with lower self-assessed Spanish

---

5. However, the use of flag elements near other language strings has been explored elsewhere for this group of speakers (Varra, 2018; Varra, 2020; Varra, to appear).

6. Repede (2002), for example, examined sociolinguistic variation in the use of attenuators in semi-formal interviews with 24 Spanish-speakers (from the PRESEEA-Sevilla corpus). For that study, attenuators did not include fillers and false starts, but rather mechanisms like vagueness in the content of a proposition, laughter or using 'impersonalization' (e.g. general 'you') or the use of corrective discourse markers like *bueno* 'well', *o sea* 'that is/I mean', *pues* 'then', *hombre* 'man').

proficiency will flag more than those with higher Spanish proficiency. Relatedly, given that declining cognitive states tend to be associated with older individuals, it could also have been expected that flagging will be more frequent among older age groups in the corpus, as has been documented elsewhere (see §3). Finally, the fact that bilinguals seem to use flagging elements in their bilingual stretches of discourse more frequently than in monolingual speech (e.g. Varra, to appear) suggests to the researcher that, insofar as this engages flags for a purpose not relevant to monolinguals, flagging among bilinguals might generally pattern differently and, in turn, be associated with distinct or special functions. What those functions might be is still a matter of ongoing investigation.

4. Methodology

4.1 Informants and independent variables

Data for this study came from the Otheguy-Zentella Corpus of Spanish in New York City (OZC).[7] The OZC is comprised of 146 sociolinguistic interviews (Labov, 1966) conducted in Spanish with Spanish speakers (some functionally monolingual, some bilingual) in New York City in the 1990s and early 2000s. The OZC includes 98 first generation individuals and 48 second generation individuals (those who were born or came to the U.S. at or after age 3). For the current study, a subset of these interviews produced by speakers considered to be 'bilingual' in Spanish and English were used ($n=115$).[8] The interviews of the corpus include variables found to be predictors of language behavior generally-speaking, such as age, sex, education level and social class (e.g. Labov, 2001). It also includes several variables that are often related to language variation among Spanish speakers and bilinguals in the United States, including ethnonational affiliation of the speaker, generation, language proficiency, regional origin, and others mentioned below and which are fully listed in footnote 11. The corpus is stratified according to these variables, so that there are nearly equal numbers of individuals for each of a variable's factors (see Appendix A). That is, there are nearly equal numbers of informants identifying as Puerto Rican, Dominican,

---

7. The corpus was developed with funding by National Science Foundation grant number 0004133.
8. The bilingual speakers of this corpus of Spanish were defined as those who were either born in the U.S., who came to the U.S. prior to age 19 or who, being an adult immigrant, rated their English as either 'pasable', 'bueno' or 'excelente'. That is, adult immigrants who reported their English to be 'poor' ($n=31$) were excluded from this study.

Cuban, Mexican, Ecuadorian and Colombian, equal numbers of individuals from Caribbean regions and the Latin American mainland, equal numbers of males and females and a proportional number of individuals from different social classes. In addition, informants are stratified according to arrival age to the U.S., age, number of years in the U.S., education level, self-rated English skills and self-rated Spanish skills, with relatively proportional numbers of individuals in each factor for these secondary stratification variables (see Otheguy & Zentella, 2012). Further, a derived variable called 'language dominance' was examined in this study. This variable was defined using the difference of an informant's self-rated score in Spanish on the one hand and English on the other. If an informant gave equivalent ratings to their Spanish and English, regardless of whether that score was 'passable' for both or 'excellent' for both, they were classified as 'balanced' in terms of language dominance. If a participant rated their Spanish as higher than their English at the time of their interview, they were classified as 'Spanish-dominant'. If they gave their English a higher rating than their Spanish, they were classified as 'English-dominant'.

4.2 Interviews

Interviews included three components: an oral narrative, a lexical survey and a sociodemographic questionnaire. The interviews were transcribed using standard Spanish orthographic and punctuation conventions, with some exceptions (e.g. *para atrás* was rendered as *pa'trás* where uttered as such). Interviews were conducted in Spanish, but there was no explicit requirement stating that speakers should speak Spanish or not use other languages. Interviewees did make use of English loanwords or codeswitches. These segments of English were transcribed according to standard English orthography.

Transcriptions were done near the time of data collection, in the early 2000s. Transcribers were under instructions to render speech as uttered, as is convention. Fillers, false starts and repetitions are rendered throughout the interviews. Fillers are transcribed in ways that are conventionally associated with their sound, such as *em, ehm, eee, este, um, uhm* and *uh*. Breath-length pauses and longer pauses are indicated in the transcriptions with a comma ',' and a period '.', respectively. These pauses have not been examined in this study, but pauses that were perceived as interrupting the flow of speech *are* of interest here. These pauses are annotated using orthographic ellipsis ('..' and '...') (Otheguy & Zentella, 2012, p. 41). Transcription conventions for the corpus indicate that double periods '..' are used when the pause occurs as a result of a false start of a phrase — what here would be called 'mid-constituent false start and repetition'. Triple periods '...' are used when the speaker restarts a phrase after the pause — what would here be called 'mid-constituent false start and reformulation'. However, for each instance of an interruptive pause (wherever '..' or '...' occurred), the author coded the data herself, noting which interruptive pauses were accompanied by a repetition (using the same linguistic forms) or a reformulation (using different linguistic forms or opting for a new message) (see § 4.3 "Data").

Note that the duration of pauses was not measured at the time of transcription nor taken into account for this study. Instead, the decision was made to take transcribers' representation of pauses in the speakers' discourses as either interruptive or not (rather than from the measured length of a pause in milliseconds) because the transcriber's own interpretation of what they heard and rendered in the transcription is itself data that suggests that such pauses were noteworthy to a listener. This decision also aligns with the purpose of this study which was to examine possible sociolinguistic 'meanings' of flags; if some sociolinguistic meaning is associated with flagging, it stands to reason that it would be detectable by a hearer. Further, while a great deal stands to be learned from the temporal measurement of pauses, it was felt that the exploratory nature of the study and the large size of the corpus did not warrant the massive undertaking of measuring pause durations for 115 interviews at this juncture. It is hoped that the reader agrees that the large size of the corpus itself lends robustness to the results obtained, where studies that document pause duration and other details generally utilize much smaller corpora. Finally, note that for discourse quoted from these conversations in this paper a three-period ellipsis in square brackets at the beginning or ending of an excerpt ('[...]') does not indicate a longer pause, but rather that the excerpt was taken from the middle of a longer speaking turn.

4.3 Data

Data were obtained from only the oral narrative portion of the interviews. The data included extended, unfilled, silent pauses ('pauses' for short), non-lexicalized filled pauses (*ah, eh, um, uhm, este, desto, mm, hm*; called 'fillers' for short) and lexical false starts (partially articulated words; called 'false starts') in monolingual segments of discourse, as in Excerpts (1–5).

(1) ...pero bueno, la gente aquí sale a más temprana edad se enfrenta a cosas más rápido, crecen más rápido, también meten la pata muchas veces, eh, de esa forma pues son más independientes... en el caso de las mujeres: son más abiertas...   308M
'...but well, the people here leave [their parents' home] at an earlier age they face things faster, they grow up faster, they also screw up a lot, eh, so in that way they are more independent... in the case of women: they are more open...

(2) Yo creo que **en el..** en el caso de mi mamá sea la cosa esta [la tendencia para defender irresponsibilidad financiera del papá], porque somos una familia muy conservativa.   037D
'I think that **in the..** in the case of my mom is where that thing is [the tendency to defend the financial irresponsibility of the father], because we are a very conservative family.'

(3) ...yo lloraba, yo me acuerdo que mi papá **me...** nos decía si se portan mal yo les mando para el Ecuador...   300E
'...I used to cry, I remember that my dad **to me...** he would tell us if you misbehave I'm sending you to Ecuador...'

(4) ...sí yo estaba en costura **eh...** muñecos, me gustaba esa.. coser muñecos porque eran unas.. piececitas chiquititas...   065P
'.. yeah I was in sewing **eh...** dolls, I liked that.. sewing dolls because they were some.. delicate pieces...'

(5) Yo sí lo creo que es **natu**, sobrenatural y sí creo que hay algo, que exista sobre eso porque me ha pasado mi familia.   009U
'I yeah I think it is **natu**, supernatural and yes I believe that there is something, that exists about that because it has happened to me [in] my family.'

In the first three excerpts, transcribers indicated noticeable pauses with '..' and '...'. In (1), the Mexican speaker, talking about differences between people in the U.S. and people in Mexico, notes that young people in the U.S. are *más independientes* 'more independent', and then pauses as indicated by '..' . He then continues speaking by initiating the new constituent *en el caso de* 'in the case of'. This pause was coded as an unfilled pause occurring at a constituent juncture. It is not coded as being followed by a reformulation or a repetition. The latter, in this study, means that there has been a repetition of linguistic elements prior to and after the pause. Examples (2) and (3) differ in that they contain pauses that occur mid-constituent. In (2), the Dominican speaker makes a noticeable pause after *en el* 'in the'. She then uses the same words *en el* to reinitiate her speech after the pause. This is classified as a mid-constituent pause with repetition. In (3), the Ecuadorian makes a pause after *que mi papá me* 'that my dad to me'. She then resumes her utterance with different linguistic elements: *nos decía* 'would tell us'. This is classified as a mid-constituent pause with a reformulation. In (4), a Puerto Rican woman inserts *eh* after *en costura* 'in sewing'. This filler co-occurs with a noticeable pause, indicated by '..' ; however, this moment in discourse was counted as a single instance of a flag (that is, a filled pause). That is, when fillers co-occur with pauses, these are considered single instances of flagging. Later in excerpt (4), there are two brief pauses, one after *esa* 'that' and one after *unas* 'some'. These were counted as two additional instances of flagging for this informant. Finally, (5) contains an instance of a lexical false start. The Cuban informant begins a word *natu-*, which is later reinitiated and completed as *sobrenatural* 'supernatural'. This is counted as one instance of a lexical false start.

Because this study is concerned with determining the extent to which such phenomena might be linked with aspects of speaker identity (rather than discursive or physiological needs), not all occurrences of fillers, unfilled pauses and false starts were included in flag counts. Breathing pauses, or those that might be construed as such (indicated by ' , ' or ' . ' in the transcriptions), are not counted as flags, as in Example (6).

(6) Aquí se cansa uno de comer pollo porque **es**, es simple.   021C
'Here one gets tired of eating chicken because **it's**, it's simple.'

In (6), the Colombian speaker begins to say *es simple* 'it's simple', stops after the first articulation of *es* 'it's' and takes a breath-length pause indicated by ' , ' . She then continues speaking by rearticulating *es* 'it's' and then finishes the sentence. The short pause indicated by ' , ' is not counted as an unfilled pause in this study. Further, in many typologies, the mid-constituent repetition of linguistic material (*es* 'it's') is classified as a false start. In this study, mid-constituent false starts were **not** counted in the flagging tallies unless they co-occurred with noticeable pause, indicated by '..' or '...' . This choice was taken (i) so as not to inflate the number of what speakers or listeners might consider meaningful flags and (ii) because there is a fair chance that the pause occurred due to the physiological need to breathe, as suggested by the fact that this pause was transcribed with a comma ' , ' , rather than double or triple periods.

Likewise, pauses and fillers that occurred in locations that might be considered discursively obligatory were not included in the flag count. For instance, fillers, such as *ah* or *eh* may be used at the beginning of a talk turn in order to hold the floor (presumably while a speaker plans their impending verbal contribution) (Stenström, 2011; but see Fruewald, 2016 who found no effect for 'same/other speaker' just prior to the use of *uhm*). These fillers were not included in the flag count in this study. Also not counted were pauses at the end of a turn as these often function to indicate that the speaker is done with their turn (Jaffe & Feldstein, 1970; Levinson, 2002). Furthermore, while lexical discourse markers (such as *entonces, tú sabes, bueno, pues, yo no sé*) may not require co-occurring adjacent pauses to function as intended, these often do occur with pauses (Levinson, 2002, p. 375), thus appearing to realize a substantive role in the functioning of such discourse markers. Thus, when a pause follows a discourse marker, it was not counted as a flag. Likewise, pauses adjacent to affirmations (*sí, no*) or quoted speech are not counted for similar reasons. Saying this again: flags that might have otherwise been included in this study (i.e. pauses and fillers) are not counted when their position in discourse indicates that they are likely functioning to manage the flow of discourse.[9] Finally, flags near English-origin strings were not included,[10] as the present analysis is concerned with the social determinants of these elements overall in monolingual Spanish segments of discourse. Further, flags near English-origin strings have been examined elsewhere for this same group of speakers (Varra, 2018; Varra, 2020; Varra, to appear).

4.4 Dependent measures

For each informant, all flagging elements of interest in this study (extended pauses, fillers and false starts) were identified and tallied for each speaker. The total number of content words used during the oral narrative part of the interview was tallied after having removed all Spanish language articles, determiners, prepositions, pronouns and conjunctions. For each informant a (monolingual) flagging rate was calculated by dividing the total number of their flagging elements by their total number of content words, resulting in a percentage. So, for instance, if a speaker used 145 flags in an interview where they uttered 6,400 content words, their flagging rate would be $\frac{145}{6400}$ or 2.3 percent. Flagging rates are rounded to the nearest tenth of a percentage point in presentation of results for this paper, but not for statistical analysis.

Several additional notes are in order. First, the choice to calculate a rate based on content words (rather than including functional words) was so that flagging rates in monolingual discourse would be somewhat more comparable to flagging rates for segments of bilingual mixed speech, since those most often involve instances of content lexicon (e.g. Haugen, 1950; Varra, 2018; Zentella, 1997). Second, although flagging elements can co-occur with each other (e.g. pauses can

---

[9] Also not examined in this study are several phenomena that other researchers have included as instances of 'hesitation phenomena', 'hesitation and monitoring phenomena' (HMP), 'temporal speech variables' or as part of the study of 'pausology', including: lexicalized filled pauses (e.g. *tú sabes, pues, como* 'like'; see Hlavac, 2011; Stenström, 2011), paralinguistic markers (e.g. laughter or coughing; see Hlavac, 2011), equivalents (e.g. using a synonym or translation to say the same as what was just said) (see Hlavac, 2011; Varra, 2020) and metalinguistic commentary (e.g. *como dicen* 'as they say') (see Varra, 2018; Varra, 2020). Other finer grained characterizations of flags have also not been considered in this study, such as the difference between *uh* and *uhm* (e.g. Clark & Fox Tree, 2002), short and long pauses (e.g. Boomer, 1965; Heike & O'Connell, 1983) or the precise syntactic, lexical or phonemic juncture at which a flagging element occurs (e.g. Boomer, 1965; Hlavac, 2011; Lounsbury, 1954; Maclay & Osgood, 1959).

[10] Previous research with this corpus indicates that flagging in the vicinity of other-language strings is in fact more frequent than in monolingual stretches of speech and may serve as a means to highlight something for a listener that a speaker perceives may need acknowledgement (Varra, to appear).

co-occur with fillers or false starts), counts of each subtype of flag considered the occurrence of a filler as a 'filler' and a false start as a 'false start' whether these occurred with a pause or not. Third, note that when elements occurred in close succession (e.g. *lo.. lo.. eh lo importante es que...*), each element was counted as one flag. That is, in the parenthetical example, there are two pauses and a filler, or three total flagging elements. Finally, note that the flag rate is a combined rate for all three elements: unfilled pauses, fillers and lexical false starts. This is a choice made with respect to the fact that all three phenomena tend to be associated with 'disfluency' in nascent and fluent bilinguals. It is expected that, in the future, separate analysis of each of these (and other phenomena) might show that speakers use these for distinct purposes.

4.5 Analysis

SPSS was used to examine the relationship between the flagging rate (dependent variable) and the social variables (independent variables) of the study. Descriptive and visualization tools were used to exclude outliers prior to statistical analysis. ANOVA and Pearson correlations were used to examine the relationship between flagging rate and categorical or else continuous independent variables, respectively. The probability value was set at $p<.05$. However, as this is an exploratory study, 'marginally significant' results, defined as $p<.10$, are also reported to give the reader a maximally informative overview of what factors may be influencing flagging rates. The researcher felt this to be important in that the current study reports on an infrequently-examined phenomenon (flagging) in an infrequently-approached way (intracommunity variation). Reporting results with $p<.10$ has also been done elsewhere to support the interpretation of the data where relevant and to give a reader as complete an understanding as possible of the phenomena at hand (e.g. Otheguy & Zentella, 2012, pp. 137–139). Further, reporting marginally significant factors does not weaken the significance of the principle and most significant findings of the current study and might be helpful in designing future studies. In other words, the choice to present 'marginally significant' findings was made in the service of comprehensiveness, illuminating statistically-significant results and suggesting additional avenues for investigation, and not for the purpose of inflating the results or the significance of the current study.

The reader will note that, in interpreting findings, special attention was given to entertaining proficiency-related explanations for specific results or patterns of results. This was done in order to counteract the researcher's bias against deficit-related interpretations of bilingual speech behavior. In other words, the researcher intentionally sought out and considered interpretations of the data that went against her current implicit bias against proficiency-related interpretations for flagging.

5. Results

5.1 Overview of flagging in the database

Table 1 provides an overview of the frequency of flagging in the corpus. Flagging counts from persons with outlying flagging rates are included in the table so as to provide an overview of flagging in the corpus as a whole.

Table 1. Words and flags uttered by New York City Spanish-speaking bilinguals in monolingual Spanish discourse in the corpus as a whole

	#	Average	Median	SD	% Of content words	% Of total words
flags ($n^{informants}$=115)	14,396	125	84	136	4.2	2.6
content words	336,407	2,925	2,834	1371	100	62
total words	546,535	4,752	4,556	2,257	–	100

Beginning with the last row of the table, it can be seen that the bilingual individuals of the corpus uttered 546,535 total words during their interviews, which included functional words like prepositions, determiners, etc., but did not include fillers like *uh* or *eh*. This total also includes any words that might have been uttered in English. The average length of an interview was about 4,700 words and the median length of the interviews was about 4,500 words. Although some interviews contained as few as 526 words and others as much as 13,546 words, the relative similarity of these measures of central tendency indicates a fairly normal distribution of interview lengths. That is, 50 percent of interviews were between 4,000 and 6,000 words. (76 percent were between 3,000 and 7,000 words.) Flagging rates for participants are, however, calculated over the number of content words they uttered. Table 1 shows that participants uttered over 336,000 content words in their interviews. This accounts for 62 percent of the total interview words uttered.

Moving to the top row, Table 1 shows that our bilinguals used 14,396 flagging elements. This amounts to a flagging rate of 4.2 percent for the corpus as a whole. If we calculated flagging over total words, both content and functional, that flagging rate would be lower: 2.6 percent. It will be noted that the standard deviation ($SD=136$) for the flagging count is large compared to the average number of flags across all interviews ($\bar{x}=125$). This likely reflects the facts that (i) flagging can be a highly individualized verbal behavior, being very frequent or infrequent depending on the affective state of the speaker (e.g. Kasl & Mahl, 1965) or the idiolect of the speaker (e.g. Maclay & Osgood, 1959) and (ii) the number of words in interviews varied greatly in some cases.

Table 2 provides the count of extended pauses, fillers and false starts. Pauses are further subdivided into those that occurred at constituent boundaries and those that did not. Those that did not occur at constituent boundaries are further subdivided into those that were followed by a repetition of the constituent with no change to the linguistic form and those pauses that were followed by a reformulation of the linguistic form(s) uttered prior to the pause.

Table 2. Types of flags used in Spanish discourse by OZC bilinguals

	Unfilled pauses			Fillers	Lexical false starts	Total count
	Constituent boundary	Mid-constituent				
		Restart-repetition	Restart-reformulate			
count	3,486	3,923	4,197	1,866	924	14,396
percent of category	30	34	36	100	100	–
percent of total count	24	27	29	13	6	100

Of the 14,396 flags used by 115 bilingual individuals, the vast majority were noticeable unfilled pauses, accounting for 80 percent (24% + 27% +29%) of the flags examined here. Another 13 percent were filler words (which may have occurred with a pause or not). Finally, six percent of the flags were lexical false starts in mid-articulation of a word. Returning to unfilled pauses, Table 2 shows that just under one-third (30%) of these occurred at a constituent boundary; about one-third (34%) occurred mid-constituent and involved a restart of the constituent using the same words just previously uttered. Slightly more than a third (36%) occurred at mid-constituent and involved a restart of speech with a reformulated message or linguistic form.

5.2 Sociodemographically-conditioned flagging

Several demographic variables were tested to examine their relationship to flagging frequency (see § 4.1). These variables were the independent variables according to which flagging rates, excluding outlying rates, were examined using both ANOVA and Pearson correlations. Of the 15 variables examined, only ethnonational affiliation reached significance at the $p<.05$ level. However, one other independent measure, daily Spanish use, is also reported because it reached a probability value of $p<.10$, which was the value set to indicate 'marginal significance'.[11]

The inclusion of 'marginally significant' results is motivated by the desire for a comprehensive view of flagging and to remain attuned to potentially significant predictors of this behavior, even if the predictor does not appear to be a primary determinant of flagging. Considering that p-values indicate the probability of making a Type I error — the error of obtaining a false positive — I consider that, in this exploratory study, reporting results that have just a 10 percent chance that observed differences are due to chance, rather than to real differences between groups (i.e. that the null hypothesis is true), is methodologically justified at this stage in the research.

Ethnonational affiliation significantly interacts with flagging rates ($F(106) = 5.49, p < .001$). Results are in Table 3.

Table 3. Monolingual flagging rates by ethnonational affiliation (outliers excluded)[†]

	Mean percent (%)	SD
Mexico ($n=20$)	1.7	0.8
Puerto Rico ($n=21$)	2.9	1.9
Dominican Republic ($n=17$)	3.8	3.1
Cuba ($n=13$)	4.6	3.6
Colombia ($n=17$)	4.9	3.4
Ecuador ($n=19$)	5.7	2.8
Total ($n=107$)	3.8	2.9
$F(106) = 5.49$	$p = .001$	

† There were eight individuals with outlying flagging rates, determined to be > 13%.

In Table 3, the average flagging rates for each ethnonational group are arranged from the lowest to the highest. Note, first, that the overall average flagging rate in this corpus, 3.8 percent, seems to be lower than the estimated rate of six percent 'disfluencies' across various studies of monolingual (English) speech

---

11. Other variables explored were not significant predictors of flagging: dialect area $F(106) = .034, p = .855$; region $F(106) = .377, p = .540$; sex $F(106) = .225, p = .637$; generation $F(106) = .352, p = .787$; social class $F(102) = .389, p = .679$; socioeconomic status $F(103) = .987, p = 402$; level of education $F(106) = .315, p = .814$; English skills $F(106) = 1.44, p = .241$; Spanish skills $F(105) = .863, p = .463$; Spanish use $F(106) = 3.116, p = .080$; age $F(106) = .440, p = .725$ and $r = .031, p = .751, n = 106$; age of arrival $F(106) = .409, p = .747$ and $r = -.054, p = .583, n = 107$; years in the U.S. $F(106) = .391, p = .760$ and $r = .162, p = .204, n = 63$; language dominance $F(105) = 2.34, p = .101$.

(Fox Tree, 1995).[12] Informants identifying as Mexican on average flag less often than others ($\bar{x}=1.7\%$), using just under two flags per 100 content words uttered (or 2 flags for every 120 content words uttered). Puerto Ricans use about 3 flags per 100 content words. Of all the ethnonational groups, Ecuadorians flag most often, using just under 6 flags per 100 content words.

In order to determine which of these ethnonational groups differs from others, a Tukey's post-hoc analysis was done (Table 4).

Table 4. Post hoc analysis of ethnonational affiliation for flagging

		Mean diff	p
Mexico	PR	−1.26	.664
	DR	−2.14	.164
	Cuba	−2.90	.037*
	Colombia	−3.20	.006*
	Ecuador	−4.00	< .001**
Ecuador	PR	2.73	.022*
	DR	1.85	.317
	Cuba	1.09	.868
	Colombia	0.79	.950
Colombia	PR	1.93	.247
	DR	1.06	.861
	Cuba	0.30	1.000
Cuba	PR	1.63	.525
	DR	0.75	.973
DR	PR	0.87	.918

Table 4 shows that Mexicans flag at rates that are statistically lower than Cubans, Colombians and Ecuadorians. Ecuadorians differ significantly from Puerto Ricans and Mexicans. In other words, the two stand-out groups in New York in terms of flagging rates are Ecuadorians who flag at rates that are much higher than average and Mexicans who flag at rates much lower than average and much lower than other ethnonational groups.

---

12. Fox Tree's (1995) estimated average rate across various studies does not include pauses, which are included in this study. She further notes that estimates can be as high as 26 percent, if pauses are included.

Several interpretations of this finding are possible. One is that flagging differences according to ethnonational group are in fact a reflection of processing and fluency differences that may covary with the ethnonational affiliation of speakers. It would be expected, thus, that Mexicans tend to be 'more fluent' in some way than Ecuadorians, or that the Ecuadorians of this corpus are in some way 'less fluent' than other groups. A chi-squared test was done to see if this was the case (Table 5).

Table 5. Cross-tabs of ethnonational affiliation and Spanish skills

	Passable	Good	Excellent
Mexico ($n=20$)	1	7	12
Puerto Rico ($n=21$)	2	5	13
Dominican Republic ($n=16$)	5	6	5
Colombia ($n=17$)	1	10	6
Cuba ($n=13$)	2	6	5
Ecuador ($n=19$)	2	11	6
Total ($n=105$)	13	45	47
$X^2=(10, n=105)=14.9$ $\quad p=.134$			

An initial look at the distribution of individuals in Table 5 seems to show a slight skewing. The majority of Mexicans ($n=12$) report 'excellent' Spanish skills as compared to Ecuadorians ($n=6$). Likewise, Puerto Rican speakers, with the next lowest flagging rate and from whom Mexicans do not differ significantly, are also skewed toward having more 'excellent' speakers among them in this sample ($n=13$). Despite this, results for the chi-squared analysis show these differences are not significant ($p=.134$). Further, if proficiency were an important determinant of flagging tendencies in this sample, it would be expected that the Spanish skills variable would have evidenced a significant correlation with flagging rate, which did not occur ($F(105)=.863, p=.463$). It appears then that proficiency-related explanations for different flagging rates by ethnonational group cannot be supported.

Although a conclusive interpretation for ethnonationally differentiated flagging rates, particularly for those that flag the least and the most, cannot be offered, some speculative explanations for this finding can be. The most obvious interpretation for this result might be that Mexicans and Puerto Ricans, on the one hand, and Ecuadorians, on the other, are using flags to indicate ethnonational identity or some personal attribute/aspect of identity with which these speakers relate ethnonational identity. For instance, it might be the case that flagging is associated with being thoughtful and careful while speaking and that this group of Ecuadorians desires to be distinguishable from others this basis. Or, it could be that flagging behaviors are seen as 'friendly' or indicating 'authenticity' and that Ecuadorians prioritize this value and attempt to convey it in conversation more than other. On the other hand, speakers might associate fewer flags with being intelligent or quick-witted. It may be the case that our Mexicans value such traits as a group and attempt to convey this through linguistic devices, such as flagging. All these interpretations, of course, are speculation. Additional evidence in the form of focus groups, perceptual studies or attitude studies could shed light on speaker interpretations of flagging behavior and if it is associated with particular ethnonational groups.

Alternatively, flagging might in fact be related to speech rate, itself a reflection of sociolinguistic norms for speaking of among different language and variety groups. For instance, there are perceptions in the U.S. that some groups, such as Puerto Ricans or Dominicans, speak Spanish faster than others. One can imagine that pauses and fillers would be fewer (and pause duration shorter) for Spanish varieties or ethnonational groups where speakers commonly articulate a greater number of syllables per minute (although see Borges Mota, 2003 for findings in L2 speech that may contradict this). If so, it might be the case that the speech rate of Ecuadorians or Mexicans in this study differs from others and that flagging is a behavior where this fact manifests. The relationship between flagging and speech rate can, of course, be explored in the future with data from the corpus.

Table 6 provides the results for flagging rates by tendencies to use Spanish on a daily basis, which was found to be a marginally significant predictor of flagging in monolingual speech ($p = .080$).

Table 6. Monolingual flagging rates by daily Spanish use (outliers excluded)[†]

	Mean percent (%)	SD
some ($n=53$)	3.3	1.4
more ($n=54$)	4.3	1.9
Total ($n=107$)	3.8	1.7
$F(106) = 3.11\ p < .080$		

[†] There were eight individuals with outlying flagging rates, determined to be > 13%.

Table 5 shows that, on average, those that use Spanish more or less on a daily basis differ in the extent to which they flag while speaking Spanish. Those that use Spanish most flag at higher rates (4.3 percent) than those that use Spanish less often (3.3 percent). If it were the case that flagging in this sample were indicative of disfluency, it would be tempting to interpret Spanish use as an indirect measure of a person's skills in Spanish or the extent to which Spanish is 'activated' for them (Grosjean, 1997). In this case, it would be expected that those that use Spanish less might experience delayed word recall more often than those that use Spanish more, and subsequently would flag more often. However, results are inverse of what would be expected if results for daily Spanish use were tapping into aspects of language processing or activation. This suggests that Spanish daily use is **not** a proxy for fluency. Although a data-driven reason for why those that use Spanish more often also flag more often cannot be offered here, it will be worth examining this marginal trend more closely. For instance, it may be that those that speak Spanish most feel less self-conscious about the form of their language production and therefore do not attempt to edit out fillers or false starts. Conversely, perhaps those that use Spanish less on a daily basis feel more self-conscious about the occurrence of these elements and therefore plan their messages more carefully before beginning to articulate a thought. Evidence for this explanation would be supported if, for instance, a study were to explore temporal differences in the use of pauses or the use of pauses at particular syntactic junctures. For instance, perhaps those that use less Spanish daily in fact tend to pause at constituent boundaries and for longer periods of time. Again, this interpretation is merely speculative, but offers avenues for a deeper understanding of how bilinguals deploy temporal elements of discourse in their languages and avenues for exploration in future studies.

Note that, of the predictors of flagging frequency uncovered in this study, neither immigrant generation ($p=.787$), nor English proficiency ($p=.241$) nor Spanish proficiency ($p<.463$) were significantly related to flagging. Further, it would have been reasonable to anticipate that, in this study of flagging in monolingual Spanish discourse, English-dominant individuals would use more of these 'monitoring and hesitation' phenomena in monolingual stretches of Spanish. However, results obtained showed that language dominance, or the difference between a speaker's proficiency rating in English and in Spanish, did not reach the established 'marginally-significant' p-value threshold ($p<.100$). However, the p-value for ANOVA analysis of language dominance was not far from the marginally-significant threshold ($p=.101$), it may be worth continuing to explore this variable in the future. Finally, while the use of pauses and fillers have elsewhere been found to vary with age and sex (e.g. Bortfeld *et al.*, 2001; Tottie, 2001), neither age ($p=.751$) nor sex ($p=.637$) were significant predictors of flagging behavior. This lack of correlation between overall flagging and age, on the one hand, and sex, on the other, is provocative. It may be that age- and sex/gender-correlated flagging involves one particular type of flag type (e.g. fillers) or occurs mainly at particular discourse junctures, such as the beginning of a turn (where fillers for this study were excluded). An additional study that breaks down flagging in terms of flagging type might be instructive. It might also be that the lack of results for age and sex indicate that bilinguals in 'other-language' majority contexts employ flagging elements differently than they would, say, in a Spanish-majority environment or differently than monolingual Spanish speakers would. A comparative study including variables like majority language context and type of Spanish-speaker (i.e. bilingual or monolingual) would help shed light on this.

6. Conclusions

6.1 Summary and discussion

The use of what may appear to be 'disfluent' elements in speech, such as pauses, fillers and false starts, has been shown to respond to a complex interplay of physiological, cognitive, affective, discursive, pragmatic and communicative factors in the speech of monolinguals. Investigation of these elements along sociolinguistic dimensions, as well as among bilinguals, has been lacking. This study attempts to remedy these investigative lacunae with a sociolinguistic examination of intra-group variation among bilingual Spanish-English speakers in New York City, whose hours of conversation provided a notably large corpus with which to conduct an investigation of this sort.

In particular, this study investigated the use of extended pauses, non-lexical fillers and lexical false starts (here considered hyponymic to the term 'flag') by bilinguals in monolingual speech (i) to determine whether these behaviors, often associated with linguistic processing and interpreted as indications of 'disfluency' for bilinguals, communicate or index social meaning and (ii) to obtain a more comprehensive understanding of flagging behavior. With respect to the first question, it was found that New York Spanish-English bilinguals flag during monolingual stretches of discourse in accordance with their ethnonational affiliation. Furthermore, daily Spanish may marginally influence flagging. The marginally significant results for daily Spanish use were such that those that use Spanish more actually flag more often. This result, while not reaching the statistically significant cut-off of $p < .05$, nonetheless provided insight into the functions that flagging might realize for bilinguals and suggests avenues for further investigation. Strikingly, it was found that Mexicans (and to some extent Puerto Ricans) tend to flag at statistically lower rates than several other groups. Ecuadorians flag most often, and significantly more often than Mexicans and Puerto Ricans. What is striking about these results is that ethnonational affiliation is the strongest predictor of flagging and that other attested predictive variables for the use of flagging elements among monolinguals, like age and sex, were not predictive in this study. The absence of effects in flagging that correlate with such variables suggests that there could be differences in the way that bilinguals manage these discourse elements in their two languages or in different majority language contexts.

With respect to the second question, results of this study generate lessons for understanding flagging behavior more generally. First, results herein support studies that show that the use of 'disfluency' phenomena can be both (a) an idiosyncratic behavior, as well as (b) reflective of community norms. That it can be an idiosyncratic behavior was reflected here in the large standard deviations within factor groups. High inter-speaker variability in the use of phenomena such as pauses and fillers has been observed by Maclay and Osgood (1959), Seliger (1980) and Raupauch (1980). On other hand, the fact that ethnonational identity was the main and only statistically significant predictor of flagging behaviors here suggests that apparently 'disruptive' elements of a discourse may be employed in accordance with variety- or community-sanctioned norms for their use. This finding is in line with studies demonstrating that aspects of these discourse phenomena vary regularly by speaker group or language community, such as vocalic quality of a filler (Candea, Vasilescu & Adda-Decker, 2005) or the type of filler 'permitted' in the language (e.g. *uh* or *um* in English compared to *este* in Spanish) (*cf.* Tottie, 2011, p. 176). Second, and importantly, the current study highlights a function of flagging behaviors that has not been widely explored for bilingual individuals in the past, particularly that flagging may in fact be a marker of (ethnolinguistic) identity within a larger bilingual linguistic community where dialect contact is present.

6.2 Implications

That flagging is not merely an indicator of processing difficulty or language proficiency when used by bilinguals, but (as found here) may be employed in sociodexical ways and in relation to ethnonational group has implications for bilingual speech research as well as teaching and learning. With respect to studies of bilingual discourse, it would be ideal to obtain a comprehensive picture of the contour of their use within any group before they are employed as diagnostics for classifying data (e.g. as 'codeswitches', 'borrowings' or as 'belonging to a language' or not; also see Varra, to appear). A flag **may** be used because something in language is difficult for the speaker, but they may also be used in ways that conform to sociocultural norms for a particular language group or for a particular ethnonational group (as well as any of the other discursive, pragmatic and listener-oriented ways mentioned in §3).

With respect to teaching and learning, insofar as some use of flags embody conscious decisions on the part of a speaker, and in light of the fact that some aspects of flagging (such as frequency, as seen here, or else type of filler employed as seen elsewhere, e.g. Candea, Vasilescu & Adda-Decker, 2005) are indicative of different varieties of Spanish, it would be instructive to not only gain a more nuanced understanding of which aspects of flagging are particular to certain varieties of Spanish, but also to inform learners of these tendencies (see e.g. Lindqvist, 2017).[13] In fact, in instructing learners that flags may be used intentionally and strategically to convey different messages, learners may be empowered to embrace these discourse elements purposefully, lending a greater sense of control and intentionality to their speaking.

6.3 Limitations and future studies

The current study was carried out using data from transcripts that faithfully represented normal breath-length pauses, extended pauses, fillers (e.g. *uh, ah, um, eh*) and lexical false starts, as well as other discursive behaviors such as repetitions (e.g. ...*se se se nota que yo soy el hijo de mi papa.* 427P) and reformulations (e.g ...*entonces cuando nos, cuando empezamos a vivir juntos hubo el choque.* 308M). However, pauses duration was not measured or accounted for in the transcriptions or at this stage of the research. The literature suggests that the length of pause may be associated with different motivations for its use. For instance, Goldman-Eisler (1972) uses a cut-off of 50 ms to distinguish between fluent transitions and hesitant transitions (such as might be related to message planning), although other studies use other cut-offs (see Zhang, 2020). A future study might take pause duration into consideration, examining whether and how it may be related to various functions, such as message planning, discourse organization or, as here, as a sociolinguistic marker among bilinguals. As mentioned earlier, a more detailed look at pausing in and of itself, given that they account for significant portions of the overall data, may help interpret trends found in the data (e.g. for daily Spanish use).

Furthermore, in this study, flags occurring in bilingual stretches of discourse or those occurring in positions known to have extant discourse-organization functions were explicitly excluded. It would also be instructive to carry out a detailed examination of all occurrences of pauses and fillers, alongside other phenomena such as discourse markers, repetitions, metalinguistic commentary and the like, in order to gain an in-depth understanding of the range of functions —

---

13. Lindqvist (2017), in examining metadiscourse markers used by L2 Spanish (including pauses, fillers, false starts, repetitions, reformulations and vowel lengthening), found that "learners who show the strongest development [in] fluency and conversational participation are also found to exhibit the most salient development of metadiscourse markers" (p. 1).

physiological, message planning, conversational organizing, pragmatic and social — that each of these phenomena play both in bilingual discourse modes and in monolingual discourse produced by bilinguals.

Funding

Otheguy-Zentella Corpus of Spanish in New York. (1999–2004). Developed under the direction of Ricardo Otheguy of the Graduate Center, CUNY and Ana Celia Zentella of the University of California at San Diego. Funded by the National Science Foundation, grant number 004133.

References

Baars, B. (1980). On the current understanding of temporal variables in speech. In H. W. Dechert & M. Raupach (Eds.), *Temporal Variables in Speech: Studies in Honour of Frieda Goldman-Eisler* (pp. 325–340). De Gruyter.

Ballmer, T. T. (1980). The role of pauses and suprasegmentals in a grammar. In H. W. Dechert & M. Raupach (Eds.), *Temporal Variables in Speech: Studies in Honour of Frieda Goldman-Eisler* (pp. 211–220). De Gruyter. http://ebookcentral.proquest.com/lib/cwm/detail.action?docID=929306.

Bilous, F. R., & Krauss, R. M. (1988). Dominance and accommodation in the conversational behaviours of same- and mixed-gender dyads. *Language and Communiction, 8*, 183–194.

Boomer, D. S. (1965). Hesitation and grammatical encoding. *Lang Speech, 8*(3), 148–58.

Borges Mota, M. (2003). Working memory capacity and fluency, accuracy, complexity and lexical density in L2 speech production. *Fragmentos, 24*, 69–104.

Bortfeld, H., Leon, S., Boom, J., Schober, M., & Brennan, S. (2001). Disfluency Rates in Conversation: Effects of Age, Relationship, Topic, Role, and Gender. *Language and Speech, 443*(32), 123–147.

Candea, M., Vasilescu, I., & Adda-Decker, M. (2005). Inter- and intra-linguistic acoustic analysis of autonomous fillers. *Proceedings of DiSS'05, Disfluency in Spontaneous Speech Workshop*, 47–51. http://www.isca-speech.org/archive

Chafe, W. (1980). *The pear stories.* Ablex.

Chapnik Smith, M. (1997). How do bilinguals access lexical information? In A. M. B. de Groot & J. Kroll (Eds.), *Tutorials in bilingualism: Psycholinguistic perspectives* (pp. 145–167). Lawrence Erlbaum Associates.

Clark, H. H., & Fox Tree, J. E. (2002). Using *uh* and *um* in spontaneous speaking. *Cognition, 84*, 73–111.

Clyne, M. (1997). Some things trilinguals do. *International Journal of Bilingualism, 1*(2), 95–116.

Clyne, M. (2003). *The dynamics of language contact.* Cambridge University Press.

Cook, V. J. (1980). Some neglected aspects of intonation. In H. W. Dechert & M. Raupach (Eds.), *Temporal Variables in Speech: Studies in Honour of Frieda Goldman-Eisler* (pp. 207–210). De Gruyter. http://ebookcentral.proquest.com/lib/cwm/detail.action?docID=929306.

Crible, L. (2018). *Discourse Markers And (Dis)fluency: Forms and Functions Across Languages and Registers*. John Benjamins Publishing Company. http://ebookcentral.proquest.com/lib/cwm/detail.action?docID=5291758.

Deschamps, A. (1980). The syntactical distribution of pauses in English spoken as a second language by French students." In H. W. Dechert & M. Raupach (Eds.), *Temporal Variables in Speech: Studies in Honour of Frieda Goldman-Eisler* (pp. 255–262). De Gruyter. http://ebookcentral.proquest.com/lib/cwm/detail.action?docID=929306.

Fox Tree, J. E. (1995). The effects of false starts and repetitions on the processing of subsequent words in spontaneous speech. *Journal of Memory and Language, 34,* 709–738.

Fox Tree, J. E. (2003). Disfluencies in Spoken Language. In L. Nadel (Ed.), *Encyclopedia of Cognitive Science* (Vol. 1, pp. 983–986). Nature Publishing Group.

Fruehwald, J. (2016). Filled Pause Choice as a Sociolinguistic Variable. *Selected Papers from New Ways of Analyzing Variation* (NWAV 44), 22(2), 41–49. [Also *University of Pennsylvania Working Papers in Linguistics*, 22(2), Article 6. https://repository.upenn.edu/pwpl/vol22/iss2/6.]

Gardner-Chloros, P., & Edwards, M. (2004). Assumption behind grammatical approaches to code-switching: When the blueprint is a red herring. *Transactions of the Philological Society, 102*(1). 103–129.

Gardner-Chloros, P., McEntee-Atalianis, L., & Paraskeva, M. (2013). Code-switching and pausing: An interdisciplinary study. *International Journal of Multilingualism, 10*(1), 1–26.

Goldman-Eisler, F. (1967). Sequential temporal patterns and cognitive processes in speech. *Lang Speech, 10*(2), 122–32.

Goldman-Eisler, F. (1972). Pauses, clauses and sentences. *Language and Speech, 15,* 103–113.

Grosjean, F. (1997). Processing mixed languages: Issues, findings and models. In A. M. B. de Groot & J. Kroll (Eds.), *Tutorials in bilingualism: Psycholinguistic perspectives* (pp. 225–254). Lawrence Erlbaum Associates.

Grosjean, J., & Deschamps, A. (1975). Analyse contrastive des variables temporelles de l'anglais et du français: Vitesse de parole et variables composantes, phénomènes d'hésitation. *Phonetica, 31,* 144–184.

Haugen, E. (1950). The analysis of linguistic borrowing. *Language, 26*(2), 210–231.

Heike, A. E. & O'Connell, D. C. (1983). The trouble with 'articulatory' pauses. *Language and Speech, 26*(3), 203–214.

Hlavac, J. (2011). Hesitation and monitoring phenomena in bilingual speech: A consequence of code-switching or a strategy to facilitate its incorporation. *Journal of Pragmatics, 43,* 3793–3806.

Jaffe, J. & Feldstein, S. (1970). *Rhythms of dialogue*. Academic Press.

Jaworski, A. (1993). *The Power of Silence. Social and Pragmatic Perspectives*. Sage Publications.

Kasl, S. V., & Mahl, G. F. (1965). The relationship of disturbances and hesitations in spontaneous speech to anxiety. *Journal of Personality and Social Psychology, 1*(5), 425–433.

Kroll, J. & de Groot, A. M. B. (1997). Lexical and conceptual memory in the bilingual: Mapping form to meaning in two languages. In A. M. B. de Groot & J. Kroll (Eds.), *Tutorials in bilingualism: Psycholinguistic perspectives* (pp. 169–199). Lawrence Erlbaum Associates.

Labov, W. (1966). *The social stratification of English in New York City*. Center for Applied Linguistics.

Labov, W. (2001). *Principles of linguistic change, volume 2: Social factors*. Blackwell.

Lennon, P. (1990). Investigating Fluency in EFL: A quantitative approach. *Language Learning, 40*(3), 387–417.

Levelt, W. (1989). *Speaking: From intention to articulation*. MIT Press.

Levinson, S. C. (2002). *Pragmatics*. [Cambridge Textbooks in Linguistics.] Cambridge University Press.

Lindqvist, H. (2017). Marcadores Metadiscursivos, fluidez y participación conversacional en español L2: La evolución de la competencia comunicativa durante la estancia en una comunidad de la lengua meta. [Doctoral dissertation, Stockholm University].

Lounsbury, F. G. (1954). Transitional probability, linguistic structure and systems of habit-family hierarchies. In C. E. Osgood & T. A. Sebeok (Eds.), *Psycholinguistics: A survey of theory and research problems* (pp. 93–101). Indiana University Press.

Maclay, H., & Osgood, C. E. (1959). Hesitation phenomena in spontaneous English speech. *Word, 15*, 19–44.

Muysken, Pieter. 2000. *Bilingual speech: A typology of code-mixing*. Cambridge University Press.

O'Connel, D. C., & S. Kowal. (1980). Prospectus for a science of pausology. In H. W. Dechert & M. Raupach (Eds.), *Temporal Variables in Speech: Studies in Honour of Frieda Goldman-Eisler* (pp. 3–12). De Gruyter. http://ebookcentral.proquest.com/lib/cwm/detail.action?docID=929306.

Olynik, M., D'Anglejan, A., & Sankoff, D. (1987). A quantitative and qualitative analysis of speech markers in the native and second language speech of bilinguals. *Applied Psycholinguistics, 8*, 121–136.

Otheguy-Zentella Corpus of Spanish in New York. (1999'2004). Developed under the direction of R. Otheguy of the Graduate Center, CUNY and A.C. Zentella of the University of California at San Diego. Funded by the National Science Foundation, grant number 004133.

Otheguy, R., & Zentella, A. C. (2012). *Spanish in New York: Language Contact, Dialectal Leveling, and Structural Continuity*. [Oxford Studies in Sociolinguistics.] Oxford University Press.

Pfaff, C. (1979). Constraints on language mixing: Intrasentential code-switching and borrowing in Spanish/English. *Language, 55*(2), 291–318.

Poplack, S. (1985). Contrasting patterns of code-switching in two communities. *Papers from the 5th International Conference on Methods in Dialectology, University of Victoria (BC)*. http://hdl.handle.net/10315/6618

Poplack, S., Sankoff, D., & Miller, C. (1988). The social correlates and linguistic consequences of lexical borrowing and assimilation. *Linguistics, 26*, 47–104.

Poplack, S., Wheeler, S., & Westwood, A. (1987). Distinguishing language-contact phenomena: Evidence from Finnish-English bilingualism. In P. Lilius & M. Saari (Eds.), *The Nordic Languages and Modern Linguistics, 6* (pp. 33–56). (*Proceedings of the Sixth International Conference of Nordic and General Linguistics in Helsinki, 1986 August 18'22*.) Helsinki University Press. [Also: (1989). *World Englishes, 8*(3), 389–406.]

Poplack, S. (1987). Contrasting patterns of code-switching in two communities. In E. Wande, J. Anward, B. Nordberg, L. Steensland, & M. Thelander (Eds.), *Aspects of Multilingualism* (pp. 51–77). Borgströms.

Poulisse, N. (1997). Language production in bilinguals." In A. M. B. de Groot & J. Kroll (Eds.), *Tutorials in bilingualism: Psycholinguistic perspectives* (pp. 201–224). Lawrence Erlbaum Associates.

Raupach, M. (1980). Cross-linguistic descriptions of speech performance as a contribution to 'Contrastive Linguistics'. In H. W. Dechert & M. Raupach (Eds.), *Towards a cross-linguistic assessment of speech production* (pp. 9–22). Lang.

Repede, D. (2002). Estudio sociopragmático de los mecanismos atenuadores en el corpus oral PRESEEA-Sevilla. *Círculo de Lingüística Aplicada a la Comunicación (CLAC)*, 92, 153–166.

Rosignoli, A. (2011). Flagging in English-Italian code-switching. [Doctoral dissertation, Bangor University.]

Seliger, H. W. (1980). Utterance planning and correction behavior: its function in the grammar construction process for second language learners. In H. W. Dechert & M. Raupach (Eds.) *Towards a cross-linguistic assessment of speech production* (pp. 87–99). Lang.

Shriberg, E. (2001). To 'errr' is human: ecology and acoustics of speech disfluencies. *Journal of the International Phonetic Association*, 31(1), 153–169.

Stenström, A.-B. (2011). Pauses and hesitations." In G. Andersen & K. Aijmer (Eds.), *Pragmatics of Society* (pp. 537–567). De Gruyter Mouton.

Tannen, D. (1984). *Conversational Style. Analyzing Talk among Friends*. Ablex Press.

Temple, L. (1992). Disfluencies in learner speech. *Australian Review of Applied Linguistics*, 15, 29–44.

Teschner, R. V. (1972). Anglicism in Spanish: A cross-referenced guide to previous findings, together with English lexical influence on Chicago Mexican Spanish. [Doctoral dissertation, University of Wisconsin, Madison.]

Toribio, A. J. (2001). Accessing bilingual code-switching competence. *International Journal of Bilingualism*, 5(4), 403–436.

Tottie, G. (2011). *Uh* and *um* as sociolinguistic markers in British English. *International Journal of Corpus Linguistics*, 16(2), 173–197.

Van Der Wege, M. M., & Ragatz, E. C. (2004). Learning To Be Fluently Disfluent. *Proceedings of the Annual Meeting of the Cognitive Science Society*, 26(26), 1647.

Varra, R. (2018). *Lexical borrowing and deborrowing in Spanish in New York City: Towards a synthesis of the social correlates of lexical use and diffusion in immigrant contexts*. Routledge.

Varra, R. (2020). "Conversational recasting in New York City: Making Global Processes Local. In Andrew Lynch (Ed.), *Spanish in the Global City* (pp. 105–137). Routledge.

Varra, R. (to appear). 'Disfluency' features in bilingual speech: Meaning and methodology. *Studies in Hispanic and Lusophone Linguistics*.

Wiese, R. (1984). Language production in foreign and native languages: same of different? In H. W. Dechert, D. Möhle, & M. Raupach (Eds.), *Second language production* (pp. 11–25). Gunter Narr.

Wray, A. (2002). *Formulaic language and the lexicon*. Cambridge University Press.

Zentella, A.C. (1997). *Growing up Bilingual: Puerto Rican Children in New York*. Blackwell Publishers.

Zhang, H. (2020). The distribution of disfluencies in spontaneous speech: empirical observations and theoretical implications. [Doctoral dissertation, University of Pennsylvania.]

Appendix A. Sociodemographic characteristics of the sample

Ethnonational affiliation was determined by (a) place of birth if an informant was born outside of the U.S. or (b) if the informant was U.S.-born, self-identification with one of six Spanish-speaking nations.

	n
Colombia	18
Ecuador	19
Mexico	21
Dominican Republic	19
Puerto Rico	21
Cuba	17

Region refers to whether an informant's ethonational affiliation is based in the Caribbean ($n=60$) or the Latin American mainland ($n=55$).

Areal is whether the informant comes from an inland or coastal region.

	n
Lowlands or coast	71
Highlands or interior	46

Sex means biological sex.

	n
Male	59
Female	56

Age is the age of the informant at the time of the interview.

	n
Teens (from 13–19 inclusive)	15
Young adults (from 20–39 inclusive)	77
Middle-age adults (from 40–59 inclusive)	20
60 plus-ers (age 60 and above)	3

Age of arrival is the age at which the informant came to the United States. Other groupings of this variable were looked at, but this division resulted in the most significant correlations with lexical transfer behavior.

	n
U.S.-born	29
U.S.-born or arrive ≤ age 3	
Child arrivals	19
arrived from ages 4 to 12	
Teenager	25
arrived from age 13–19	
Older arrivals	42
arrived ≥ age 20	

Years in the U.S. refers to the amount of time the informant had spent in the United States up to the time of the interview.

	n
15 years or less	54
Recent (0–2 years in U.S.) [12]	
Long (3–15 years in U.S. [42]	
Over 15 years + Native	61
16 years+ [23]	
Native (any 5 of first 8 years of education in U.S.) [38]	

Social Class means self-ascribed social class.

	n
Middle (+High)	70
Working	41
Unknown	4

Socioeconomic status (SES) was a classification of informants based on the more objective criteria of occupation and income: *level A*, the highest rating ($n=1$), *level B* ($n=35$), *level C* ($n=53$), *level D* ($n=22$) and unknown ($n=4$).

Level of education was determined by the highest level of education attended, though not necessarily completed.

	n
Elementary school	4
High school	35
College	54
Graduate	21
not disclosed	1

English skills is a qualitative self-assessment of an informant's ability in English. Informants rated their English according to a four-point descriptive scale, later condensed into two.

	n
Non-excellent	68
Poor [1]	
Passable [33]	
Good [34]	
Excellent	46
unrated	1

Spanish skills is a qualitative self-assessment of an informant's ability in Spanish using the same four-point descriptive scale.

	n
Non-excellent	63
Poor [2]	
Passable [15]	
'Good' [46]	
Excellent	51
unrated	1

Language dominance is a condensation of the Spanish skills minus English skills composite.

	n
Balanced	36
Spanish dominant	44
English dominant	32

Spanish use in general

	n
None	13
Low	43
Mid	41
High	17
undisclosed	1

CHAPTER 3

El code-switching is hitting la aldea
Evidence from Loíza, Puerto Rico

Piero Visconte
The University of Texas at Austin

As a result of the United States' acquisition of Puerto Rico in 1898, there have been extensive economic and cultural exchanges between the two countries (Orama-López, 2012), alongside decades of language disputes driven by political purposes (Millán, 2012). This persistent linguistic contact situation has encouraged the study of code-switching (CS), a phenomenon widely examined from the perspective of its social determinants (Myers-Scotton, 2002; Gardner-Chloros, 2009). There have been several sociolinguistic studies conducted in Puerto Rican diasporas in the United States over the past decades (Torres, 1997, 2002; Flores-Ferrán, 2014; etc.); nevertheless, CS has received relatively little attention within the island (Dupey, 2012; Guzzardo et al., 2019; Acosta-Santiago, 2020). The present paper examines CS in Loíza, an isolated Afro-Hispanic community (Rivera-Rideau, 2015) where English is increasing its presence. The focus is on the category of bilingual discourse markers (DMs) (*so/entonces, you know/tú sabes, like/como que, etc.*), which are ubiquitous in the colloquial speech of Puerto Ricans (Flores-Ferrán, 2014). Data were collected in Loíza through semi-directed sociolinguistic interviews and analyzed within the framework of Variational Pragmatics (Schneider & Barron, 2008) to examine patterns of variation in the use of DMs, as well as to determine the social variables that trigger CS. Findings show evidence of how English, after 127 years of presence on the island, is spreading even in rural communities such as Loíza. Nonetheless, Spanish remains overwhelmingly the language of life and everyday affairs among all members of Puerto Rican society (Denton, 2014).

Keywords: code-switching, discourse markers, Loíza, Puerto Rico

1. Introduction

In the Puerto Rican context, code-switching (CS) is particularly significant as it reflects the complex linguistic and cultural history of the island. Since the United States acquired Puerto Rico in 1898, economic and cultural exchanges between the two countries have been evident in the alternation of Spanish and English within conversations and speech (Negrón-de Montilla, 1990; Pousada, 1999; Orama-López, 2012). At the same time, decades of politically-motivated language struggles followed (Academia Puertorriqueña de la Lengua Española, 2000; Kerkhof, 2001; Millán, 2012): on the one hand, the United States' attempt to impose English in Puerto Rico "as part of a heavy-handed Americanization plan" (Pousada, 1996, p. 499); on the other hand, the maintenance of Spanish as a symbol of Puerto Rican identity in contrast to the prolonged US military and economic intervention (Sepúlveda Muñoz, 1993).

Puerto Ricans constantly experience a large amount of information in English (through television, highway billboards, supermarkets, even in some textbooks, etc.) (Barreto, 2001), which would suggest a deep and prolonged situation of linguistic contact. Nonetheless, according to recent US Census data (2021), Spanish remains the native and primary language for the majority of Puerto Ricans (94%), with English as a secondary language (5.5%). Furthermore, fewer than 25% of Puerto Ricans reported speaking English "very well," and 96% of the population indicated that they use Spanish daily. Therefore, the persistance of Puerto Rico's predominately monolingual society should be analyzed beyond issues of identity and resistance. Pousada (2000), for example, highlighted the inadequate English teacher preparation, a situation exacerbated by socioeconomic disparities that split the Puerto Rican society and frequently make young Puerto Ricans' English proficiency dependent on their educational institutions.

This linguistic coexistence invites scholarly attention to CS, which has been extensively studied concerning its social determinants (Sankoff & Poplack, 1981; Swigart, 1994; Myers-Scotton, 2002; Gardner-Chloros, 2009). A comprehensive definition of CS has been proposed by many authors:

> Codeswitching is the use of words and structures from more than one language or linguistic variety by the same speaker within the same speech situation, conversation or utterance. Conversational codeswitching refers to the use of two languages by the same speaker within the same speech event. Codeswitching may occur at inter- and intrasentential levels and may consist of single words or phrases.
> (Callahan, 2004, p. 5)

> Code-switching will be referred to as single-word borrowings that have not been adapted to the language, phrasal-level utterances and sentence-level utterances which changes the original language to the other will also be regarded as code-switching. [...] Intrasentential code-switching takes place by introducing a word or a phrase in a different language than is being spoken. Intersentential code-switching is ending a sentence in one language and resuming the other sentence in another language (possibly going back to the other language in the next sentence) (Acosta-Santiago, 2020, p. 4)

With this broad descriptive definition, Callahan summarizes under the same category several phenomena that are classified individually by other scholars: for instance, Muysken (2000) clearly distinguishes between *code-mixing* (alternation within the same sentence) and *code-switching* (inter-sentential alternation). Other linguists have sought to distinguish between single word insertions as CS or established borrowings (Hadei, 2016 for an overview). To close the circle, Callahan's definition even encompasses *translanguaging*, term aimed to the conceptualization of bilinguals' two languages as clearly distinct systems normally deployed separately, pointing instead to their possible implementation in alternating, closed succession under a practice known as CS (Otheguy et al., 2015).

CS is a widespread phenomenon in the speech of bilinguals, who alternate their codes in their verbal interactions with specific pragmatic purposes for communication (Silva-Corvalán, 2001; F. Gimeno-Menéndez & M.V. Gimeno-Menéndez, 2003; Klee & Lynch, 2009). Scholars have long argued that language mixing is not random or indicative of lack of linguistic proficiency, but it follows systematic patterns. (Timm, 1975; Poplack, 1980). In this regard, Bullock and Toribio (2009, p. 1) state:

> Broadly defined, C[ode] S[witching] is the ability on the part of bilinguals to alternate effortlessly between their two languages. This capacity is truly remarkable and invites scientific and scholarly analysis from professionals, but, at the same time, generates a great deal of pointed discussion that reflect popular misperceptions of the nature of CS in particular and bilinguals more generally. While CS is viewed as an index of bilingual proficiency among linguists, it is more commonly perceived by the general public as indicative of language degeneration.

1.1 Research questions and objectives

Within the enduring situation of linguistic contact that characterizes Puerto Rico, the category of bilingual DMs (*so, entonces, you know, tú sabes, like, como que, etc.*) has garnered increasing attention in discourse analysis. While several sociolinguistic works have been conducted in the Puerto Rican diaspora in the United States over last forty years (Poplack, 1980; Torres, 1997, 2002; Pousada, 1999;

Lipski, 2005; Flores-Ferrán, 2014; etc.), relatively few have examined CS on the Caribbean island (Dupey, 2012; Guzzardo et al., 2019; Acosta-Santiago, 2020).

The present paper examines CS in Loíza, an Afro-Hispanic community (Rivera-Rideau, 2015) where English usage is increasing. Specifically, it focuses on bilingual DMs, which are ubiquitous in the colloquial speech of *boricuas*[1] (Jiménez & Flores-Ferrán, 2018) — as in (1):

(1) *If she catches me,* ***tú sabes****, acaba conmigo.* ***Like****, she's gonna kill me!*
    If she catches me, **you know**, she will finish me. **Like**, she's gonna kill me!

Focusing on a specific speech community, the main objectives of this work can be addressed through the following research questions (RQs):

RQ1: Which DMs are most likely to trigger CS (from Spanish to English or vice versa) in contexts of oral interaction in Spanish?

RQ2: How do extralinguistic variables (e.g., gender, age, level of education of the participants and degree of formality of the linguistic environment) influence the use of bilingual DMs among Loíza speakers?

RQ3: To what extent is the effect of linguistic contact between Spanish and English in Puerto Rico evident in the presence or absence of monolingual versus bilingual DMs?

The chapter is structured as follows: Section 2 reviews relevant literature on CS and DMs. Section 3 outlines study methodology, data and participants. Section 4 presents the results. Section 5 answers the research questions. Finally, Section 6 summarizes the main findings and provides the concluding remarks.

2. Background literature

Studies related to CS includes spontaneous speech (Auer, 1998; Zentella, 1982, 1997), sociolinguistic interviews (García, 2009), as well as oral narratives (Álvarez, 1991), stories (Toribio, 2000), and literary texts (Torres, 2007; Díaz, 2012). Over the past four decades, this linguistic phenomenon has been approached from different perspectives, including structuralist (Timm, 1975; Poplack, 1980) and generativist methodologies (D'Introno, 1996; Toribio & Rubin, 1996), as well as the Matrix Language Frame theory (Myers-Scotton, 1993; Callahan, 2002 and, 2004). Additionally, some studies have also approached CS from psycholinguistic (Bullock & Toribio, 2009) and pedagogical perspectives (Carvalho, 2012).

---

1. Puerto Ricans.

Concerning DMs, these spontaneous linguistic expressions constitute a heterogeneous class of generally invariable words or expressions that are "syntactically and semantically independent of the surrounding discourse" (Travis, 2006, p. 224). Likewise, they represent much more than simple morphemes, trespassing into the category of markers, connectors, particles, discursive signals, and of which almost all languages have a wide repertoire (Garachana-Camarero & Artigas, 2012). The growing academic interest in this topic has made it difficult to establish a universal definition (Rivas & Brown, 2009). However, the most commonly used terms are *discourse markers* (Schiffrin, 1987; Jucker & Ziv, 1998) and *pragmatic markers* (Brinton, 1996), with the latter preferred when markers primarily serve a pragmatic rather than a structural function in discourse. In addition, two other terms are worth mentioning: *discourse particle* (Hansen, 1998; Aijmer, 2002) and *pragmatic particle* (Östman, 1995), whose alternation is based on the difference between a *marker*, "a (larger) signpost instructing the hearer how the message should be interpreted", and a *particle*, "a well-established (short) grammatical term for a part-of-speech" (Andersen & Fretheim, 2000, p. 1).

In contexts of interaction, some scholars have emphasized that DMs are essential not only for linking expressions and sentences but also for "indicating something about the attitude of the speaker regarding the content of the message and the recipient" (Travis, 2006, p. 224). Other proposals have explored the role of DMs in guiding listeners to make correct deductions (Acín Villa, 2000; Martín-Zorraquino & Portolés-Lázaro, 1999). In this regard, DMs have been also defined as "windows through which one can make deductions about the speaker's attitudes and opinions" (Östman, 1995, p. 100).

A substantial body of research on linguistic contact has identified significant correlations between the use of DMs and various linguistic and extralinguistic variables (Sankoff et al., 1997; Torres, 2002). The presence of DMs in bilingual speech has also been explored across different varieties and language pairs (see Aaron, 2004 for details).

As for Puerto Ricans, being one of the oldest Spanish-speaking diasporic groups in the New York area (Henríquez-Ureña, 1921), Spanish-English contact have often been studied (Poplack, 1980; Torres, 1997, 2002; Pousada, 1999; Lipski, 2005; Flores-Ferrán, 2014). Poplack (1980) suggested that the cosmopolitan environment of New York City may have played a fundamental role in the frequency of bilingual DMs in Spanish conversations. Meanwhile, Torres (2002) argued that the constant overlap of bilingual DMs in Spanish conversations could be considered as a typical characteristic of this diasporic variety of Puerto Rican Spanish, often referred to as *nuyorriqueño* (Duany, 2000). According to Duany (2018, p. 2), this term captures "the hybrid identities of Puerto Rican migrants" who "imply a basic geographic, linguistic, and cultural split between Puerto Ricans living on the island and in the United States".

Most research has focused almost exclusively on *nuyorriqueño*, reaffirming the distinctive socio-historical ties between the Caribbean island and the American metropolis, a topic that remains a subject of debate (Torres, 2002). However, these studies lack the autochthonous context of the analyzed participants, that is, the archipelago of Puerto Rico itself. The present paper shifts the geographic focus of analysis to Puerto Rico, specifically to the Afro-Hispanic community of Loíza, to examine the effect of language contact in the context of oral interaction, particularly within the category of DMs.

3. Methodology

It is a well-known fact that language use (pragmatics) varies under the influence of socio-cultural factors, including contextual elements, such as the relationship between participants in an interaction, as well as identity-related factors (García, 2008).

The present study is based on Schneider and Barron's (2008) model of *Variational Pragmatics*, a new field at the interface of pragmatics and sociolinguistics (or, more specifically, dialectology) that systematically investigate the effect of pragmatic variation on language in action (Schneider & Barron, 2008).[2] This framework allows for the examination of the patterns of variation in the use of DMs, as well as determining the social variables that trigger CS.

The main goal of Variational Pragmatics is to determine and examine how macro-social factors (e.g., region, social class, ethnicity, gender, and age) influence language in interaction (Barron, 2005). Subsequently, it analyzes the interplay between macro-social and micro-social factors (e.g., power, distance, and other situational factors), distinguishing between individual speakers and subcategories of speakers (Schneider & Barron, 2008). Ultimately, it considers other factors, such as discourse style, community of practice, and levels of formality.

The study of pragmatic variation dates back to the late 1970s and early 1980s, initially focusing on cross-linguistic pragmatic differences rather than variation within a single language (García, 2008). Later, attention shifted towards pragmatic variation within varieties of the same language (Clyne, 1992; Wolfram, 1998),

---

2. As stated in Schneider and Barron (2008), the first time the term "*Variational Pragmatics*" was presented as a new discipline was in 2005, at the 9th International Pragmatics Conference held in Riva del Garda, Italy, titled "*Variational pragmatics: Cross-cultural approaches*". The focus of this panel was on regional variation on the national and sub- national level.

while more recent proposals have carried out research on pragmatic variation both in L1-L2 interaction contexts (Félix-Brasdefer & Koike, 2012) and among native speakers of the same language (Wolfram & Schilling-Estes, 2006). In this regard, Spanish has become the language with the most research on the pragmatic variation of its regional varieties (Félix-Brasdefer, 2008), as reported by Placencia's (2012, pp. 87–88) chronological overview (Table 1).

Variational Pragmatics is one of the sub-disciplines of *Intercultural Pragmatics*, a broad category which investigates intra-linguistic differences, that is, speakers who share the same native language but not necessarily the same culture. Since language use is shaped by cultural values, speakers of the same language may exhibit both pragmatic similarities and significant differences across regional varieties of the same language (Schneider & Barron, 2008). This is the case of Puerto Rico, where Spanish and English share the linguistic landscape of the U.S. territory, despite relatively low levels of bilingualism (Pousada, 1999).[3]

Table 1. Studies on regional pragmatic variation in Spanish (Placencia, 2012: 87–88)*

Author(s)	Year	Focus	AS	ChS	DoS	ES	MxS	PnS	PvS	UrS	USS	VS
Placencia	1994	Telephone management requests				✓		✓				
Fant	1996	Turn delivery and turn-taking features in business negotiation					✓	✓				
Puga Larraín	1997	Mitigation	✓					✓				
Bravo	1998	Laughter in business negotiation					✓	✓				
Cured	1998	Requests & mitigation					✓	✓				
Placencia	1998	Requests in service encounters				✓		✓				
Puga Larraín	1999	Mitigation	✓					✓				
Wagner	1999	Apologies					✓	✓				
Grindsted	2000	Markers of social proximity/distance					✓	✓				
De los Heros	2001	Compliments								2 subvars.		

---

3. In 1898, Puerto Rico ceased to be a Spanish colony and came under the control of the United States, but only with the establishment of the *Estado Libre Asociado (ELA)* in 1952 English and Spanish were recognized as co-official languages for the first time (Orama-López, 2012).

Table 1. *(continued)*

Author(s)	Year	Focus	AS	ChS	DoS	ES	MxS	PnS	PvS	UrS	USS	VS
Hardin	2001	Pragmatic features of television commercials	✓				✓			✓		
Cureó & de Fina	2002	Requests & mitigation					✓	✓				
Márquez Reiter	2002	Requests in various situations					✓			✓		
Márquez Reiter	2003	Requests in various situations					✓			✓		
García	2004	Reprimands & responses							✓			✓
Márquez Reiter & Placencia	2004	Openings & closings of service encounters: selling strategies				✓			✓			
Placencia	2005	Requests in service encounters				✓	✓					
Alba Juez	2008	Impolite actions	✓				✓					
Albelda Marco	2008	Mitigation in youth talk	✓				✓					
Félix-Brasdefer	2008a	Refusals to various directives			✓		✓					
Félix-Brasdefer	2008b	Requests			✓		✓					
Garcés-Conejos Blitvich & Bou Franch	2008	Internet-based service encounters					✓			✓		
García	2008	Invitations	✓									✓
Jorgensen	2008	Discourse markers in youth talk	✓				✓					
Martínez Camino	2008	Television advertising				✓	✓					
Placencia	2008	Requests: small talk in service encounters				2 subvars.						
García	2009	Reprimands	✓						✓			✓

* AS = Argentinian Spanish; ChS = Chilean Spanish; DoS = Dominican Spanish; ES = Peninsular Spanish; MxS = Mexican Spanish; PnS = Paraguayan Spanish; PvS = Peruvian Spanish; UrS = Uruguayan Spanish; VS = Venezuelan Spanish.

This study focuses on the social factors influencing language choice, particularly in the use of DMs. A novel aspect of this research is its analysis of the linguistic and social variables of Puerto Ricans residing in Puerto Rico within the theoretical framework of Variational Pragmatics. This framework emphasizes that regional variation is a particular type of social variation in which regional relationships and identities are reflected in language use (García, 2008).

3.1 Data collection procedure

Labov (1972) posits that approaching research topics from a variety of aspects is what provides a unique and multidisciplinary perspective, taking into account the evolution of modern sociolinguistics and its ongoing search for the optimal sort of data or method for linguistic study. This study follows a Labovian approach by collecting data on language use in a specific setting. As a result, information about the speakers' traits and linguistic relationships can be learned through interviews. Additionally, sociolinguistic interviews were conducted to gather insights into speakers' linguistic behaviors, attitudes, and intuitions (Cornips & Poletto, 2005).

Twelve Afro-Puerto Rican participants (six men and six women), 22 to 78, as seen in Table 2 and educational background (from illiterate to speakers with a college degree), took part in Spanish-language sociolinguistic interviews (Table 2). All the informants were life-long residents of Loíza, a marginalized community located east of San Juan.

Table 2. Study participants (gender, age, and educational level)

	Younger speakers			Older speakers	
	Age	Education		Age	Education
M1	22	BA*	M4	44	High School
F1	22	BA*	F4	48	High School
M2	24	BA*	M5	55	High School
F2	25	MA*	F5	58	High School**
M3	26	BA*	M6	78	High School**
F3	28	MA*	F6	65	High School

* in progress ** not completed

The interviews were conducted during 2019 and 2020 in Loíza in informal settings such as bars, houses, and parks to measure the Spanish-English variation of DMs in L1 Spanish speakers from Loíza in contexts of oral interaction. The interviews followed Labov's (1984) "Principle of Tangential Shift" (p. 37) in a network of topics[4] that first raised less-personal questions for the informants and then gradually delved deeper into more intimate and sensitive topics. In this way, minimum attention will be paid to speech (Labov, 1972) while the impact of extralinguistic elements on oral interaction situations is measured.

As a result, the research succesfully mitigated Labov's "Observer Paradox", which states that "to obtain the most important data for linguistic theory, we have to observe how people speak when they are not being observed" (1972, p. 113).

The collected data consists of roughly six hours of recording conversations between individual informants and the interviewer, and took place in quiet environments with visible recording equipment to ensure high-quality data while maintaining speech patterns.

4. Results and discussion

This section illustrates the results of the data extracted from the sociolinguistic interviews conducted with Loíza speakers and is developed into main parts. First, the total number of discourse markers (DMs) in both languages is presented. Second, the frequency of DMs that trigger code-switching (CS) is analyzed, highlighting the five most commonly used markers and examining the influence of gender, age, and education. Third, a linguistic analysis of the most frequent DMs is provided.

The total number of English and Spanish DMs extracted from the twelve interviews amounts to 174 tokens, with female participants using slightly more DMs than males (respectively 92 vs. 82, for a total percentage of 53% vs. 47%). Notably bilingual DMs were produced only by younger speakers who have already obtained or are in process of obtaining their college degree. This finding supports the view that Puerto Rico is still *un territorio monolingüe hispanohablante* ('a monolingual Spanish-speaking territory') (Meléndez, 1993, pp. 9–10) and that Puerto Ricans perceive their mother tongue as a reflection of their national identity (Zentella, 1990). In this regard, Acosta-Santiago (2020) reported an anonymous excerpt from her interviews:

> *Odio tener que hablar inglés. Es el idioma que estos gringos[5] le imponen al mundo; mientras que paises tienen que aprenderlo, ellos ni se molestan en aprender lo básico del español, francés o chino. Simplemente me niego a hablarlo y solo lo estu-*

---

4. The most common topics include family, work, African heritage in Puerto Rico, Puerto Rican traditions, catastrophic natural events that have affected the region, local festivals, sports, food, etc.

5. English-speaking Anglo-Americans.

dio por los cursos en la iupi. Yo hablo españoool no engrishh. Ese es el idioma de mi patria. ('I hate having to speak English. It's the language that those gringos impose to the world; while other countries have to learn it, they don't bother learning the basics of Spanish, French or Chinese. Simply put, I refuse to speak it and I only study because of the iupi (University of Puerto Rico-Río Piedras campus) courses. I speak Spaniiish not Engrishh. That is the language of my country.')

Of the 174 DMs extracted from the Loíza corpus, 108 result in the five most frequent ones (Table 3): *tú sabes* (2a–b), *pues* (3), *so* (4a–b), *like* (5a–b), and *como que* (6a–b):

Table 3. Top 5 most used DMs (*n* = 108)

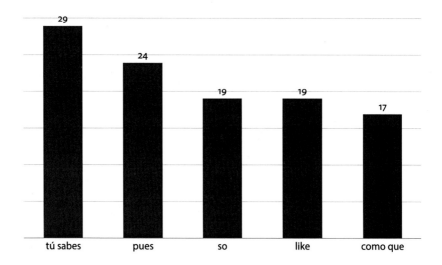

(2) a. *I'm in, **tú sabes**, a mí me encantan estas cosas!*
    (Spanish DM triggering CS) (M2)
    I'am in, **you know**, I love these things!
  b. *El trabajo, **tú sabes**, tengo a un nieto que criar.*
    (Spanish DM not triggering CS) (F4)
    Work, **you know**, I have a grandson to raise.

(3) *La verdad es que, **pues**, nadie me ha ayudado a mí.*
    (Spanish DM not triggering CS) (F3)
    The truth is that, **well**, nobody has helped me.

(4) a. *Hablo de más, **so** feel free to interrupt me.*
    (English DM triggering CS) (M3)
    I talk too much, **so** feel free to interrupt me.

b. *Le dije: "te fuiste, **so** ahora bregas con eso!"*
(English DM not triggering CS) (F3)
I told him: "you left, **so** now you deal with it!"

(5) a. *Me casaría mañana mismo, **like**, I love him.*
(English DM triggering CS) (F2)
I would get married tomorrow, like, I love him!
b. *Y yo **like**, no me lo podía creer.* (English DM not triggering CS) (F1)
And I, **like**, I couldn't believe it.

(6) a. *Y yo dije: "Esa jugada **como que** te salió mal.*
(Spanish DM triggering CS) (M3)
And I said: "It looks **like** this play went wrong".
b. *Eso me tiene **como que** sick and tired.*
(Spanish DM not triggering CS) (M1)
That got me **like** sick and tired.

Within these 108 tokens, 43 triggered CS from one language to another, accounting for 40% of occurrences (Table 4). Interestingly, *pues* never triggered CS and was thus excluded from further analysis. Conversely, *tú sabes*, the most common DM among the twelve participants, was also the least likely to switch to English (2a–b). Additionally, older speakers did not switch from Spanish to English at all, suggesting that lower educational attainment or reduced exposure to English may be influencing this behavior.

Table 4. DMs triggering CS (from Spanish to English and vice versa)

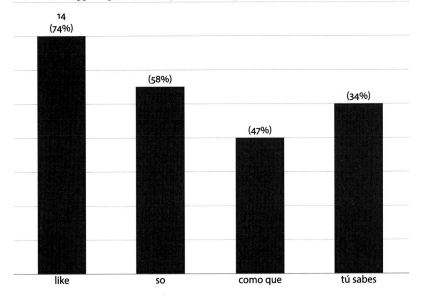

Table 3 and Table 4 can be summarized as follows:

TOP 5 MOST USED DMs (by all participants)	DMs TRIGGERING CS
tú sabes (29)	*like* (74%)
pues (24)	*so* (58%)
so (19)	*como que* (47%)
like (19)	*tú sabes* (34%)
como que (17)	*pues* (0%)

Regarding gender, the findings indicate that this variable plays a role in CS. Female participants code-switched more frequently than male speakers: of the total of 43 DMs triggering CS, 27 (63%) were produced by female speakers, while only 16 (37%) were produced by males.

Concerning age and education, this study proposes that CS is typical of younger speakers, who accounted for 100% of the occurrences in this dataset. The same six young speakers engaged in CS were also those who have obtained or were obtaining their university degree, reinforcing education as a significant variable in this phenomenon.

The following part of this section offers a linguistic analysis of the DMs that have resulted more prone to trigger CS: *like, so, como que*, and *tú sabes*.

4.1 Discourse marker *like*

Previous research has identified *like* as one of the most frequently used DMs in the oral discourse of younger participants (Ferrara & Bell, 1995; Romaine & Lange, 1991). While Romaine and Lange (1991) focused on participants' age and gender, Ferrara and Bell (1995) have also measured informants' ethnicity and their socioeconomical status. Both proposals reported the extensive use of *like* to transmit certain ideas, stories, or anecdotes with greater emotion and affectivity.

In this study conducted in Spanish, *like* was produced exclusively by the youngest participants and it triggered CS in 74% of cases. Three distinct pattern involving *like* were identified

i. English DM *like* triggering CS, following the sequence "Spanish + *like* + English" (7);
ii. English DM *like* without triggering CS, with the sequence "Spanish + *like* + Spanish" (8);

iii. monolingual use of English DM *like*, following the sequence "English + *like* + English" (9).

(7) *Así es mi vida, **like**, this is who I really am.* (F3)
This is my life, **like**, this is who I really am.

(8) *Es como mi tía de Guaynabo, **like**, una gringa wannabe.* (M2)
She is like my aunt from Guaynabo, **like**, una gringa wannabe.

(9) *Salí con mis amigas y he was there, **like**, I couldn't believe it.* (F2)
I went out with my friends and he was there, **like**, I couldn't believe it.

4.2 Discourse marker *so*

A number of proposals have labeled the DM *so* in different ways: *integrated loan* (Torres, 2002), *integrated borrowing* (as a sequence "*Spanish-Spanish-Spanish*") (Aaron, 2004), and *intra-sentential CS* ("*Spanish-English-Spanish*") (Lipski, 2005), even if "qualitatively different from the CS patterns normally studied in the Spanish-English bilingual community in the US" (Lipski, 2005, p. 11). Nonetheless, the phonological realization of *so* could determine "whether it is produced as an English word or as an assimilated borrowing into Spanish," since "the tense vowel /o/ in English is realized as a diphthong, while Spanish /o/ is never diphthongized" (Lipski, 2005, p. 6).

In the analysis of Loíza speech, *so* frequently appears as a borrowed element, in line with other studies indicating that this DM often emerges "surrounded by entirely Spanish discourse, and appears only very rarely [...] as part of a code-switched sequence" (Torres & Potowski 2008, p. 277–on Chicago Spanish). In dataset, *so* was primarily perceived as an English DM due to its phonological characteristics and its tendency to trigger CS. It was functionally equivalent to the Spanish DM *entonces* ('consequently, then, therefore') (Torres, 1997, 2002; Aaron, 2004; Lipski, 2004) — as in (10a–b):

(10) a. *Ese tipo no sirve, **so** it is what it is.* (F3)
That man is useless, **so** it is what it is.
b. *Él pega más bueno [mejor] que yo, **so** juega él.* (Lipski, 2005, p. 4)
He hits better than me, **so** he plays.

In a few cases, *so* was also phonologically perceived as an adapted Spanish DM. This is the case of older participants, who do not often switch from Spanish to English and vice versa (11), and who adopt this DM as a case of "momentary code-switching" (Lipski, 2005, p. 6):

(11) *Ay, mijo, puedo ser tu abuela, **so** suelta.* (F6)
Oh, boy, I can be your grandmother, **so** tell me.

As claimed by Lipski (2005, p. 6):

> The fact that the *so*-insertion often occurs in discourse with no other English elements, and is used by individuals who do not normally engage in intrasentential code-switching leaves little doubt that the sentences are produced in Spanish with English *so* embedded at appropriate points.

Among Loíza speakers, *so* can be classified as a nonce-borrowing, or word-borrowing, that is, a single borrowed word adapted to Spanish phonology and orthography (Zentella, 1997). Importantly, it does not fill a lexical gap, as equivalent Spanish expressions exist (*e.g., entonces, así que, por lo tanto,* etc.).

On the other hand, *so* cannot be considered a case of CS (aside from Lipski's "*momentary code-switching*" mentioned above), since it does "not mark a point of transition to a switch to English or Spanish, but rather a punctuation of a discourse realized entirely in Spanish" (Lipski, 2005, p. 13). Despite its "*hybrid status*" and being perceived as an English or Spanish DM, in the present study *so* was used by all participants, regardless of age, gender, and education, and it only triggered CS in youngest speaker (58%). It should be noted that when appearing phrase-internally, it was often "set off by at least a slight pause" (12a–b), as also reported in the literature (12):

(12) a. *Aquí hay buenos cafés, pero no me gusta el sabor. So what can I do?* (F2)
There are good coffees here, but I don't like the taste. **So** what can I do?
b. *Había gente que Fidel soltó de la cárcel. So había de todo.* (Lipski, 2005, p. 11)
There were people that Fidel released from jail. **So**, there was everything.

Conversely, when *so* occurred as a single element at the end of the sentence, it signaled a relinquishing of the speaker's turn (13). As claimed by Lipski (2005, p. 10), "what follows [this use of *so*] is usually a pause or hesitation" (14):

(13) *Yo espero que después que yo me vaya, pues que pase lo que sea. So.* (M1)
I hope that after I leave [die], then no matter what happens. **So**.

(14) *También puede trabajar, so ##* (Lipski, 2005, p. 10)
He/She can also work, **so**...

4.3 Discourse marker *como que*

Regarding *como que*, scholars have taken two different paths: considering it a closed unit (Moreno-Ayora, 1991) or analyzing it as "*adverb + que*" (Trujillo, 1990). Some studies also highlight its function as a "*vagueness mitigator*" to avoid being too straightforward when talking about serious topics or when to express thoughts, feelings, and emotions that were not clear in the speakers' minds (Janney, 2002).

In Latin American Spanish varieties, *como que* often alternates with *como*, the former viewed as a lexicalized variant of the latter (Flores-Ferrán, 2014). In this study, *como que* was found across all participants regardless age, gender, and education, and it triggers CS in 47% of cases (15).

(15) *On Thanksgiving we get together, we have dinner, **como que** huele a Navidad.*
(M2)
On Thanksgiving we get together, we have dinner, it **kind of** smells like Christmas.

4.4 Discourse marker *tú sabes*

According to the literature (Schiffrin, 1987), DM *tú sabes* is used with two main functions: as a discursive progression (16) and as a conclusion (17):

(16) ***Tú sabes**, una oportunidad para mí.* (F5)
You know, an opportunity for me.

(17) *El viento se lo llevó todo, **tú sabes**.* (M6)
The wind took it all, **you know**.

In (16), *tú sabes* elaborates on a topic in response to a question asked during the interview. It literally means '*you know the information X*', even if sometimes the information provided by the speaker is not shared by the listener. *Tú sabes* also functions as a conclusion marker (17) signaling the end of a speaker's turn and inviting the interlocutor to take over (turn-taking strategy).

The DM *tú sabes* was documented among participants regardless of age, gender, or educational level. It triggered CS "in" "*only*" 34% of cases, a relatively low percentage compared to the other DMs "analyzed" (18).

(18) *She's ninety-two, **tú sabes**, está viejita.*
She is ninety-two, **you know**, she is old. (M3)

5. Answering the research questions

Bringing back the RQs asked at the beginning of this work:

RQ1:	Which DMs are more likely to trigger CS (from Spanish to English or vice versa) in contexts of oral interaction in Spanish?

Among the five most common DMs identified in the analysis of 12 sociolinguistic interviews (Table 3), *like, so, como que,* and *tú sabes* emerged as the most frequently occurring. Conversely, *pues* did not trigger CS in any instance and was therefore excluded from further analysis.

> RQ2: Do extralinguistic variables (gender, age, and level of education of the participants) influence the use of bilingual DMs in Loíza speakers?

The findings of this study suggest that they do. However, a more balanced participant sample would clarify how gender, age, and level of education are independently influencing the use of DMs. This would help mitigate overlap caused by: (i) the fact that all participants under the age of 28 had at least a bachelor's degree or were in process of obtaining one; (ii) that all participants over the age of 44 have at most a high school diploma or have not completed high school.

Likewise, the frequency of bilingual DMs could depend on other factors considered in this study but relevant for future research. These include level of education, years of exposure to English, frequent trips to English-speaking countries, and access to English-language media such as satellite TV, social networks, and newspapers.

> RQ3: To what extent is the effect of linguistic contact between Spanish and English in Puerto Rico reflected in the presence/absence of monolingual/bilingual DMs?

The unique political and social relationship between Puerto Rico and the United States is reflected at the linguistic level in the alternation between Spanish and English. This alternation strongly favors Spanish, the native and primary language of 94% of Puerto Ricans residing in Puerto Rico. English is limited to single-word insertions (e.g., the DM *so*) or to intra- and inter-sentential CS. In the first case, it is "non-assimilated L2 functional elements — particularly conjunctions — in the midst of L1 discourse. If such insertion becomes frequent, full grammaticalization of the borrowed functional item may be the end result" (Lipski, 2005, p. 2). As far as CS is concerned, *intra-sentential CS* occurs when a word or phrase from another language is introduced within a sentence, whereas *intersentential CS* involves completing a sentence in one language, summarizing in another and potentially returning to the original language in the next sentence (Zentella, 1997; Acosta-Santiago, 2020).

6. Conclusions

This study has provided empirical data to discuss how bilingual DMs trigger CS in the spontaneous speech of Loíza speakers, a topic strictly related to Puerto Rico's complex political and economic relationship with the United States (Negrón-de Montilla, 1990; Pousada, 1999; Orama-López, 2012). In the Caribbean territory, Spanish and English are the main protagonists of a *pugna lingüística* ('linguistics struggle') that lasts for more than 125 years (Academia Puertorriqueña de la Lengua Española, 2000; Kerkhof, 2001), in which Spanish continues to be the dominant language in everyday life across Puerto Rican society (Denton, 2014).

The constant exposure to English among monolingual Spanish speakers in Loíza affects not only their pronunciation and vocabulary, but also their use of language in contexts of interaction. This proposal has focused on DMs variation in context of spontaneous sociolinguistic interviews. After identifying the most common DMs in the speech of *loiceños*, these spontaneous linguistic expressions were analyzed with respect to extralinguistic variables such as gender, age, and educational level.

Findings show that all these variables significantly influence the frequency of bilingual DMs and consequent CS in Loíza speakers. Older participants from Loíza, both male and female, who lack a college degree, are predominantly monolingual Spanish speakers. Their occasional use of English words (e.g., lexical items, DM *so*, etc.) does not necessarily indicate proficiency in this language. In contrast, CS is more frequent among younger generations of Loíza speakers, particularly those who have obtained or are pursuing a university degree.

However, the frequency of bilingual DMs and the occurrences of CS may also be influenced by other factors, such as years of exposure to English, trips to the United States, consumption of English-language media (satellite TV, social networks, newspapers, etc.), and internal factors related to pragmatics (e.g., common conversational topics among younger speakers, interlocutor relationships).

The present study contributes to the ongoing discussion on DMs (Torres, 2002; Aaron, 2004; Lipski, 2005; Flores-Ferrán, 2014), recalling Poplack's expression of "emblematic switches" (1980, p. 614) that "are found in the speech of bilinguals who are strongly based in one language and make 'emblematic forays' into the second language" (Brody, 1987, p. 609). This is particularly relevant in Puerto Rico, where English, despite holding a degree of prestige due to its association with job opportunities, "is not necessary to survive" in the daily life of almost all Puerto Ricans (Acosta-Santiago, 2020, p. 27).

The data analyzed in this study have shown how *loiceños*, who in recent years have been receiving more attention from government authorities and have even been included in the metropolitan area of San Juan due to its proximity to the

Puerto Rican capital (The White House Bulletin, 2017–2023), have been *"opening up"* to the rest of Puerto Rico. This has facilitated increased exposure to English, leading to instances of CS and linguistic borrowing among younger generations.

Future research should expand the scope of this study by analyzing these variables on a larger scale to obtain more robust empirical results. Additionally, further investigations could incorporate other sociocultural factors such as ethnicity, socioeconomic status (income level, living conditions, profession, lifestyle), identity, and linguistic attitudes toward English. Understanding why Puerto Ricans, after more than 125 years of American colonial rule, have not achieved widespread bilingual proficiency remains a key area for future exploration.

References

Aaron, J. E. (2004). So respetamos un tradición del uno al otro: So and entonces in New Mexican bilingual discourse. *Spanish in Context*, 1(2), 161–179.

Academia Puertorriqueña de la Lengua Española. (2000). *La enseñanza del español y del inglés en Puerto Rico: Una polemica de cien años*. Academia Puertorriqueña de la Lengua Española.

Acín-Villa, E. (2000). El marcador discursivo por lo demás. *RILCE*, 16 (2), 197–212.

Acosta-Santiago, J. M. (2020). *Politics and its Impact on Code-switching in Puerto Rico*. MA in Linguistics Final Projects. 11. https://digitalcommons.fiu.edu/linguistics_ma/11

Aijmer, K. (2002). *English discourse particles: Evidence from a corpus*. John Benjamins Publishing.

Álvarez, C. (1991). Code-Switching in Narrative Performance: Social, Structural and Pragmatic Function in the Puerto Rican Speech Community of East Harlem. In C.A. Klee & L.A. Ramos García (Eds.), *Sociolinguistics of the Spanish-Speaking World: Iberia, Latin America, United States* (pp. 271–298). Bilingual Press/Editorial Bilingüe.

Andersen, G., & Fretheim, T. (Eds.). (2000). *Pragmatic markers and propositional attitude*. John Benjamins Publishing.

Auer, P. (1998). *Code-Switching in Conversation: Language, Interaction and Identity*. Routledge.

Barreto, A. A. (2001). *The politics of language in Puerto Rico*. University Press of Florida.

Barron, A. (2005). Variational pragmatics in the foreign language classroom. *System* 33(3), 519–536.

Brinton, L. (1996). *Pragmatic Markers in English: Grammaticalization and Discourse Functions*. De Gruyter Mouton.

Brody, J. (1987). Particles borrowed from Spanish as discourse markers in Mayan language. *Anthropological Linguistics*, 29(4), 507–521.

Bullock, B. E., & Toribio, A. J. (2009). *The Cambridge Handbook of Linguistic Code-switching*. Cambridge University Press.

Callahan, L. (2002). The Matrix Language Frame Model and Spanish/English Codeswitching in Fiction. *Language and Communication* 22, 1–16.

Callahan, L. (2004). *Spanish/English Codeswitching in a Written Corpus*. John Benjamins Publishing Company.

Carvalho, A. M. (2012). Code-Switching: From Theoretical to Pedagogical Considerations. In S. M. Beaudrie & M. Fairclough (Eds.), *Spanish as a Heritage Language in the United States: The State of the Field* (pp. 139–157). Georgetown University Press.

Clyne, M. (1992). German as a Pluricentric Language. In M. Clyne (Ed.), *Pluricentric Languages* (pp. 56–72). De Gruyter Mouton.

Cornips, L. & C. Poletto. 2005. On standardising syntactic elicitation techniques (Part 1). *Lingua* 115, 939–957.

Denton, R. A. (2014). Hablo Español, You Know? Language and Identity in the Puerto Rican Diaspora. [Master's Thesis, University of Tennessee]. https://trace.tennessee.edu/utk_gradthes/2807

Díaz, J. (2012). *This is how you lose her*. Riverhead Books.

D'Introno, F. (1996). Spanish-English Code-Switching: Conditions on Movement. In A. Roca & J. B. Jensen (Eds.), *Spanish in Contact: Issues in Bilingualism* (pp. 187–201). Cascadilla Press.

Duany, J. (2000). Nation on the move: The construction of cultural identities in Puerto Rico and the diaspora. *American Ethnologist*, 27(1), 5–30.

Duany, J. (2018). *Puerto Rico: What Everyone Needs to Know*. Oxford University Press.

Dupey, R. (2012). Multiple perspectives of code-switching behavior in bilingual University of Puerto Rico students: Attitudes, domains, and interlocutors. *20th Anniversary Conference Monograph Series* (pp. 1,067–1,084). National Association of African American Studies.

Félix-Brasdefer, J. C. (2008). Sociopragmatic variation: dispreferred responses in Mexican and Dominican Spanish. *Journal of Politeness Research*, 4(1), 81–110.

Félix-Brasdefer, J. C., & Koike, D. A. (Eds.). (2012). *Pragmatic variation in first and second language contexts: Methodological issues* (Vol. 31). John Benjamins Publishing.

Ferrara, K., & Bell, B. (1995). Sociolinguistic variation and discourse function of constructed dialogue introducers: The case of be + like. *American Speech*, 70(3), 265–290.

Flores-Ferrán, N. (2014). So pues entonces: An examination of bilingual discourse markers in Spanish oral narratives of personal experience of New York City-born Puerto Ricans. *Sociolinguistic Studies*, 8(1), 57–83.

Garachana-Camarero, M., & Artigas, E. (2012). Corpus digitalizados y palabras gramaticales. *Scriptum Digital*, 1, 37–65.

García, C. (2008). Different realization of solidarity politeness: Comparing Venezuelan and Argentinean invitations. In P. Schneider & A. Barron (Eds.), *Variational pragmatics* (pp. 269–305). John Benjamins Publishing.

García, M. E. (2009). Code-Switching and Discourse Style in a Chicano Community. In M. Lacorte & J. Leeman (Eds.), *Español en Estados Unidos y otros contextos de contacto: Sociolingüística, ideología y pedagogía / Spanish in the United States and Other Contact Environments: Sociolinguistics, Ideology, and Pedagogy* (pp. 137–156) Iberoamericana/Vervuert.

Gardner-Chloros, P. (2009). Sociolinguistic factors in code-switching. In B. E. Bullock & A. J. Toribio (Eds.), *The handbook of code-switching* (pp. 97–113). Cambridge University Press.

Gimeno-Menéndez, F. & Gimeno-Menéndez, M. V. (2003). *El desplazamiento lingüístico del español por el inglés*. Cátedra.

Guzzardo-Tamargo, R. E., Loureiro-Rodríguez, V., Fidan-Acar, E., & Vélez-Avilés, J. (2019). Attitudes in Progress: Puerto Rican Youth's Opinions on Monolingual and Code-switched Language Varieties. *Journal of Multilingual and Multicultural Development*, 40(4), 304–321.

Hadei, M. (2016). Single Word Insertions as Code-Switching or Established Borrowing? *International Journal of Linguistics*, 8(1), 14.

Hansen, M. B. M. (1998). The semantic status of discourse markers. *Lingua*, 104(3‑4), 235–260.

Henríquez Ureña, P. (1921). Observaciones sobre el español de América. *Revista de filología española*, 8, 357–390.

Janney, R. W. (2002). Context as context: Vague answers in court. *Language & Communication*, 22(4), 457–475.

Jiménez, A. & Flores-Ferrán, N. (2018). The Functions of the Spanish Approximators Como and Como Que in Institutional and Non-Institutional Discursive Contexts. *Pragmática Sociocultural / Sociocultural Pragmatics*, 6(2), 145–171.

Jucker, A. H., & Ziv, Y. (Eds.). (1998). *Discourse markers: Descriptions and theory*. John Benjamins Publishing.

Kerkhof, E. (2001). The myth of the dumb Puerto Rican: Circular migration and language struggle in Puerto Rico. *New West Indian Guide/Nieuwe West-Indische Gids*, 75(3‑4), 257–288.

Klee, C. A. & Lynch, A. (2009). *El español en contacto con otras lenguas*. Georgetown University Press.

Labov, W. (1972). Some principles of linguistic methodology. *Language in Society*, 1, 97–120.

Labov, W. (1984). Field methods of the project on linguistic change and variation. In J. Baugh & J. Sherzer (Eds), *Language in Use: Readings in Sociolinguistics* (pp. 28–53). Prentice Hall.

Lipski, J. (2004). Is "Spanglish" the third language of the South?: Truth and fantasy about US Spanish. *3rd Language Variation in the South (LAVIS III) Conference*, Tuscaloosa, AL.

Lipski, J. M. (2005). Code-switching or borrowing? No sé so no puedo decir, you know. In L. Sayahi & M. Westermoreland (Eds), *Selected Proceedings of the Second Workshop on Spanish Sociolinguistics* (pp. 1–15). Cascadilla Proceedings Project.

Martín Zorraquino, M. A., & Portolés Lázaro, J. (1999). Los marcadores del discurso. In I. Bosque & V. Demonte (Dirs.), *Gramática descriptiva de la lengua española* (pp. 4051–4213). Espasa.

Meléndez, E. (1993). *Movimiento anexionista en Puerto Rico*. Universidad de Puerto Rico.

Millán, Y. (2012, May 27). Piden fuera a la politización del inglés. *El Vocero*.

Moreno-Ayora, A. (1991). *Sintaxis y semántica de como*. Editorial Librería Agora.

Muysken, P. (2000). *Bilingual Speech: A Typology of Code-Mixing*. Cambridge University Press.

Myers-Scotton, C. (2002). *Contact linguistics: bilingual encounters and grammatical outcomes*. Oxford University Press.

Negrón de Montilla, A. (1990). *La americanización de Puerto Rico y el sistema de instrucción pública 1900'1930*. Editorial de la Universidad de Puerto Rico.

Orama López, C. I. (2012). Puerto Rico y sus pugnas político-lingüísticas. *Lenguas en contacto y bilingüismo: revista digital*, 4, 1–23.

Östman, J. O. (1995). Pragmatic particles twenty years after. *Organization in discourse*, 14, 95–108.

Otheguy, R., García, O., & Reid, W. (2015). Clarifying translanguaging and deconstructing named languages: A perspective from linguistics. *Applied Linguistics Review 2015*, 6(3), 281–307.

Placencia, M. E. (2012). Regional pragmatic variation. In Andersen, G. & K. Aijmer (Eds.), *Pragmatics of Society* (pp. 79–114). De Gruyter Mouton.

Poplack, S. (1980). Sometimes I'll start a sentence in Spanish y termino en espanol: toward a typology of code switching. *Linguistics*, 18(7'8), 581–618.

Pousada, A. (1996). Puerto Rico: On the Horns of a Language Planning Dilemma. *Tesol Quarterly*, 30(3), 499–510.

Pousada, A. (1999). The singularly strange story of the English language in Puerto Rico. *Milenio*, 3, 33–60.

Pousada, A. (2000). The competent bilingual in Puerto Rico. *International Journal of the Sociology of Language*, 2000(142), 103–118.

Rivas, J. & Brown, E. L. (2009). No sé as a discourse marker in Spanish: a corpus-based approach to a cross-dialectal comparison. In P. Cantos Gómez & A. Sánchez Pérez (Eds.), *A Survey on Corpus-Based Research. Panorama de investigaciones basadas en corpus* (pp. 631–645). AELINCO.

Rivera-Rideau, P. R. (2015). *Remixing reggaetón. The cultural politics of race in Puerto Rico*. Duke University Press.

Romaine, S., & Lange, D. (1991). The use of like as a marker of reported speech and thought: A case of grammaticalization in progress. *American speech*, 66(3), 227–279.

Sankoff, D. & Poplack, S. (1981). A formal grammar for code-switching. *Linguistics*, 14(1), 3–45.

Sankoff, G., Thibault, P., Nagy, N., Blondeau, H., Fonollosa, M. O., & Gagnon, L. (1997). Variation in the use of discourse markers in a language contact situation. *Language variation and change*, 9(2), 191–217.

Schiffrin, D. (1987). *Discourse Markers*. Cambridge University Press.

Schneider, K. & Barron, A. (2008). *Variational Pragmatics*. John Benjamins.

Sepúlveda-Muñoz, I. (1993). Identificación nacional mediante la defensa del idioma: El caso de Puerto Rico. *Espacio, Tiempo y Forma. Serie V, Historia Contemporánea*, 6, 461–500.

Silva-Corvalán, C. (2001). *Sociolingüística y pragmática del español* (con Ejercicios de Reflexión de Andrés Enrique-Arias). Georgetown University Press.

Swigart, L. (1994). Cultural creolisation and language use in post-colonial Africa: the case of Senegal. *Africa*, 64(2), 175–189.

The White House Bulletin (2017'2023). Office of Management and Budget, Washington D. C. https://obamawhitehouse.archives.gov/sites/default/files/omb/bulletins/2013/b13-01

Timm, L. A. (1975). Spanish-English Code Switching: El Porqué y How Not To". *Romance Philology*, 28(4), 473–482.

Toribio, A. J. (2000). 'Once upon a time en un lugar muy lejano...' Spanish-English Code-Switching across Fairy Tales Narratives. In A. Roca (Ed.), *Research on Spanish in the United States: Linguistic Issues and Challenges* (pp. 184–203). Cascadilla Press.

Toribio, A. J., & Rubin, E. J. (1996). Code-Switching in Generative Grammar. In A. Roca & J. B. Jensen (Eds.), *Spanish in Contact: Issues in Bilingualism* (pp. 203–226). Cascadilla Press.

Torres, L. (1997). *Puerto Rican discourse: A sociolinguistic study of a New York suburb.* Psychology Press.

Torres, L. (2002). Bilingual discourse markers in Puerto Rican Spanish. *Language in society*, 31(1), 65–83.

Torres, L. (2007). In the Contact Zone: Code-Switching Strategies by Latino/a Writers, *MELUS* 32(1), 75–96.

Torres, L., & Potowski, K. (2008). A comparative study of bilingual discourse markers in Chicago Mexican, Puerto Rican, and MexiRican Spanish. *International Journal of Bilingualism*, 12(4), 263–279.

Travis, C. E. (2006). The Natural Semantic Metalanguage approach to discourse markers. In K. Fischer (Ed.), *Approaches to discourse particles* (pp. 219–241). Elsevier.

Trujillo, R. (1990). Sobre la explicación de algunas construcciones de como. *Verba*, 17, 249–266.

U.S. Census. (2021). Department of Commerce. Retrieved November 1, 2024 from https://www.census.gov/quickfacts/fact/table/PR/POP815221?#POP815221

Wolfram, W. (1998). Scrutinizing linguistic gratuity: Issues from the field. *Journal of Sociolinguistics*, 2(2), 271–279.

Wolfram, W., & N. Schilling-Estes. (2006). Language evolution or dying traditions: The state of American dialects. In W. Wolfram, & B. Ward (Eds.), *American Voices* (pp.1–7). Wiley-Blackwell.

Zentella, A. C. (1982). Spanish and English in Contact in the United States: The Puerto Rican Experience. *Word*, 33(1'2), 41–57.

Zentella, A. C. (1990). Returned migration, language, and identity: Puerto Rican bilinguals in dos worlds/two mundos. *International Journal of the Sociology of Language*, 1990(84): 81–100.

Zentella, A. C. (1997). *Growing Up Bilingual: Puerto Rican Children in New York.* Blackwell Publishers.

PART II

Sociolinguistic variation in the Spanish-speaking world

CHAPTER 4

Clitic placement in New York City Spanish

Kevin Martillo Viner
Bronx Community College

This variationist-sociolinguistic study analyzes the clitic position of all Spanish clitics (*me, te, se, nos, lo, los, la, las, le, les*) in the spoken Spanish of 52 New York City (NYC) participants. We address the following question: what, if any, external and internal variables influence clitic placement in this cohort of NYC Spanish speakers? A multiple linear regression revealed that, of the eight external variables identified for this study (generation, national origin, region, age, sex, socioeconomic status (SES), Spanish skill, English skill), only SES influenced clitic placement: participants with a lower SES employed proclisis (e.g., *te voy a llamar* 'I'm going to call you') significantly more (79%) than did participants with a higher SES (70%). Regarding conditioning linguistic factors, of nine internal variables (clause type, tense, person, number, pronominality, grammatical mood, negation, clitic type, finite verb), four reached statistical significance for proclisis. A logistic regression ranked them thusly: pronominality, specifically non-reflexivity; person (2nd > 1st > 3rd); clitic type (*me, te, nos > se > lo/s, la/s, le/s*); and clause type (gerund > infinitive). In its broadest sense, this study contributes to research surrounding languages in contact and subordinate languages. Its narrower implications involve the study of Spanish in the U.S. as both an immigrant and heritage language.

Keywords: Spanish in US, Spanish clitics, variationist-sociolinguistics, Languages in contact, Spanish syntax, heritage Spanish

1. Introduction

Clitic placement in the Spanish language is variable, occurring as either proclitic (e.g., *lo quiero comprar* 'I want to buy it'), or enclitic (e.g., *quiero comprarlo* 'I want to buy it'). This variability has been studied by many scholars (e.g., Limerick, 2022, 2018; Viner, 2021; Shin, Rodríguez, Armijo, & Perara-Lunde, 2019; Shin, Requena, & Kemp, 2017; Schwenter & Torres Cacoullos, 2014; Peace, 2012; Gutiérrez, 2008; Darwich, 2007; Gudmestad, 2006; Torres Cacoullos, 1999; Davies, 1995; Silva-Corvalán & Gutiérrez, 1995; Silva-Corvalán, 1994), in both

https://doi.org/10.1075/ihll.42.04vin
© 2025 John Benjamins Publishing Company

monolingual and bilingual language settings, and all have found the proclitic position (proclisis) to be the most frequent. The aim of this variationist-sociolinguist study is to advance current understanding on the syntactic placement of Spanish clitics (*me, te, se, nos, lo, la, le, los, las, les*) by analyzing external and internal independent variables. The data for this investigation are from the naturalistic speech of New York City (NYC) Spanish speakers ($n=52$). Two primary research questions guide the present study:

1. What, if any, external variables influence clitic placement in this cohort of NYC Spanish speakers?
2. What, if any, internal variables influence clitic placement in this cohort of NYC Spanish speakers?

In keeping with current variationist-sociolinguistic practices, we rely on results stemming from quantitative analyses in order to answer these research questions by accepting or rejecting their corresponding null hypotheses. We now turn to previous research surrounding clitic position in Spanish.

1.1 Previous research

What follows is a brief, yet concise, review of the relevant literature on the topic of Spanish clitic placement. In order to avoid unnecessary repetition, the presentation and discussion of the specific findings from previous research are reserved for the present paper's *Findings and Discussion* section, wherein we analyze all pertinent results thoroughly.

Prior to the mid-1990s, the study of clitic placement in Spanish centered primarily on written texts (e.g., Keniston, 1937; Myhill, 1988). Davies (1995) published the first work considering both written and spoken use of Spanish clitics, finding proclisis as the dominate position. Since that study, numerous scholars have researched clitic placement in Spanish monolingual and bilingual settings (e.g., Limerick, 2022, 2018; Viner, 2021; Shin et al., 2019; Shin et al., 2017; Schwenter & Torres Cacoullos, 2014; Peace, 2012; Gutiérrez, 2008; Darwich, 2007; Gudmestad, 2006; Torres Cacoullos, 1999; Davies, 1995; Silva-Corvalán & Gutiérrez, 1995; Silva-Corvalán, 1994) and, like Davies, proclisis has continually emerged the most frequent. For example, in Shin et al. (2017), the scholars compared several studies on clitic placement in different Spanish-speaking areas, specifically: Mexico by Schwenter and Torres Cacoullos (2014) and Requena and Miller (2014); Argentina by Requena (2015); Venezuela by Gudmestad (2006); Houston, Texas by Gutiérrez (2008); Los Angeles, California by Silva-Corvalán and Gutiérrez (1995); Massachusetts by Peace (2012); New York City by Darwich (2007). Their meta-analysis found that rates of proclisis for adults from Latin

America and the U.S. were near identical, at 75% and 73%, respectively. Moreover, Shin et al. (2017) reported similar results in their own study, to wit, 61% monolingual adult vs. 73% bilingual adult proclisis rates. More recent U.S.-focused studies also corroborate a clear preference for the proclitic position (e.g., Limerick, 2022, 2018; Viner, 2021), the details of which will be discussed later.

Regarding the study of variables associated with clitic placement, until recently, internal variables have been the crux of clitic placement investigation (e.g., Shin et al. 2017; Schwenter & Torres Cacoullos, 2014; Davies, 1995; Myhill, 1988), with a heavy focus on the influence from specific finite verbs (e.g., *ir, querer, poder, deber* and *esperar*) and construction (e.g., *ir a, estar* + gerund, *tener que*). Other internal variables studied, and reported as having an effect on placement, include verb reflexivity (Viner, 2021; Gutiérrez, 2008), animacy, multiple clitic use, and register (Davies, 1995), topic persistence (Schwenter & Torres Cacoullos, 2014), and specific clitic and presence of pause (Limerick, 2022).

Finally, external variables have only recently begun to be examined in association with clitic placement in Spanish (Limerick, 2022). In fact, of the studies mentioned thus far, a mere handful consider external variables (Limerick, 2022, 2018; Viner, 2021; Peace, 2012; Gudmestad, 2006), where social factors such as generation, sex, and social status, among others, are measured. The present study expands on these previous investigations by analyzing a total of 12 external variables, which we present below in the *Methodology* section.

1.2 The corpus

We use the Otheguy-Zentella corpus, commonly referred to as the OZC, as the data source. This stratified corpus has been used for many publications (e.g., Viner, 2020, 2018, 2017, 2016; Erker & Otheguy, 2016; Shin & Erker, 2015; Shin & Otheguy, 2013; Otheguy & Zentella, 2012), consisting of transcribed conversations with Spanish-speaking participants of different generations and national origins.[1] These casual sociolinguistic conversations were recorded, typically in the participants' homes, and lasted around 60 minutes. All efforts were made to pair participants with interviewers of the same national origins in order to control for linguistic accommodation (Giles & Ogay, 2006).

---

1. For an exhaustive description of the OZC, see Otheguy & Zentella (2012).

1.3 The participants

Of the 52 participants included in the present study, half (*n* = 26) belong to what we identified as the first-generation group (G1), the other half (*n* = 26) to the second-generation group (G2). Following Viner (2020, 2018, 2017, 2016) and Otheguy and Zentella (2012), participants from the G1 cohort immigrated to the U.S. from one of six Latin American countries (Puerto Rico, Dominican Republic, Cuba, Mexico, Ecuador, Colombia) at age 17 or older and had lived in the U.S. for no more than six years at the time of the interview. The rationale behind these criteria is that these participants fully acquired the monolingual variety from their respective country prior to their U.S. arrival and had spent an insufficient amount of time in the U.S. to be susceptible to substantial contact-induced changes, thus representing the variety from their country of origin.[2] G2 participants, on the other hand, were either born in or brought to the U.S. by no later than age three, thus representing a bilingual cohort whose Spanish was acquired in a contact setting where English was the dominant language. Like G1 participants, G2 participants have national roots from the same six Latin American countries listed above. The idea behind this generational and national stratification is the potential effect those external variables might have on clitic placement. Table 1 enumerates national origin by generation.

Table 1. National origin, by generation

	G1	G2
Puerto Rico	6	6
Dominican Republic	4	4
Cuba	4	4
Mexico	4	4
Colombia	4	4
Ecuador	4	4
Total	26	26

The decision to include more participants with Puerto Rican origins was deliberate — at the time of the development of this corpus, circa 2007, Puerto

---

[2]. We acknowledge that this rationale is not without its own shortcomings, i.e., it is possible that *some* contact-based influence occurs in six years or less. Nevertheless, we believe that these criteria are sound for our purposes here, especially as it has to do with fundamental grammatical aspects, such as syntactic positioning of clitics, which are essentially impervious to contact-induced or influenced changes after a mere few years in a contact setting.

Ricans made up the largest Hispanic group in NYC. According to the 2020 census, however, Dominicans have now surpassed Puerto Ricans in NYC, though not by a large number. The rest of the participants represent the other Spanish-speaking peoples with the largest Hispanic populations in NYC.

2. Methodology

The dependent variable for this study is clitic placement. To qualify for inclusion, the token must be situated in a syntactic environment where either proclisis or enclisis is entirely possible, which in Spanish is limited to verbal periphrasis, i.e., an inflected verb coupled with an impersonal verb form, specifically an infinitive or present participle. What follows are examples of the syntactic structures that permit both positions and, thusly, qualify for the study.[3]

(1) G1-198P:
*No **nos** querían creer* 'They didn't want to believe us'
*No querían creer**nos*** 'They didn't want to believe us'
G1-435P:
***Lo** tuvimos que dejar* 'We had to leave it/him'
*Tengo que buscar**lo*** 'I have to look for it/him'
G1-042U:
***Te** voy a llamar* 'I'm going to call you'
*Voy a llamar**te*** 'I'm going to call you'

(2) G2-206U:
***Me** quiero casar* 'I want to get married'
*Quiero casar**me*** 'I want to get married'
G2-311C:
***Le** voy a decir* 'I'm going to tell her/him'
*Voy a decir**le*** 'I'm going to tell her/him'
G2-315M:
***La** tengo que proteger* 'I have to protect her/it'
*Tengo que ayudar**la** a ella* 'I have to help her/it'
G2-092P:
***Se** están descartando* 'They are being rejected'
*Está derrumbándo**se*** 'It/he/she is collapsing'

---

3. Anonymous participant codes include the following: generation (G1 or G2), an identification number (e.g., 435, 092, 315, etc.), and national origin (P = Puerto Rico, D = Dominican Republic, U = Cuba, M = Mexico, C = Colombia, E = Ecuador). Thus, G1-198P is a first-generation Puerto Rican; G2-206U is a second-generation Cuban, and so on.

The first set of examples are from G1 participants and the second set are from G2 participants. These tokens demonstrate the verbal periphrases that allow variation of the dependent variable. Further, several of the utterances are linguistically very similar (G1-198P, G1-042U, G2-206U, and G2-311C), thus highlighting variation very clearly.

Regarding exclusion, the following clitics did not qualify for inclusion in the present study: invariable enclitic constructions *hay + que* (e.g., *hay que hacerlo* 'one must do it'), *ser* + adjective + infinitive (e.g., *es difícil decirte* 'it's difficult to tell you'), and affirmative imperatives (e.g., *pásalo* 'pass it'); invariable proclitic constructions, i.e., clitics presenting with a single inflected verb (e.g., *lo tengo* 'I have it'), and negative imperatives (e.g., *no lo pases* 'don't pass it'). To be sure, these exclusions are not based on any sort of prescriptive norm, but rather on the total absence of variation amongst these syntactic structures in the dataset. Additionally, for the integrity of quantification, we excluded clitics with a very low token count, specifically: double clitics (e.g., *se lo va a decir* 'S/he is going to tell it to her/him/them/you all'; *estoy explicándotelo* 'I'm explaining it to you'); very rare instances of duplicated use of the same clitic (e.g., *el Señor me está llamándome* 'God is calling me', G2-428P), and "floating clitics" (e.g., *por eso estaba pensando en me casar* 'for that reason I was thinking of getting married', G2-311C).

Concerning the collection process, once the envelope of variation was established, i.e., the tokens to be included in the study, each participant's transcript was thoroughly examined and all instances of verbal periphrases presenting with a single clitic were extracted and grouped according to the clitic used in the utterance (*me, te, se, nos, lo, la, le, los, las, les*). Once all tokens were collected (final token count $n = 1692$), each token was coded for external and internal variables, which we present now.

External variables:
- Generation (G1 or G2)
- National origin (Colombia, Dominican Republic, Ecuador, Mexico, Puerto Rico, Cuba)
- Region (Caribbean: Dominican Republic, Puerto Rico, Cuba; Mainland: Mexico Colombia, Ecuador)
- Sex (Male or Female)
- Age, expressed in categories (13–19, 20–39, 40–59, 60+)
- Spanish skill (poor/passable, good/excellent)
- English skill (poor/passable, good/excellent)
- Socioeconomic status (SES) (1–4 points, 5–8 points)

Internal variables:
- Clause type (infinitive, gerund)
- Tense (present, past)
- Person (first, second, third)
- Number (singular, plural)
- Pronominality (pronominal, non-pronominal)
- Grammatical mood (indicative, subjunctive)
- Negation (negated, affirmative)
- Clitic type (*se, lo/s, la/s, le/s, me/te/nos*)
- Finite verb (*deber, ir+a, tener+que, estar, poder,* other)

After all qualified tokens were coded, we ran a series of statistical tests. For the external variables, we used one-way ANOVA tests for each of the external variables, then a multiple linear regression. For internal variables, we ran individual Pearson's chi-square tests, followed by a logistic regression.

3. Findings and discussion

3.1 Descriptive results

In an effort to lay the groundwork for the results from statistical tests, we first briefly consider the data through a purely descriptive lens, presented in Tables 2a–2c.

Table 2a. Total tokens

Proclitic	1206 (71%)
Enclitic	486 (29%)
Total	1692 (100%)

Table 2b. Token by generation

	G1	G2
Proclitic	704 (71%)	502 (72%)
Enclitic	293 (29%)	193 (28%)
Total	997 (100%)	695 (100%)

Taking into consideration all tokens collected ($n=1692$), Table 2a shows a clear preference of the proclitic position ($n=1206$, 71%). Compared to other U.S.-based studies centered on clitic placement, Gutiérrez (2008) found the exact same rate of proclisis (71%) in Spanish spoken in Houston, Texas. Silva-Corvalán

Table 2c. Tokens by region

	Mainland	Caribbean
Proclitic	569 (69%)	637 (73%)
Enclitic	250 (31%)	236 (27%)
Total	819 (100%)	873 (100%)

and Gutiérrez (1995), however, reported a proclisis rate of 63% in Spanish spoken in Los Angeles, California.

This pattern remains largely intact when we look at clitic position across generation, as illustrated in Table 2b. Here we see the same percentile distribution amongst the G1 participants (71% proclitic and 29% enclitic). G2 also displays very similar usage, though the proclitic position is favored slightly more, gaining one percentage point, at 72%. It bears pointing out, however, the rather large difference in token production between the two generations: 997 for G1 vs. 695 for G2. There could be numerous reasons for this difference, especially given the free-flowing nature of the conversations from which the tokens originated, i.e., because discussion topics varied greatly, perhaps some topics naturally triggered more frequent use of clitics, while others did not. It is also possible that G2 participants employed some type of avoidance strategy, resulting in a reduction of tokens (Viner, 2018; Bookhamer, 2013; Lantolf, 1978). This claim, however, would be near impossible to substantiate and is thus merely mentioned in passing as a possible factor.

Limerick (2018) reported similar results for his U.S.-born participants with 74% in the proclitic position, but quite different for his recent arrivals with a proclisis rate of 48%. This discrepancy, however, could in part be due to the fact that his participants were in two entirely different areas (Arizona and Georgia), whereas our participants all live in NYC and are in constant contact with one another. Nevertheless, we do observe a pattern between these two studies wherein the G2 use the proclitic position *more* than do their G1 counterparts.

Finally, we observe in Table 2c that when considered by regional groupings (**Mainland**: Mexico, Colombia, Ecuador; **Caribbean**: Puerto Rico, Dominican Republic, Cuba), though still more homogenous than not, the most notable difference emerges: 69% Mainland proclitic placement vs. 73% Caribbean, a difference of four percentage points. However, because these findings are descriptive only, we must turn to the ANOVA test results in order to see if these, or any other external variables, are statistically significant.[4]

---

4. Out of curiosity, we did run chi-square tests on Generation and Region, but neither reached significance ($p = .469$ and $p = .113$, respectively).

3.2 External variables

One-way ANOVAs were performed on each external variable and the results are presented in Table 3a.

Table 3a. External variables, by ANOVA results

External variable	ANOVA results
Generation	$F(1, 50) = .004, p = .947$
National origin	$F(5, 46) = .445, p = .815$
Region	$F(1, 50) = .087, p = .769$
Areal	$F(1, 50) = .117, p = .734$
Sex	$F(1, 50) = .356, p = .553$
Age	$F(3, 48) = 2.089, p = .114$
Years in U.S.	$F(3, 48) = 1.303, p = .284$
Class	$F(2, 49) = .155, p = .857$
Education	$F(3, 48) = 1.048, p = .380$
Spanish skill	$F(1, 50) = .008, p = .928$
English skill	$F(1, 50) = .271, p = .605$
SES	$F(1, 50) = 6.678, p = .013$

The ANOVA test results reveal that there was not a significant difference in clitic placement (the dependent variable) between any of the external variable except for SES, which we will discuss shortly. These results suggest that this cohort of 52 Spanish-speaking New Yorkers is largely homogenous with regard to proclitic placement.[5] This is especially surprising given the substantial effect that generation has had with regard to subject pronoun and grammatical mood amongst these same participants (e.g., Viner, 2020, 2018, 2017, 2016; Otheguy & Zentella, 2012), not to mention its significant role in placement of clitic *se* in Viner (2021), wherein G2 produced significantly more proclisis than their G1 counterparts (78% vs. 68%, respectively). It warrants mention, however, that because that study analyzed clitic *se* alone, the dataset was considerably smaller ($n = 420$ vs. $n = 1692$

---

5. We acknowledge that sex has returned significant results in previous studies (Limerick, 2022; Peace, 2012; Gudmestad, 2006). The results of those studies, however, do not point in one unison direction. To wit, Limerick (2022) found men favored proclisis (75% vs. 59% women), whereas both Gudmestad (2006) and Peace (2012) reported that women favored proclisis. Sex did not reach statistical significance in the present study, but women did use the proclitic position slightly more (71.8% women vs. 70.9% men).

for the present study). With a near identical token count ($n=417$) to Viner (2021), Limerick (2018) found age of arrival (AOA) had a significant effect on proclisis, namely in that those born in the U.S. used it significantly more than did recent, older arrivals (74% vs. 48%, respectively). On the other hand, in his more recent study (Limerick, 2022), consisting of an even smaller dataset ($n=306$), AOA did not produce a statistically significant effect. Peace (2012), with a similar token count ($n=454$), reported an effect based on AOA wherein those who arrived at age 40+ had a significantly lower proclitic production rate (70%) compared to those born in the U.S. (78%). On the other hand, in Gutiérrez (2008), whose token count ($n=1689$) and findings (69.6% for his G_1; 71.6% for his G_2) most closely resemble our own, generation failed to reach significance. Lastly, Shin et al. (2017) reported very similar patterns amongst monolingual and bilingual adults and children, all of whom overwhelming preferred the proclitic position.

Returning now to the one external variable that reached significance, SES, Table 3b provides a detailed description of it by showing the mean and standard deviation of the values.

Table 3b. Descriptives of SES

SES	N	Mean	Std. deviation	Std. error	95% confidence lower bound	Interval for mean upper bound
Points 1–4	17	78.65	11.451	2.777	72.76	84.53
Points 5–8	35	69.69	11.859	2.005	65.61	73.76
Total	52	72.62	12.366	1.715	69.17	76.06

A few words on the makeup of SES. Identical to the composite measure developed in Otheguy and Zentella (2012), each participant was assigned points based on their level of education (elementary 1 point; secondary 2 points; college 3 points; graduate education 4 points) and occupation (little/no skill work 1 point; blue-collar or white-collar clerical work 2 points; store owner or store manager 3 points; doctor, lawyer, or accountant 4 points). These points were then added to provide the general SES of each participant. That said, we observe in Table 3b that the 17 participants who belong to the 1–4 total points cohort, i.e., those with lower socioeconomic status, tend to employ proclisis more than do the 35 participants from the 5–8 total points cohort (78.65 mean vs. 69.69 mean). Indeed, we will want to consider how this external variable stacks up against all of the other external variables in the regression model before accepting or dismissing these results here, but the large *F* value (6.68) coupled with the significant *p* value close to .01 does point toward a rejection of the null hypothesis associated with this external variable.

3.3 Linear regression

For the sake of thoroughness, we ran a multiple linear regression using all of the external variables identified for the present study even though only one tested at significance in the bivariate analyses above. That said, with such weak *F* and *p* values from the ANOVAs, we did not expect any profound changes in the results. Table 4 presents the findings from the multiple linear regression.

Table 4. Multiple linear regression, external variables

External variable	Unstandardized coefficients		Standardized coefficients	t	Sig.
	B	Std. error	Beta		
Region	1.474	3.959	.060	.372	.711
Sex	2.815	3.514	.114	.801	.428
Age	−4.626	2.794	−.228	−1.656	.105
SES	−11.247	3.769	−.431	−2.984	.005
Nationality	.864	1.198	.119	.721	.475
Spanish skill	.933	4.687	.034	.199	.843
English skill	6.917	4.937	.277	1.401	.168
Generation	−2.665	5.426	−.109	−.491	.626

Before we consider these results, a rationale for the exclusion of several external variables from the model is warranted. Many of the variables shared very similar information, which would result in a problem of multicollinearity, and, as such, they needed to be removed for a more precise model. The variables left out of the regression were: class, education, years in US, and areal. The first two, class and education, were used to create the point factors for SES; years in US would certainly correlate with generation, given our stratification criteria; and areal is closely linked to nationality.

Concerning these results, as we suspected, the regression model sheds little additional light on external predictor variables. However, SES again reaches statistical significance, only now it emerges *more* significant than previously ($p = .005$ from the regression model), suggesting an even stronger effect on proclisis than we might have concluded based on the ANOVA alone. According to this finding, the *lower* the level of the two SES factors (education and work), the *higher* the occurrence of the proclitic position in spoken Spanish.

In studying subject pronoun usage from the same corpus, Otheguy and Zentella (2012) discovered a similar result concerning SES wherein the pronoun rate was higher amongst participants with a lower SES score, and lower amongst those with a higher score (p. 71). The bivariate test on pronoun rate against SES did not quite reach significance, but it did in the regressions run for that study. On the other hand, this same external variable did not yield significant results in Viner's studies on grammatical mood (2020, 2018, 2017, 2016) nor in Viner's analysis of clitic *se* placement (2021), both of which used the same participants as the present study. Indeed, comparing results between considerably different grammatical features is ultimately of little use, but it is worth noting, especially since we are analyzing the exact same participants across studies.

To our knowledge, the only other study centered on Spanish clitic placement that considers SES as a social factor is Gudmestad (2006), which examines clitic placement with regard to *querer* 'to want' and *ir* 'to go', exclusively. Like our SES, Gudmestad's socioeconomic level, which also included occupation and level of education, reached significance for the verb *querer*, namely in that participants of the lower class used proclisis significantly more. The scholar argued that a possible explanation for this difference is that enclisis is the more conservative of the two and, as such, a decrease in it, and a subsequent increase in proclisis, occurs as the socioeconomic level lowers. To be sure, that study merely examined occurrences associated with two finite verbs and is therefore quite different from the present study. Its findings on SES, however, are relevant here given the scarcity of studies wherein this social factor is included.

3.4 Internal variables

For our first step in examining potential relationships between clitic placement and linguistic variables, we performed chi-square tests for each internal variable, from which four of the nine reached significance. The results for these four are presented in Tables 5a and 5b.

Table 5a. Chi-square results, internal variables

Internal variable	Chi-square results
Clause type	$X^2 (1, 1692) = 28.508, p < .001$
Clitic type	$X^2 (2, 1692) = 17.093, p < .001$
Pronominality	$X^2 (1, 1692) = 50.201, p < .001$
Person	$X^2 (2, 1692) = 14.718, p = .001$

Focusing on the proclitic position because of its dominance in spoken Spanish, these findings suggest the following: the gerund has a stronger effect than does an infinitive across all clitics; *me, te, nos* have a stronger effect than the other

Table 5b. Descriptives of significant internal variables

Clause type	Infinitive	Gerund		Total
Proclitic	981 (69%)	225 (85%)		1206
Enclitic	446	40		486
Total	1427	265		1692
Clitic type	Se	Lo/s, La/s, Le/s	Me, Te, Nos	Total
Proclitic	303 (72%)	359 (65%)	544 (75%)	1206
Enclitic	117	193	176	486
Total	420	552	720	1692
Pronominality	Reflexive	Non-reflexive		Total
Proclitic	357 (61%)	849 (77%)		1206
Enclitic	232	254		486
Total	589	1103		1692
Person	First	Second	Third	Total
Proclitic	377 (74%)	168 (80%)	661 (68%)	1206
Enclitic	135	41	310	486
Total	512	209	971	1692

clitics;[6] non-reflexivity has a stronger effect than does reflexivity; second-person clitics have a stronger effect than do first or third person.

These results corroborate the following findings from previous studies centered on clitic placement:

- clitics presenting with the gerund favored the proclitic position in Myhill (1988), Silva-Corvalán and Gutiérrez (1995), Gutiérrez (2008), Limerick (2018), and Viner (2021)
- non-reflexive verbs correlated with proclisis in Davies (1995), Gutiérrez (2008), and Viner (2021)
- second-person clitics were found to appear in the proclitic position the most, followed by first-person, then third-person, in both Myhill (1988) and Gudmestad (2006); Torres Cacoullos (1999) reported that both first- and second-person clitics occurred most often in the proclitic position; Limerick (2022) also found that *te* favored proclisis, but also *se* and *me* (though *me* only slightly, with a proclisis rate of 66%)

---

6. In order to analyze a robust number of tokens, and following Torres Cacoullos (1999), we collapsed the present study's clitic types into three levels: 1. *se*; 2. *lo/s, la/s, le/s*; 3. *me, te, nos*

To be sure, not all of the above investigations were based on U.S. Spanish, but the similarity in findings across all of them is important in the context of the present study.

A word on the internal variable *finite verb*. This variable has consistently emerged significant across most research on Spanish clitic placement (e.g., Limerick, 2022, 2018; Viner, 2021; Shin et al., 2017; Schwenter & Torres Cacoullos, 2014; Torres Cacoullos & Schwenter, 2009; Gutiérrez, 2008; Silva-Corvalán & Gutiérrez, 1995). For the studies centered on U.S. Spanish, a pattern with regard to the specific verb appears to emerge, i.e., in Limerick (2022, 2018), *ir a* and *poder* showed to have the strongest effect on proclisis; Viner (2021) found that *ir a, poder,* and *estar* favored proclisis, but only for the G1 participants; Shin et al. (2017) reported *ir a* and *estar* as carrying the most weight; Gutiérrez (2008) reported *estar, ir a,* and *poder* as the conditioning finite verbs. What varies considerably, however, is the number of tokens available for analysis in each of the aforementioned studies. The following summarizes these numbers:

- Limerick (2022): 306 tokens
- Limerick (2018): 417 tokens
- Viner (2021): 420 tokens
- Shin et al. (2017), for U.S. adults: 140 tokens
- Gutiérrez (2008): 1,689 tokens

The present study yielded 1,692 tokens, yet *finite verb* failed to show an effect on clitic placement (X^2 (5, 1692) = 6.570, p = .255). Table 5c details the distribution of the tokens across the most frequently used finite verbs amongst our participants.[7]

Table 5c. Clitic position by finite verb

Finite verb	Proclitic position	Enclitic position
Tener que	N = 145 (74%)	N = 51 (26%)
Poder	N = 287 (73%)	N = 106 (27%)
Ir a	N = 307 (69%)	N = 137 (31%)
Deber	N = 41 (67%)	N = 20 (33%)
Estar	N = 140 (66%)	N = 71 (34%)
Other	N = 286 (74%)	N = 101 (26%)

---

7. We ran a separate chi-square test excluding "Other", but the results were still insignificant at p = .308.

We are unable to state with certainty why our study returned such differing results compared to others, but one might suspect that, with the exception of Gutiérrez (2008), the small number of tokens in the other investigations had some impact. What differed greatly between Gutiérrez (2008) and the present investigation, however, was the number of finite verbs analyzed in Gutiérrez's, to wit: 18 finite verbs, some of which had as few as *one* token (Table 6, p. 310, 2008) vs. the five most frequent finite verbs for the present study. As such, we decided to replicate our analysis, using the same five finite verbs with Gutiérrez's tokens, the results of which are presented below in Table 5d.

Table 5d. Clitic position by finite verb, modified from Gutiérrez (2008)

Finite verb	Proclitic position	Enclitic position
Tener que	N=61 (58%)	N=44 (42%)
Poder	N=141 (76%)	N=45 (24%)
Ir a	N=228 (87%)	N=34 (13%)
Deber	N=18 (56%)	N=14 (44%)
Estar	N=144 (88%)	N=20 (12%)

Yet even when modified to match the present investigation, i.e., grouped together, as opposed to by generation like Gutiérrez (2008), and reduced to the same five finite verbs, this analysis still delivers significant results (X^2 (4, 749) = 56.69, $p < .001$). Of course, the reduction of finite verbs resulted in a reduced token count ($n = 749$), less than half of the entire token count in the original Gutiérrez study ($n = 1,689$), but the findings still appear sound. Regarding proclisis, except for *poder* (76% for Gutiérrez, 73% for present study), the rates are strikingly different between the two investigations: 58% Gutiérrez vs. 74% present study for *tener que*; 87% Gutiérrez vs. 69% present study for *ir a*; 56% Gutiérrez vs. 67% present study for *deber*; 88% Gutiérrez vs. 66% present study for *estar*. The reason behind these sizeable differences is uncertain, but a plausible reason could be attributed to distinct study designs and overall methodologies (e.g., collection processes, envelope of variation, participant demographics, location of the study, etc.).

3.5 Logistic regression

In an effort to better comprehend the effect of these internal variables, a logistic regression was run to determine the weight of each linguistic factor when considered *en masse*. Table 6 presents the hierarchy of these four internal variables.[8]

Table 6. Logistic regression, internal variables

Internal variable	Wald	Significance
Pronominality	89.158	$p<.001$
Person	50.209	$p<.001$
Clitic type	30.036	$p<.001$
Clause type	23.314	$p<.001$

The variables are ranked based on the strength of their given Wald statistical value, all of which are significant at $p<.001$. This regression informs us that pronominality, specifically non-reflexivity, has by far the strongest effect with regard to proclisis. From there, person (2nd > 1st > 3rd), clitic type (*me, te, nos > se > lo/s, la/s, le/s*), and clause type (gerund > infinitive).

To our knowledge, Limerick (2022, 2018) is the only other scholar to utilize a multivariate analysis for clitic placement in U.S. Spanish. In his 2018 study, whose internal variables most closely resemble those of the present study, he included four linguistic variables in the model: non-finite verb form (gerund or infinitive), construction (*ir a*+ infinitive, *poder* + infinitive, *querer* + infinitive), reflexivity (non-reflexive or reflexive), and frequency (constructions with 30 or greater = more frequent; 30 or less = less frequent). Of those four variables, construction and non-finite returned significant results in his study, whereas only non-finite (clause type here) reached significance in ours.

---

8. For the sake of thoroughness, we also ran a model in which we included *all* internal variables, but the results were unchanged: the same four internal variables reached significance. *Finite verb* did return a slightly stronger *p* value ($p=.133$), but still not within the bounds of statistical significance. *Tense*, on the other hand, approached significance with $p=.056$, wherein the present tense produced 72% of all clitics in the proclitic position, and the past tense 68%.

4. Conclusion

This study explored clitic placement tendencies across a cohort of 52 Spanish-speaking New Yorkers. Two research questions guided the investigation, both aimed at broadening our understanding of the complex linguistic composition of Spanish situated in NYC.

The first research question centered on external variables in order to determine whether or not separate autonomous groups, or subgroups, existed within the sample. We were particularly interested in generation and region since these two external variables have had an effect on other grammatical features analyzed using the same corpus (e.g., subject pronouns in Otheguy and Zentella, 2012, and grammatical mood in Viner, 2020, 2018, 2017, 2016). However, the null hypotheses associated with all but one external variable, SES, were accepted, verified by both bivariate (ANOVA) and multivariate (linear regression) means of analyses. In other words, the proclitic position is the dominant placement irrespective of the participants' age, sex, generation, national origin, region, years spent living in the U.S., or Spanish / English skills. The only variable that appears to affect this is the speaker's socioeconomic status, specifically in that those with a higher score use enclisis more than those with a lower score, albeit still far less than proclisis (69.69% average proclisis for higher scores vs. 78.65% with lower scores, Table 3b above).

This generational similarity is likely the most important finding of this investigation because, as we stated before, measurable linguistic differences have been, and continue to be, discovered between G1 and G2 Spanish speakers in NYC. Yet with regard to this particular linguistic feature, which happens to be very high in frequency and thus quite relevant, the generational differences cease to exist. In other words, concepts that sometimes surround studies centered on bilinguals and heritage speakers, things like simplification (Lynch, 1999), incomplete acquisition (Montrul, 2009), and/or other English-influenced "non-monolingual" like features, are inapplicable here.

The focus of the second research question rested on internal linguistic variables. Having established the homogenous nature of this study's participants, we analyzed these internal variables across all 52 participants as a single sample. Bivariate analyses pinpointed four significant internal variables (Pronominality, Person, Clitic type, Clause type), followed by a logistic regression that revealed the hierarchy of these variables in terms of their strength, i.e., those which had the *most* influence on proclisis. We can visually summarize those findings thusly: pronominaltiy > person > clitic type > clause type.

In sum, the proclitic position is undeniably the preferred position for this group of NYC Spanish speakers, irrespective of external and internal variables. That is, no matter the linguistic factors, a clitic will appear in the proclitic position far more often than in the enclitic. However, four internal variables are significantly more influential on proclisis. Naturally, the question arises — just these four? From the nine internal variables that were identified for this study, yes. However, we acknowledge that there are likely other linguistic variables that affect clitic placement. We leave that question to future undertakings.

References

Bookhamer, K. M. (2013). The Variable Grammar of the Spanish Subjunctive in Second-Generation Bilinguals in New York City. [Doctoral dissertation, The City University of New York].

Darwich, B. (2007). Los clíticos *lo, la, los* y *las* en situación de contacto: datos sobre el español en Nueva York. *LLJournal*, 2(2).

Davies, M. (1995). Analyzing syntactic variation with computer-based corpora: e case of modern Spanish clitic climbing. *Hispania*, 78, 370–380.

Erker, D., & Otheguy, R. (2016). Contact and coherence: Dialectal leveling and structural convergence in NYC Spanish. *Lingua*, 172–173, 131–146.

Giles, H., & Ogay, T. (2006). *Communication accommodation theory*. In B. B. Whaley & W. Samter (Eds.), *Explaining communication: Contemporary theories and exemplars* (pp. 293–310). Routledge.

Gudmestad, A. (2006). Clitic climbing in Caracas Spanish: A sociolinguistic study of *ir* and *querer*. *IULC Working Papers Online*, 06–03.

Gutiérrez, M. J. (2008). Restringiendo la subida de clíticos: Reflexividad, modalidad verbal y contacto lingüístico en el español de Houston. *Hispanic Research Journal*, 9(4), 299–313.

Keniston, H. (1937). *Spanish syntax list*. Henry Holt and Company.

Lantolf, J. (1978). The variable constraints on mood in Puerto Rican-American Spanish. In M. Suñer (Ed.), *Contemporary Studies in Romance Linguistics* (pp. 193–217). Georgetown University Press.

Limerick, P. (2018). Variable clitic placement in US Spanish. In J. MacDonald (Ed.), *Contemporary Trends in Hispanic and Lusophone Linguistics: Selected papers from the Hispanic Linguistic Symposium 2015* (pp. 49–70). John Benjamins.

Limerick, P. (2022). New considerations for variable clitic placement in Spanish: Findings from Atlanta, Georgia. Amsterdam: John Benjamins. *Revista Española de Lingüística Aplicada*, 35(2), 650-674.

Lynch, A. (1999). The subjunctive in Miami Cuban Spanish: Bilingualism, contact, and language variability. [Doctoral dissertation, University of Minnesota].

Montrul, S. (2009). Knowledge of tense-aspect and mood in Spanish heritage speakers. *International Journal of Bilingualism* 13(2), 239–69.

Myhill, J. (1988). Variation in Spanish clitic climbing. *Georgetown University Round Table on Language and Linguistics*, 227–250.

Otheguy, R., & Zentella, A. C. (2012). *Spanish in New York: Language contact, dialectal leveling and structural continuity*. Oxford University Press.

Peace, M.M. (2012). ¿Lo puedo subir o puedo subirlo? La subida del clítico en el español del oeste de Massachusetts. *International Journal Lasso, 31*(1), 131-160.

Requena, P.E. (2015). Direct object clitic placement preferences in Argentine child Spanish. [Doctoral dissertation, State College: Pennsylvania State University].

Requena, P.E., & Miller, K. (2014). *Constraining Spanish clitic placement variation: Evidence from child language.* Paper presented at the Hispanic Linguistic Symposium 2014, Purdue University. West Lafayette, Indiana.

Schwenter, S.A., & Torres Cacoullos, R. (2014). Competing constraints on the variable placement of direct object clitics in Mexico City Spanish. *Revista Española de Lingüística Aplicada, 27*(2), 514-536.

Shin, N.L., & Erker, D. (2015). The emergence of structured variability in morphosyntax: childhood acquisition of Spanish subject pronouns. In A. Carvalho, R. Orozco, & N.L. Shin (Eds.), *Subject pronoun expression in Spanish: a cross-dialectal perspective* (pp. 169–190). Georgetown University Press.

Shin, N.L. & Otheguy, O. (2013). Social class and gender impacting change in bilingual settings: Spanish subject pronoun use in New York. *Language in Society, 42*, 429–452.

Shin, N.L., Requena, P.E., & Kemp, A. (2017). Bilingual and Monolingual Children's Patterns of Syntactic Variation: Variable Clitic Placement in Spanish. In A. Benavides & R. Schwartz (Eds.), *Language Development and Disorders in Spanish-speaking Children. Literacy Studies* (pp. 63–88). Springer International Publishing/Springer Nature.

Shin, N.L., Rodriguez, B., Armijo, A., & Perara-Lunde, M. (2019). Child heritage speakers' production and comprehension of direct object clitic gender in Spanish. *Linguistic Approaches to Bilingualism, 9*, 659–686.

Silva-Corvalán, C., & Gutiérrez, M.J. (1995). On transfer and simplification: Verbal clitics in Mexican-American Spanish. In P. Hashemipour, R. Maldonado, & M. van Naerssen (Eds.), *Studies in language learning and Spanish linguistics in honor of Tracy D. Terrell* (pp. 302–312). McGraw-Hill.

Silva-Corvalán, C. (1994). *Language contact and change.* New York: Oxford University Press.

Torres Cacoullos, R. (1999). Construction frequency and reductive change: Diachronic and register variation in Spanish clitic climbing. *Language Variation and Change, 14*, 143–170.

Viner, K.M. (2021). Generational Differences in the Placement of Clitic *se* in New York City Spanish. *International Journal of Bilingualism, 25*(5), 1460–1472.

Viner, K.M. (2020). Comment Clauses and Mood Choice in New York City Spanish: Generational Constraints and Innovations. *Linguistic Approaches to Bilingualism, 10*(5), 728–744.

Viner, K.M. (2018). The Optional Spanish Subjunctive Mood Grammar of New York City Heritage Bilinguals. *Lingua, 210–211*, 79–94.

Viner, K.M. (2017). Subjunctive Use in the Speech of New York City Spanish Heritage Language Bilinguals: A Variationist Analysis. *Heritage Language Journal, 14*(3), 307–333.

Viner, K.M. (2016). Second-Generation NYC Bilinguals' Use of the Spanish Subjunctive in Obligatory Contexts. *Spanish in Context, 13*(3), 343–370.

CHAPTER 5

Variation in the use of the interdental fricative in Melilla

Lotfi Sayahi & Marina Bonilla-Conejo
The State University of New York at Albany | St. John Fisher University

Several studies have shown the existence of different degrees of variation in the use of the voiceless interdental fricative phoneme in southern Spain. This includes *seseo, distinción*, and, less frequently, *ceceo*. However, in several communities the use of *seseo* or *distinción* is not categorical as the same speaker can make use of both pronunciations, even within the same sentence.

The present study offers an analysis of the use of [θ] in the autonomous city of Melilla where two ethnolinguistic communities coexist: speakers of Peninsular origin and speakers of Amazigh (Berber) origin. The objective is to determine the distribution of [θ] according to ethnic origin and gender, on the one hand, and, on the other hand, to determine the role of word class, position in the word, grapheme, and word frequency in the appearance of [θ] or [s]. Data consist of sociolinguistic interviews with 10 speakers of Amazigh origin and 10 speakers of Peninsular Spanish origin. Altogether 3,660 occurrences were analyzed with a distribution of 78% of [θ] use and 17.1% of [s] use. The results show that the two most significant factors are extralinguistic: ethnicity and gender. Men of Amazigh origin used [θ] in 60.6% of cases while men of Peninsular origin produced [θ] in 80% of the cases. In turn, women of Peninsular origin used [θ] almost categorically (97.1%), similar to Amazigh women who also showed very high level of use of [θ] (92%). Linguistic factors did not show a considerable effect in this case, leading us to conclude that the alternation between the use of both variants is a socially conditioned phenomenon present in the speech of males in both ethnic groups.

Keywords: Melilla, interdental fricative, seseo, distinción, Amazigh

1. Introduction

One of the most distinctive phonetic features of Castilian Spanish today, the voiceless interdental fricative, emerged because of a series of changes that affected the sibilant system of medieval Spanish. Before the sixteenth century, Castilian Spanish had the dental affricates /t^s/ and /d^z/ that evolved into the dental predorsal /s̪/ and then /θ/. Those changes became extended in the seventeenth century in central and northern Spain, while in Andalusia, in the south of the country, /t^s/, /d^z/, /s/ and /z/ converged into /s/ (Alvar, 1972; Hualde et al., 2020; Penny, 2000).

Although undoubtedly brought along by speakers from northern parts of Spain (Lapesa, 1956), the interdental fricative has been documented only in sporadic cases in Latin America (Caravedo, 1992; Moreno Fernández, 2005). It is true, however, that some speakers of Spanish as a second language may use this sound given the general prestige that central and northern Peninsular Spanish varieties hold. This includes speakers in Equatorial Guinea (Lipski & Sayahi, 2023), northern Morocco (Scipione & Sayahi, 2005; Sayahi, 2011), the Philippines (Lipski, 2019) and some instructed second language learners of Spanish in the United States (Ringer-Hilfinger, 2013). Nonetheless, in terms of numbers of speakers, absence of /θ/ is by far the dominant phenomenon in Spanish varieties.

Generally speaking, mainland Spain is divided into two major dialect zones: Central/northern varieties and Andalusian varieties.[1] In central/ northern varieties, the graphemes ⟨ce⟩, ⟨ci⟩, and ⟨z⟩, are articulated as [θ] while the grapheme ⟨s⟩ is produced as [s], a phenomenon known as *distinción*. Elsewhere speakers do not use the interdental fricative in such contexts and use [s] instead, leading to homophones in words such as the noun *sierra* 'saw' and the verb *cierra* 's/he closes'. The absence of the interdental fricative in Spanish varieties is referred to as *seseo*. A less common phenomenon that has been described in smaller communities of southern Spain is the absence of /s/ in favor of a voiceless dental-alveolar sibilant, which could be transcribed as [s̪^{θ}], even with graphemic ⟨s⟩, a phenomenon known as *ceceo* [θeθeo]. In the case of *ceceo*, both *sierra* and *cierra* are articulated with an interdental fricative sound (see Table 1).

However, in communities where both *distinción* and *seseo* are present, users may show intra-speaker variation, a phenomenon referred to as *alternancia*. They can alternate between both *distinción* and *seseo* thus realizing ⟨ce⟩, ⟨ci⟩, and ⟨z⟩ as either [s] or [θ], sometimes in the same utterance as in (1). Table 1 summarizes the phenomena described thus far and their general geographical distribution.

---

1. The Spanish islands are also different from each other when it comes to the use of the interdental fricative: in the Balearic Islands the use of *distinción* is predominant while in the Canary Islands *seseo* is the norm (Hualde et al., 2020).

Table 1. Use of the interdental fricative in Spanish

	Articulation of the noun *sierra* 'saw'	Articulation of the verb *cierra* 's/he closes'	Geographical distribution
Seseo	[s]ierra	[s]ierra	Latin America, Southern Spain, Canary Islands, United States
Distinción	[s]ierra	[θ]ierra	Central and northern Spain, parts of southern Spain, Balearic Islands, parts of North Africa, Equatorial Guinea
Ceceo	[s̪θ]ierra	[θ]ierra	Parts of southern Spain
Alternancia	[s]ierra	[s]ierra or [θ]ierra	Parts of southern Spain

In the current study, we look at the factors that condition the distribution of *seseo* and *distinción* in a geographically-contained context, that of the autonomous city of Melilla. Our interest is to describe what social and linguistic factors promote the use of either [s] or [θ] or the alternation between both in the speech of a group of speakers from this city. For example, in (1), the speaker articulates the grapheme ⟨ci⟩ differently in each of the two separate occurrences of the word *documentación*, first as [θ] and then as [s], as he shows intra-speaker variation in the use of [θ]. He also uses [θ] with the grapheme ⟨ci⟩ in the word *vacío*, but uses [s] with the grapheme ⟨ce⟩ in *necesidad*.

(1) "[…] documenta[θ]ión, extranjero por ejemplo, pongamos un ejemplo un holandés, ¿no? Cuando pasa el control, eso sería un poquillo un va[θ]ío legal, ¿no? Cuando pasa por el control marroquí, enseña su identidad marroquí y cuando llega a los españoles enseña su documenta[s]ión holandesa entra por la frontera de Farhana sin ne[s]esidad de sellar ningún documento."

(Male speaker, Melilla).

There has been a wide range of studies on variation in the use of the interdental fricative in Spanish over the last few decades (see for example Salvador, 1980; Villena Ponsoda, 2001; and references therein). Dalbor's (1980) early paper offers notes on what he calls "phonemic slips", based on impressionistic observations from interactions he had with speakers in Granada and Seville. He notes that in Granada "[i]n almost all speakers encountered, the mode was never absolute; that is, there was almost always a certain degree of phonemic variation or "slippage" in one direction or the other, or both." (Dalbor, 1980, p.11). As for Seville, he writes that "the speakers varied so chaotically between seseo and ceceo that it would be impossible to assign them definitively to one mode or the other without a precise statistical analysis of very long continuous stretches of their speech" (Dalbor, 1980, p. 14). Similarly, Morillo-Velarde (1997) in a comparative survey of previous studies on Andalusia also makes reference to significant variation calling it "trueque anárquico" and claiming that speakers "alternan anárquicamente ambas realizaciones" (Morillo-Velarde, 1997, p. 206). In turn, commenting on her own experience in Seville, González-Bueno (1993) proposes that access to education has encouraged the use of the interdental fricative even among speakers who are otherwise regular users of *seseo*, which at times may even lead to cases of *ceceo* as a result of hypercorrection.

More recent studies take a more quantitative approach attempting to describe the factors that condition variation in the use of the interdental sound, as opposed to just labelling it as a chaotic phenomenon (Regan, 2021). In his study on variation in the use of *ceceo* in Jerez, García-Amaya (2008) shows that the generational and educational changes that marked post-Franco Spain need to be taken into consideration to explain the decrease in the use of *ceceo* in the city, especially among younger generations. A different study by Melguizo Moreno (2007) shows that younger and university-educated migrants who settle in Granada from a rural area, the town of Pinos Puente, show higher use of *distinción* even if in their original village *ceceo* is the more dominant norm, while older migrants without higher education continue to use *ceceo* even after establishing their residence in the city of Granada. According to Melguizo Moreno (2007), education is the most significant factor to explain higher rates of the use of *distinción* both in the town of Pinos Puente and in the city of Granada itself. This study shows that speakers are able to alternate between both systems and adapt their rates of use of the interdental sound depending on the situation in which they find themselves.

Also in Granada, Moya Corral and Sosiński (2015) found that *ceceo* has more of a "residual" usage, mainly because of contact with rural areas, and that its use hovers around 5% only. These authors find a rapid increase in the use of *distinción*, from 55% in 1995 to 79.4% in 2014, while *seseo* saw a decrease in its use from 55% in 1994 to 40% in 2014 (Moya Corral & Sosiński 2015, p. 23). As a result, they affirm that "[h]oy la ciudad es distinguidora. El seseo se refugia en miembros de la tercera generación (25%) y de bajo grado de instrucción (21.6%)" (Moya Corral & Sosiński 2015, p. 24).

In Málaga, Villena Ponsoda and Requena Santos (1996) highlighted the role of gender in the use of the interdental fricative to note that the use of *distinción* is a prestigious feature that represents a change in progress in the city that is spreading at the expense of *seseo*. They also argue that the effect of gender becomes less relevant when higher levels of education are attained. While for speakers with elementary and secondary levels of education women produce almost double the percent for cases of use of *distinción*, this difference disappears at the higher education levels. They summarize their findings by arguing that: "[...] la distinción de /s/: /θ/ puede considerarse como un fenómeno relativamente reciente de las generaciones jóvenes, prestigioso y ligado fuertemente a los individuos con niveles educativos altos" (Villena Ponsoda & Requena Santos, 1996, pp. 36–38). Likewise, Regan (2020, p. 181) proposes the existence of a demerger where *ceceo* is changing into *distinción* based on read speech in Huelva and Lepe. Among the factors that he singled out as leading to the demerger are the presence of an additional same grapheme in the word and that change is led primarily by women, and younger educated speakers. He gives importance to the social change that had occurred in the region with the socioeconomic changes that brought speakers from other areas of Spain and the wide impact of mass media.

Hernández-Campoy and Villena Ponsoda (2009) in their study of the contact between standard Castilian Spanish and regional varieties of Spanish, including Murcian and Andalusian varieties, argue that as part of the convergence of eastern Andalusian Spanish towards the national standard variety, educated speakers tend to show an increased rate in the use of *distinción* to the degree that "educated speakers born after 1970 use the /s/-/θ/ distinction pattern consistently" (Hernández-Campoy & Villena Ponsoda, 2009, p. 196). This last study is particularly relevant to the present investigation as, at many levels, Melilla has more interactions with Málaga than with any other Spanish city and shares several features with it as will be discussed in the next section.

Focusing on Melilla, in her study with 20 speakers from the city, all of Peninsular origin, González Las (1991, p. 51) found that among educated speakers *distinción* is used in 89.6% of the cases, while in the case of uneducated speakers the rate of [θ] use reaches 51.1% of the cases only. She notes that ⟨z⟩ tends to be deleted in final position as happens with final ⟨s⟩. Even within this same group of Peninsular-origin speakers, González Las (1991, p. 115) finds that there is intragroup variation: "En los incultos, la realización de θ prenuclear como s predorsal es más frecuente que la modalidad interdental, aunque no la tienen como exclusiva, pues, en idéntica situación, las mujeres cultas también sesean."

In the most extensive study on Melillan Spanish, Ruiz Domínguez (1997, 1999) extracted 2379 tokens from recorded interviews with 44 participants, an average of 10 minutes per participant, to compare the use of the interdental sound by participants of Peninsular origin and participants of Amazigh origin. A striking conclusion that she reaches is that none of her Amazigh-origin participants, referred to as *musulmanes* in her study, uses *distinción* which she defines broadly as "distinción habitual" (Ruiz Domínguez, 1999, p. 129). They either use *seseo*, at a rate of 82.51%, or *alternancia* at a rate of (17.49%). With regards to the Peninsular-origin speakers, referred to as *cristianos* in her study, she shows that *distinción* is used in 53.51% of the cases, *alternancia* in 27.95% of the cases, and *seseo* in

18.54%. She states that in the case of the Amazigh-origin population "a diferencia de lo que sucede en los cristianos, no se recoge ningún caso de distinción" (Ruiz Domínguez, 1999, p.134). Another surprising result is that her Peninsular-origin male participants do not use *seseo*, while women use it at a rate of 40.17%. On the other hand, within the Amazigh-origin speakers, men use *seseo* in 96.03% of the cases and women in 65.98%, the rest are cases of *alternancia* between both as she describes it. One issue appears to be that unless the participants use *distinción* categorically, their usage is considered *alternancia* by Ruiz Domínguez.

Finally, López Fernández and Vallejos Jiménez (2010) carried out a study with 15 Peninsular-origin speakers and 15 Amazigh-origin speakers in Melilla stratified according to their "native language". They opted to use only 20 tokens per speaker resulting in a total of 600 tokens in total. They divided their participants into three groups: Spanish speakers, Tamazight speakers (referred to in their study as Chelja), and bilingual speakers. Their results show that *distinción* was used in 72.3% of the cases by those who claimed to be native Spanish speakers, 48% by those who claimed to have Tamazight as their native language, and 38% by bilingual speakers. In sum, studies on the use of the interdental fricative in Melilla claim that the Amazigh-origin population uses *seseo* predominantly regardless of gender.

2. A sociolinguistic profile of Melilla

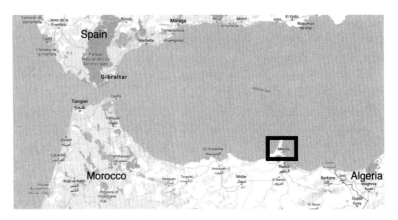

Map 1. Geographical location of Melilla (Source: map data ©2020 Inst. Geogr. Nacional)

The city of Melilla is one of two Spanish North African autonomous cities embedded in the Moroccan coast (the other is Ceuta). As shown in the map, in addition to being physically detached from Spain, Melilla has an extension of only 4.7 square miles. The Spanish occupied Melilla in 1497 and the city has remained a part of Spain since then. Before achieving the status of *ciudad autónoma* 'autonomous city' in 1995, Melilla was a municipality of the Málaga Province. Another defining aspect of Melilla is the fact that its population, some 84,000 people, is evenly divided between residents of Peninsular Spanish origin and residents of Amazigh (Berber) origin (Instituto Nacional de Estadística, 2020a). In addition to this ethnic division, religion is a factor commonly used to determine membership in one group or another by the residents themselves. The term *musulmanes* is often heard in reference to Amazigh residents while the term *cristianos* is often heard in reference to residents of Peninsular origin. In addition, historically, there has been a small presence of Jewish and Hindu populations that have seen their numbers reduced drastically in the recent decades (Sayahi & Montero Alonso, 2021). We recognize that the use of religious affiliation or national origin can be confusing as the majority of Melillans are Spanish nationals. For the sake of clarity, in the remainder of this article we will use the terms Amazigh-origin and Peninsular-origin to distinguish between the two major ethnic groups of Spanish speakers in Melilla.

With regard to language, Melilla is officially a monolingual city. All government and other official business is conducted in Spanish. Education is also imparted exclusively in Spanish with other European languages taught as foreign languages as is the case in the rest of Spain. What is interesting is that, despite the official monolingualism of the city, the population of Peninsular origin remains overwhelmingly monolingual in Spanish, but the Amazigh population is highly bilingual in Spanish and Tamazight. Tamazight is an Afro-Asiatic language that is part of the Berber languages family, or Amazigh languages, native to North Africa. The variety spoken in Melilla is the same that is spoken in the neighboring oriental region of Morocco and especially the province of Nador. Known locally as Tamazight, Tarifit, or Riffian, this variety is spoken by more than a million speakers.

In a survey of 92 residents of the city, Sayahi and Montero Alonso (2021) found that among the Amazigh participants only 11.90% claimed that they do not speak Tamazight, while the majority 52.38% claimed they have native competence, and 40.48% claimed they have some competence in the language. Residents of Amazigh origin in Melilla are exposed to Tamazight at home, in their community, and through extensive ties with Morocco to where many Melillans travel on a regular basis. They all develop competence in Spanish in the community and especially once they start formal schooling. Other languages, including Arabic, do not seem to enjoy the same type of use among the Amazigh community. Arabic is a language strongly associated with the Islamic religion practiced by the Amazigh population but is not of common use in Melilla. Sayahi and Montero (2021) also showed that Amazigh speakers have positive attitude towards both Tamazight and Spanish and would like to see Tamazight recognized as a co-official language. While Spain adheres to the *European Charter for Regional or Minority Languages* and recognizes several regional languages in the Iberian Peninsula including Catalan, Basque and Galician, Tamazight is not recognized by the Spanish State despite its widespread use among the Amazigh community of Melilla.

As a result of this ethnolinguistic composition of the city, speakers of Spanish in Melilla can be divided into three groups. The first group are speakers of Spanish of Peninsular origin. They tend to be monolingual in Spanish, with no knowledge of Tamazight. Their variety of Spanish shares strong similarities with eastern Andalusian varieties, especially that of the Málaga region, including some lexical features and a predominant final consonant weakening. The second group are speakers of Spanish of Amazigh origin who were born in Melilla or who settled there at a very early age. This group of speakers tend to be highly bilingual in Spanish and Tamazight, often showing typical phenomena of intense language contact situations such as code switching and lexical borrowing. The third group are Moroccan immigrants and cross-border workers (*trabajadores fronterizos*) who are L2 Spanish speakers with variable levels of competence in the language. The focus of this chapter is on the first two groups of speakers.

3. Methods

In order to examine the use of *distinción* in Melilla, we analyze recorded sociolinguistic interviews with 20 educated speakers: 10 Amazigh-origin speakers (5 males, 5 females), and 10 Peninsular-origin speakers (5 males, 5 females). By educated we refer to participants who at least completed their secondary education. In fact, in the present sample, all but 2 Peninsular-origin speakers had a university education. With regard to age, we included 8 speakers aged between 20 and 30, 5 aged between 31 and 50, and 7 above 51. Difficulty in contacting educated older Amazigh-origin speakers prompted us to not consider age as a factor in the current study. With an average duration of 30 minutes, the interviews have the nature of a general conversation where participants had the opportunity to talk about their childhood, education, and professions. Participants were also asked about changes they were observing in day-to-day life in Melilla and during their visits to neighboring Morocco. The interviews were conducted separately by the two researchers both of whom use *distinción* consistently, which could have led to different degrees of convergence by the participants (Giles & Powesland, 1975). The impact of the interviewers' own behavior is worthy of additional exploration in future studies on variation in the use of /θ/, as it has been for example in the case of final /s/ articulation (Corbett, 2019), but is not considered in the current study.

We set out to answer the following research questions: (1) What is the frequency and diffusion of the interdental fricative use in Melillan Spanish? What are the main factors that condition the alternation between [s] and [θ]? The social factors that we are taking into account to answer these two questions are ethnicity and gender of the speaker. With regards to the linguistic factors we considered grapheme ⟨ce, ci, z⟩, position in the word (word-initial, word-internal, word-final), position in the syllable (onset, coda), preceding segment (vowel, consonant, pause), following segment (vowel, consonant, pause), type of word (noun, verb, adjective, adverb, determinant/ number, other), syllable stress (stressed, unstressed), and existence of other sibilants (including all possible combination of sibilants in different positions). For the last factor, we looked at whether there is another [θ], as in *recepción* 'reception' or other /s/ sounds in onset and coda position as in *distancias* 'distances', among other possible combinations. Two other factors that we considered are priming (Torres Cacoullos & Travis, 2019), referring to what the speaker used in the previous context of occurrence for [θ], and frequency, referring to the relative frequency of the word compared to other words with a context of occurrence for the interdental in our corpus.

We used auditory analysis to extract all realizations of the graphemes ⟨ce⟩, ⟨ci⟩ and ⟨z⟩. We did not consider realization of the grapheme ⟨s⟩ since we did not observe any cases of *ceceo*, or the realization of graphemic ⟨s⟩ as [θ], in our corpus. Initial data analysis for descriptive statistics and chi-squared tests was carried out using the Statistical Package for Social Sciences (IBM Corp., 2020). Additional logistic regression analyses with mixed effects models that consider both fixed and random predicting variables were carried out using Rbrul (Johnson, 2022).

4. Results

In total, we extracted 3660 cases of ⟨ce⟩, ⟨ci⟩ and ⟨z⟩ where [θ] could have occurred from our data, an average of 183 per participant. As shown in Table 2, out of the total cases that we extracted, 2854 (78%) were realized as interdental, 625 (17.07%) as alveolar, 65 (1.77%) were deletions, and 116 (3.16%) were cases of voicing of the grapheme ⟨z⟩. Looking at the diffusion of [θ] among our participants, we find that all speakers used instances of [θ] at least 5 times, while 12 speakers showed no cases of *seseo* or fewer than 5 cases. What this means is that [θ] indeed forms part of the phonetic inventory of speakers in Melilla even if its use varies significantly.

Graph 1 is an illustration of the distribution of speakers according to the total percent of their use of [θ] and [s], each circle represents one speaker. It shows that, in the current sample, there is not any speaker who uses *seseo* in 100% of the

Table 2. Global realization of the graphemes ⟨ce⟩, ⟨ci⟩, and ⟨z⟩

	Interdental	Alveolar	Deletion	Voicing	Total
⟨ce⟩, ⟨ci⟩, ⟨z⟩	2854 (78%)	625 (17.07%)	65 (1.77%)	116 (3.16%)	3660 (100%)

cases with the graphemes ⟨ce⟩, ⟨ci⟩, and ⟨z⟩. On the other hand, the majority of the speakers, 15 in total, show a use of the [θ] that is between 80% and 100%. Only two speakers use [θ] categorically in all contexts. A first conclusion that can be drawn at this point, based on the percent use of [θ] for each of the twenty participants, is that in Melilla, the use of *distinción* is dominant but it is not categorical (Mean: 83.715; Standard Deviation: 24.73).

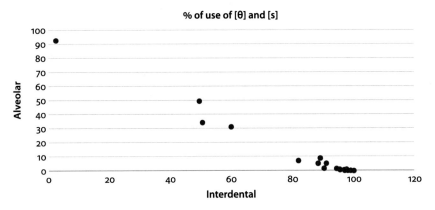

Graph 1. Individual speaker precent of use of [θ] and [s] with ⟨ce, ci, z⟩

Looking at the role of ethnicity in the use of [θ], the results in Graph 2 show that speakers of Amazigh origin use it at a rate of 72%, while Peninsular-origin speakers use it at a rate of 89.3%. The speakers of Peninsular origin clearly show a more dominant use of *distinción*, a difference of 17.3%. In addition, the range is much greater for the Amazigh-origin group. There are two outliers in each group whose use diverges significantly from the rest of the group (one Peninsular-origin speaker indicated by an asterisk and one Amazigh-origin speaker indicated by a circle in the graph). This is not totally unexpected, both because of the sociolinguistic context of Melilla and because of the fact that the presence of outliers, defined by Britain (2003, p. 191) as "individuals whose linguistic behavior for some reason falls well outside that of the wider speech community", is not uncommon.

With regards to gender, Graph 3 shows that female speakers from both ethnicities use [θ] more consistently, with female Amazigh speakers reaching a total of 92% while Peninsular female speakers reaching 97.1%. This is in line with Labov's (2001, p. 293) statement that "women conform more closely than men to socio-

Chapter 5. Variation in the use of the interdental fricative in Melilla   121

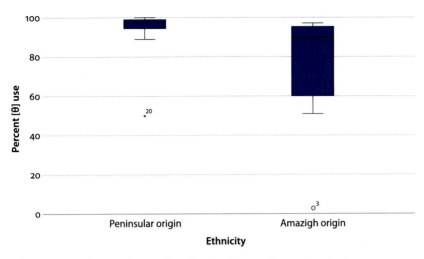

Graph 2. Use of [θ] according to ethnicity with the graphemes ⟨ce, ci, z⟩

linguistic norms that are overtly prescribed". It was mentioned above that several studies have shown that *distinción* is perceived as the more prestigious option in different communities. Awareness of the stigma surrounding the use of *seseo* is indeed high in Melilla. One participant in our study stated that people in Melilla: "[…] hablan bastante bien en comparación con otras regiones como Andalucía que también sesean mucho y eso". We will come back to the role of language attitude in the use of *distinción* in the conclusion of this chapter.

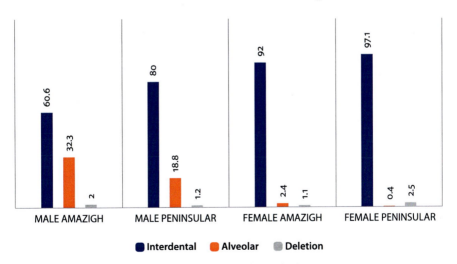

Graph 3. Use of the interdental fricative by gender and ethnicity

Peninsular-origin males on the other hand use *distinción* at a rate of 80% while Amazigh-origin males use it the least, with a rate of 60.2%. In Graph 4, we also see that the difference between males and females of the same ethnicity is larger among participants of Amazigh origin. In sum, women of both origins use the [θ] more than men with Peninsular-origin women nearing a categorical use, while Amazigh-origin men show the highest variation in their overall use of the interdental.

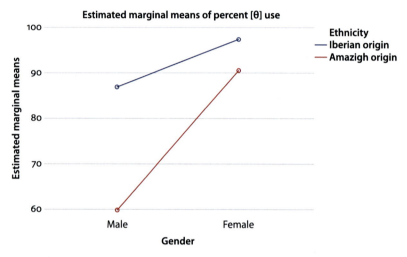

Graph 4. Estimated marginal means of the percentages of [θ] use

A one-level logistic regression analysis (Table 3) confirms that ethnicity (*p* = .00) and gender (*p* = .00) are both significant predictors of the use of *distinción*. Female speakers and Peninsular-origin speakers are the ones who use *distinción* more frequently. A positive log odds value indicates a positive correlation between the factor and the dependent variable, in this case use of [θ], while a negative log odds value indicates a disfavoring effect. In turn, factor weights range between 0 and 1, with factor weights that are higher than 0.50 indicating a positive effect while values that are lower than 0.50 show a disfavoring effect.

For the next step in our analysis, we carried out a linear mixed effects analysis in Rbrul. The factors tested were gender and ethnicity as fixed effects, with individual speaker as a random effect. The results confirm that ethnicity is highly significant (*p* = 0.011), but gender on the other hand becomes not significant (*p* = 0.075) when ethnicity of individual speakers is taken into consideration. This is so because although overall speakers of Amazigh origin use *distinción* at a lower rate, it is Amazigh men who bring the overall rate down while Amazigh women's rate of use remains high. With "speaker" as random effect the model shows the

Table 3. A one-level logistic regression analysis of the role of gender and ethnicity in [θ] use

	Factor weight	Log odds	N	% [θ] use
Female	0.734	1.017	1559	94
Male	0.266	−1.017	2101	65
Peninsular	0.620	0.489	1264	89
Amazigh	0.380	−0.489	2396	72

sizeable variation across speakers with a large standard deviation (SD=1.663). This is not surprising given that the speaker with the lowest use of *distinción*, Speaker 3 (Amazigh-origin male), used it only in 2.5% of the cases (log odds: −4.205, factor weight=0.016) while one of the speakers with highest use of *distinción*, speaker 11 (Iberian-origin male), diverges greatly from other males (log odds=2.23, factor weight: 0.91) because his categorical use of *distinción* separates him significantly from other males in the sample, especially Amazigh-origin males. The other speaker with a categorical use of *distinción* is speaker 19 (Iberian-origin female) whose numbers are lower than the male categorical user of *distinción* (log odds=0.881, factor weight=0.724) because females of both ethnic origins make an overall much higher use of *distinción* and are clustered together more closely. In sum, while variation between speakers is significant, differences exist mostly between Amazigh-origin males and the rest.

Moving on to the linguistic variables, the first factor that we looked at is the role of the grapheme. Of all tokens, the grapheme ⟨ci⟩ is the most frequent context of occurrence, representing 51% (*n*=1867) of all cases. ⟨ci⟩ was realized as [θ] in 81.2% of the times (log odds=0.450, factor weight=0.61). The next most frequent context is ⟨ce⟩, which represents 31% (*n*=1135) of the total. The interdental was used at a very similar rate to what occurred with ⟨ci⟩, in 83.3% of the cases (log odds=0.309, factor weight=0.57). Finally, in the case of ⟨z⟩, as expected, it is the least frequent context representing 18% (*n*=658) of all cases. The grapheme ⟨z⟩ was realized as [θ] only in 59.7% of the cases (log odds=−0.760, factor weight=0.31). A Pearson Chi-Square test shows a significant association between [θ] use and type of grapheme: ($X^2(6)$=859.476, *p*<.001). This confirms that ⟨ce⟩ and ⟨ci⟩ trigger a higher and similar rate of [θ] use, while ⟨z⟩ is realized as [θ] at a significantly lower rate compared to the other two graphemes, with a significant rate of the tokens being voiced (17.6%) and deleted (9.7%).

In the case of position in the word, the contexts for the occurrence of the interdental are much more frequent in word-medial position (83.6%, *n*=3061), followed by word-initial position (13.4%, *n*=489), and word-final position (3%,

$n=110$). In both initial and medial position, the use of [θ] shows similar frequency 77.1% (log odds = 0.565, factor weight = 0.63) and 79.3% (log odds = 0.434, factor weight = 0.60), but in final position the use of [θ] decreases to 44.5%, while deletion increases to 50% (log odds = −0.999, factor weight = 0.26). The reason for the higher rates of deletion in final position has to do with the tendency to weaken final consonants, and particularly final /s/, in Melillan Spanish in general (Ruiz Domínguez, 1999, p. 55). As such, position in the word is significant when the ⟨z⟩ is in final position as it tends to be deleted half the time. This result is similar to that of González Las (1991: 56) who found that in final position the grapheme ⟨z⟩ was deleted in 57% of the cases by her Peninsular-origin speakers in Melilla.

In relation to position in the syllable, contexts of [θ] occurrence in onset position represent 95% of the cases (3476/3660) of which 78.8% ($n=2738$) are realized as [θ], 17.9% ($n=621$) are realized as [s], and 3.3% ($n=116$) are realized as [z]. The rate of [θ] use in syllable-onset position reflects its overall use in the data, also 78%. What is interesting here is that the majority of the cases of voicing happened with the word *Tamazight* in the speech of Amazigh-origin men who tend to maintain the native [z], unlike other participants. In turn, contexts of [θ] occurrence in coda position represent only 5% of the tokens (184/3660) with 63% ($n=116$) realized as [θ], 34.8% ($n=64$) are deletions, and 2.2% ($n=4$) are [s]. Here again, like in word-final position, in syllable-final position we are dealing with the grapheme ⟨z⟩ which tends to be deleted frequently as is the case of other final consonants in Melillan Spanish (González Las, 1991).

Another linguistic variable that we looked at is the preceding sound. Although initially we coded for each vowel separately, the results were very similar, so we grouped them together. When the preceding sound is a vowel, [θ] was produced in 78.92% of the cases (log odds = 0.167, factor weight = 0.52), very close to when the preceding sound is a consonant (80%, log odds = 0.159, factor weight = 0.54). Although we had very few cases where the context for the occurrence of the interdental was after a pause ($n=21$), this context produced the highest rate of use of [s] (36.4%, log odds = −0.667, factor weight = 0.33).

Table 4. Use of [θ] according to preceding sound

	Frequency	Interdental use	Alveolar	Deletion
After vowels	77.1% ($n=2602$)	78.92%	17.8%	1.1%
After consonants	28% ($n=1025$)	80%	19.9%	0.1%
After pause	0.9% ($n=21$)	63.6%	36.4%	0%

With regard to syllable stress, ⟨ce⟩, ⟨ci⟩, and ⟨z⟩ occurred in stressed syllables on 1867 occasions and on 1793 occasions in unstressed syllables, with similar rates of use of [s]: 17.4% in stressed syllables and 16.7% in unstressed syllables. In unstressed syllables, [θ] was used in 80% of the cases (log odds = 0.15, factor weight = 0.53) and in stressed syllable it surfaced in 75% of the cases (log odds = −0.15, factor weight = 0.46). We also considered all possible combinations for the existence of another sibilant in the word, including other instances of the interdental and the presence of other [s] sounds. In the majority of the cases when [θ] occurred by itself in the word (*n* = 2431; 66% of the cases), only 16.4% of the tokens were produced as [s]. The second most frequent pattern is the presence of a coda /s/ that is usually deleted in Melillan Spanish, *n* = 851 (23.3%), and where 18% of the tokens for the occurrence of [θ] were produced as [s]. There were 81 cases where a word contained two contexts for the occurrence of [θ], such as in the words *ejercicio*, and *organización*, but there were no cases where a speaker showed a lack of harmony by pronouncing them differently, making the claim that some speakers alternate between *distinción* and *seseo* in the same word highly implausible. Finally, the presence of a non-coda /s/ along with [θ] led to 21.3% of usage of [s] (32/150 tokens), which is not different from the overall rates of use of [θ] in our data, leading us to conclude that the presence of an ⟨s⟩ in the word does not trigger more *seseo*, and that in general the presence of other sibilants does not lead to different rates in the use of *distinción*.

Another variable that we considered in the current study is the relative frequency of the words containing ⟨ce⟩, ⟨ci⟩, or ⟨z⟩ in our corpus. We created a scale, from 1 (very frequent) to 5 (not frequent) that reflects the frequency of these words in our dataset according to the number of occurrences and the percent that the frequency of a given word represents of the total tokens that were extracted:

1 = More frequent: 110 occurrences or more (3% or above of all tokens)
2 = Frequent: 74–109 occurrences (between 2% and 3% of all tokens)
3 = Average: 37–73 occurrences (between 1% and 2% of all tokens)
4 = Less frequent: 19–36 occurrences (between 0.5% and 1%)
5 = Not frequent: 18 occurrences or fewer (less than 0.5% of all tokens)

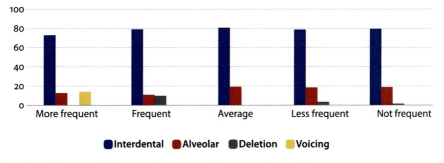

Graph 5. The use of [θ] according to word frequency in our data

As Graph 5 shows, use of [θ] is very similar regardless of frequency. Specifically, [θ] was used 73% with the more frequent words, 79.1% with frequent words, 80.8% with average frequency words, 78.8% with less frequent words, and 79.5% with words that are not very frequent. While the percent is lowest for more frequent words, 73%, it is, as mentioned above, because one of the more frequent words, Tamazight, tends to be voiced by Amazigh-origin speakers who pronounce it as it is articulated in the language. In fact, voicing reaches 14.1% of the tokens in the more frequent words category while it is non-existent in the case of the rest of the words. Table 5 below shows that the most frequent words with a context for [θ] occurrence in our data are forms of the words *decir*, 'to say', *entonces* 'so', *hacer* 'to do', *tamazight*, and *vez* 'time'. We included in the count different verb forms and plurals if they still contain a context for the occurrence of [θ]. For example, we included the word *dice* 's/he says' but not *digo* 'I say'.

Table 5. The 10 most frequent words with a context for [θ] occurrence in our data

1) Decir: 293	2) Entonces: 214	3) Hacer: 196	4) Tamazight: 128	5) Vez: 90
6) Re/conocer: 80	7) Ciudad: 72	8) Cinco: 50	9) Empezar: 44	10) Acento: 38

Finally, we considered how priming, the articulation of the previous token by the same speaker, affects the one that follows it. Based on Table 6 below, it is clear that the use of [θ] triggers more of its use. In 90.9% of the cases, the interdental was followed by another interdental (log odds = 1.591, factor weight = 0.83) and only in 5.1% it was followed by [s] (log odds = −1.856, factor weight = 0.13). On the other hand, use of [s] was followed by [θ] in 24.1% of the cases with a preference by the speakers to follow one [s] with another [s] in 70.7% of the cases. Looking at each ethnic group, participants of Peninsular origin followed one [θ] by an [s] in 42 cases only (3.7%). On the other hand, participants of Amazigh origin switched from [θ] to [s] in 105 cases (6.1%). In sum, although participants of Amazigh origin, especially men, alternated more often, the overall rate is still very low. A Pearson Chi Square test shows that there is a statistically significant relationship between the use of [θ] and the occurrence of the same sound in the previous context ($p = .00$).

5. Conclusion

The interdental fricative occurs at a frequency of 78% in Melilla. All speakers, regardless of ethnicity and gender, made use of [θ] indicating that it forms part of the phonetic inventory of all participants, but distribution varies.

Table 6. Use of [θ] according to the articulation of the preceding token

		Interdental	Alveolar	Deletion	Voicing
Previous token	Interdental	2586	147	48	65
		90.9%	5.1%	1.7%	2.3%
	Alveolar	148	435	9	23
		24.1%	70.7%	1.5%	3.7%

Ethnic origin and gender play the most significant role in this distribution as male Amazigh speakers use the interdental at the lowest rate of 60.6%, while female participants of Peninsular origin use it at a rate of 97.1%. Linguistic factors do not significantly condition the use of the interdental as rates are similar to the overall usage in each case. However, priming is a major factor as use of the interdental in a preceding context triggers additional use of [θ] for all speakers in 90.9% of the cases. Looking at the content of the interviews themselves and the type of language ideologies that can be gleaned from them, it becomes clear that negative attitudes towards *seseo* help explain the higher usage of *distinción* by women in general and males of Peninsular origin as well. For example, one female Peninsular-origin speaker mentions that "Realmente el seseo es más bien para gente de poca formación, con pocos estudios." Although we did not consider different levels of education in this study, it could be a factor, but even highly educated speakers may show cases of *seseo* as described by the following speaker: "[…] tiene estudios universitarios y todo, […] sesea mucho, pero es una manía suya porque en su casa no sesea nadie. […] Y yo me meto mucho con él porque no tiene por qué sesear. Yo le achaco más a eso, son vulgarismos."

Peninsular-origin speakers tend to perceive strong differences in the Spanish used by bilingual speakers and often ascribe divergences to their competence in Tamazight. One Peninsular-origin participant mentions that "El deje siempre lo tienen, siempre. ¿Por qué? Porque hablan su idioma en sus domicilios, en sus casas […]. Se destacan enseguida." Another speaker mentions how use of Tamazight is interfering with Spanish in Melilla to the degree that it is affecting Spanish used by speakers of Peninsular origin as well: "Los hablantes melillenses que no son de origen bereber están adaptando rasgos lingüísticos de estos que son bereberes." In fact, and in direct relevance with our study, one participant of Peninsular origin was more categorical in stating that: "Ese [sesear] es un rasgo distintivo de los bilingües."

Since using *seseo* is associated with less prestigious Spanish varieties in Melilla, it is not surprising that women, regardless of ethnicity, use *distinción* more often. Ideology indeed seems to be a determining factor in sociolinguistic variation in this case, reminiscent of Labov's (2010, p. 244) statement that "the most convincing and demonstrable determinants of language change are structural and mechanical, but we must be alert to the possibility that ideology is a driving force behind change, as well as a barrier to its further expansion." This is particularly true in Melilla, given the sharp ethnic and religious differences that mark a city of only 4.7 square miles.

References

Alvar, M. (1972). A vueltas con el seseo y el ceceo. *Romántica*, 5, 41–58.
Britain, D. (2003). Exploring the Importance of the Outlier in Sociolinguistic Dialectology. In D. Britain & J. Cheshire (Eds.), *Social Dialectology: In Honour of Peter Trudgill* (pp. 191–208). John Benjamins.
Caravedo, R. (1992). ¿Restos de la distinción /s/ /z/ en el español de Perú? *Revista de Filología Española* 72(3/4), 639–654.
Corbett, C. (2019). Short-Term Accommodation as a Function of Addressee Language Proficiency. *Spanish in Context*, 16(2), 173–93.
Dalbor, J. (1980). Observations on Present-Day Seseo and Ceceo in Southern Spain. *Hispania*, 63(1), 5–19.
García-Amaya, L. J. (2008). Variable norms in the production of /θ/ in Jerez de la Frontera, Spain. In J. F. Siegel, T. C. Nagle, A. Lorente-Lapole, & J. Auger (Eds.), *IUWPL7: Gender in Language: Classic Questions, New Contexts* (pp. 49–71). IULC Publications.
Giles, H., & Powesland, P. (1975). *Speech Style and Social Evaluation*. Academic Press.
González-Bueno, M. (1993). Variaciones en el tratamiento de las sibilante Inconsistencia en el seseo sevillano: Un enfoque sociolingüístico. *Hispania*, 76, 392–398.
González Las, C. (1991). *El español en Melilla: fonética y fonología*. Servicio de Publicaciones del Excmo. Ayuntamiento de Melilla.
Hernández-Campoy, J. & Villena Ponsoda, J. (2009). Standardness and nonstandardness in Spain. *International Journal of the Sociology of Language*, 196–197, 181–214.
Hualde, J. I., Olarrea, A., Escobar, A. M., Travis, C. E., & Sanz, C. (2020). *Introducción a la lingüística hispánica* (3rd ed.). Cambridge: Cambridge University Press.
IBM Corp. (2020). *IBM SPSS Statistics for Windows, Version 27.0*. IBM Corp.
Instituto Nacional de Estadística. 2020a. Población residente por fecha, sexo y edad. Retrieved November 1, 2024, from https://www.ine.es/jaxiT3/Datos.htm?t=31304#!tabs-tabla
Johnson, D. E. (2022). Rbrul version 3.1.6. http://www.danielezrajohnson.com/rbrul.html
Labov, W. (2001). *Principles of linguistic change, volume 2: Social factors*. Blackwell.
Lapesa, R. (1956). Sobre el ceceo y el seseo en Hispanoamérica. *Revista iberoamericana*, 21(41), 409–416.
Lipski, J. M. (2019). Spanish phonological variation. In S. Colina & F. Martínez-Gil (Eds.), *The Routledge Handbook of Spanish. Phonology* (pp. 455–469). Routledge.

Lipski, J. M. & Sayahi, L. (2023). La historia de la lengua española en África. In S. N. Dworkin, G. Clavería Nadal, & A. Octavio de Toledo y Huerta (Eds.), *Lingüística histórica del español / The Routledge Handbook of Spanish Historical Linguistics* (pp. 577–588). Routledge.

López Fernández, S. & Vallejos Jiménez, M. (2010). Los fenómenos del seseo y la distinción en el habla de Melilla. In E. T. Montoro del Arco & J. A. Moya Corral (Eds.), *El español en contexto: actas de las XV Jornadas sobre la Lengua Española y su Enseñanza* (pp. 163–174). Universidad de Granada.

Melguizo Moreno, E. (2007). La variación de /θs/: Estudio comparativo de dos muestras de población de Granada. *Estudios de Lingüística Universidad de Alicante*, 21(1), 1–16.

Moreno Fernández, F. (2005). Sobre la existencia de [z] en el español de América. In *Filología y Lingüística. Estudios ofrecidos a Antonio Quilis* (pp. 1089–1109). CSIC-UNED-Universidad de Valladolid.

Morillo-Velarde, R. (1997). Seseo, ceceo y seceo: problemas metodológicos. In A. Narbona & M. Ropero (Eds.), *El habla andaluza.* (pp. 201–21). Universidad de Sevilla.

Moya Corral, J. & Sosiński, M. (2015). La inserción social del cambio. La distinción s/θ en Granada. Análisis en tiempo aparente y en tiempo real. *Lingüística Española Actual*, 37(1), 33–72.

Penny, R. (2009). *A history of the Spanish language.* Cambridge University Press.

Penny, R. (2000). *Variation and Change in Spanish.* Cambridge University Press.

Regan, B. (2021). Analyzing Andalusian coronal fricative norms (ceceo, seseo, and distinción) using a sociophonetic Demerger Index. In M. Díaz-Campos (Ed.), *The Routledge Handbook of Variationist Approaches to Spanish* (pp. 137–158). Routledge.

Regan, B. (2020). The split of a fricative merger due to dialect contact and societal changes: A sociophonetic study on Andalusian Spanish read-speech. *Language Variation and Change*, 32(2), 159–190.

Ringer-Hilfinger, K. (2013). The acquisition of sociolinguistic variation by study abroad students: the case of American students in Madrid. [Doctoral dissertation, University at Albany].

Ruiz Domínguez, M. (1997). Estudio sociolingüístico del habla de Melilla. [Doctoral dissertation, Universidad de Alcalá de Henares].

Ruiz Domínguez, M. (1999). El seseo en el habla de la ciudad de Melilla. *Lingüística Española Actual*, 21(1), 127–148.

Salvador, F. (1980). Niveles sociolingüísticos de seseo, ceceo y distinción en la ciudad de Granada. *Español actual*, 37, 25–32

Sayahi, L. (2011). Spanish in Contact with Arabic. In M. Díaz-Campos (Ed.), *The Handbook of Spanish Sociolinguistics* (pp. 473–490). Wiley-Blackwell.

Sayahi, L. & Montero Alonso, M. (2021). Bilingualism and language attitude in Melilla (Spain). *Revista Lengua y Migración / Language & Migration*, 13(1), 55–75.

Scipione, R. & Sayahi, L. (2005). Consonantal Variation of Spanish in Northern Morocco. In L. Sayahi & M. Westmoreland (Eds.), *Selected Proceedings of the Second Workshop on Spanish Sociolinguistics*, (pp. 127–132). Cascadilla Press.

Torres Cacoullos, R. & Travis, C. E. (2019). Variationist typology: Shared probabilistic constraints across (non-)null subject languages. *Linguistics*, 57(3), 653–692.

Villena Ponsoda, J. (2001). *Continuidad Del Cambio Lingüístico: Tendencias conservadoras e innovadoras en la fonología del español a la luz de la investigación sociolingüística urbana.* Universidad de Granada.

Villena Ponsoda, J. & Requena Santos, F. (1996). Género, Educación y Uso La variación social y reticular de S y Z en la ciudad de Málaga. *Lingüística* (ALFAL), 8, 5–51.

CHAPTER 6

Does increased grammaticalization yield decreased duration?
Testing *vamos a* variants in Spanish

Javier Rivas & Esther L. Brown
University of Colorado at Boulder

This study employed naturalistic data to provide a descriptive overview of the patterns of reduction in the Spanish [*ir* (PRESENT) *a* + INFINITIVE] construction (the default future marker). A durational analysis of $N=158$ tokens of *vamos* ('we go') confirms faster rates of articulation across the [*vamos a*] construction when followed by an infinitival form than when followed by an allative complement. Results reveal that the phonological reduction of *vamos a* occurs regardless of the meaning it conveys (future, hortative, habitual). We suggest shorter durations may not reflect the meaning of futurity, but rather may be associated with those constructions in which *vamos a* has undergone a process of auxiliarization as it becomes part of the infinitival periphrastic form.

Keywords: auxiliarization, durational shortening, grammaticalization, periphrastic future, phonological reduction, Spanish in contact with Galician

1. Introduction

Empirical approaches to phonological realizations in naturally occurring discourse have identified differences in duration and degrees of lenition and deletion in purportedly homophonous linguistic forms based upon meaning. This finding has implications for theories of language variation, language change and grammaticalization, as well as models of lexical representation. These variable patterns of use are tied up with grammar as they shape meanings derived in contexts. Thus, studies that highlight quantitative differences between etymologically related forms allow for detailed synchronic snapshots of processes contributing to diachronic change.

https://doi.org/10.1075/ihll.42.06riv
© 2025 John Benjamins Publishing Company

In the field of (T)ense, (A)spect, (M)ood markers, for example, a widely studied grammaticalization process is the use in Peninsular Spanish of present perfect (*ie. he comido* lit. 'I have eaten') as a perfective marker (*e.g.*, Schwenter & Torres Cacoullos, 2008; Howe, 2013). These studies reveal the pathway of this change by identifying the contexts that contribute to the spread of the innovative form into the territory of the preterit. In addition to the grammatical changes these forms undergo, recent work (Howe, 2021) identifies a reduction in the phonological realization of the auxiliary *haber* in correlation with the meaning of perfective. This finding provides empirical support for the widely cited connection between phonological reduction and greater grammaticalization (Hopper & Traugott, 2003; Bybee, 2010).

Following this line of research, in this study we explore a previously unanalyzed potential case of divergence (Hopper, 1991) in Spanish. The construction [*ir* + *a*] 'go to' can appear in lexically transparent uses expressing 'movement towards' ([*vamos a*] + *Santiago* 'we go/are going to Santiago') as well as in constructions grammaticalized to differing degrees in which the verbal construction has become an auxiliary, for example with the periphrastic future forms ([*vamos a*] + *ser viejos*, 'we're going to be old'). This work examines durations of *vamos a* across different meanings of the construction in order to determine whether there is any correlation in durations between forms and functions. More specifically, using naturalistic data and variationist methodology (Labov, 1994; Tagliamonte, 2012), we aim to determine whether the more grammaticalized form expressing future correlates with significantly shorter durations.

2. Background

Languages commonly use more than one strategy to express future (Bybee et al., 1994, p. 243). In Spanish, for example, in certain contexts both simple present (Orozco, 2005, 2007, 2018), and present progressive (Aponte Alequín & Ortiz López, 2010; Cipria, 2021), as well as other constructions such as *estar a punto de* 'to be about to' serve to express events that will happen at a point subsequent to the speech moment. More commonly, however, the expression of future is associated with two main strategies: synthetic and periphrastic future forms. The synthetic future (*cantaré* 'I will sing'), also called morphological future, was originally a periphrastic form that became fused very early in the developmental history of Spanish (Fleischman, 1982; Penny, 1991; Company Company, 2006) and is older than the periphrastic future [*ir* (PRESENT) *a* + INFINITIVE], *voy a cantar* 'I am going to sing']. The periphrastic construction, which displayed very low frequency throughout the history of Spanish and gained traction in the 19th century (Aaron, 2010, p. 5), is now the most frequent marker of futurity, especially in spoken Spanish (Gutiérrez, 1994; Sedano, 2006). The synthetic future form, *cantaré* 'I will sing', has acquired epistemic and other modality-related meanings (see Aaron, 2014 and references therein), as is common in language for grams expressing simple future (Bybee et al., 1994, p. 279).

The grammaticalization of [*ir* (PRESENT) *a* + INFINITIVE] as a future marker is well advanced in present-day Spanish. This widely studied grammaticalization process has been considered from a diachronic (Aaron, 2006, 2010, 2014) and synchronic perspective in both monolingual (Orozco, 2005, 2018: Colombian, Serrano, 2006: Venezuelan, Giordano, 2022: Peninsular Spanish) and contact varieties (Orozco, 2007, 2018: Spanish-English, Blas Arroyo, 2008: Spanish-Catalan), as well as in second and heritage language (Gudmestad & Geeslin, 2011, de Prada Pérez et al., 2021) varieties of Spanish. Consequently, we have detailed knowledge of the grammatical, semantic, and pragmatic changes that this grammaticalization pathway entails.

For example, at the grammatical level, the construction undergoes a gradual increase in unit-hood as *ir* becomes an auxiliary verb. Concurrently, *ir* also goes through a process of desemanticization from a more concrete meaning of 'motion' to a more abstract meaning of 'futurity'. This change takes place in a very specific context: constructions in which *ir* is followed by an infinitival clause of purpose headed by *a* (e.g., *voy a España a visitar a mi familia* 'I am going to Spain to visit my family'). It is in this context that the construction undergoes a pragmatic change because purposive constructions have an inference of 'futurity' (Hopper & Traugott, 2003, p. 3).

In addition to changes at the morphosyntactic, semantic, and pragmatic levels, grammaticalization processes often entail phonological reduction (Hopper & Traugott, 2003; Brinton & Traugott, 2005; Bybee 2010, 2015). Phonological reduction includes syllable and segment lenition, syllable and segment elision, and durational shortening of segments and words. Perhaps the area in which phonological reduction has been more closely considered is in the case of discourse markers. Studies across multiple languages report greater degrees of reduction in discourse markers compared to their lexical sources [*e.g.*, English: *you know* (Schubotz et al., 2015), Spanish: *o sea* 'I mean' (Bybee et al., 2016; Martínez Gómez & Ibarra Zetter, 2017), Dutch: *eigenlikjkin* 'actually' (Plug, 2005; Ernestus & Smith, 2018), Hebrew: *axshav* 'now' (Gonen et al., 2015)].

Studies contrasting etymologically related words with different functions produce results that support an Exemplar Model of lexical representation (Bybee, 2001). Separate lexical representations in memory emerge for the different lexical units (*e.g.* discourse marker, non-discourse marker) reflecting their unique variability of form and meaning derived from contexts of use. That is, the lexical items, although historically related, through an accumulation of experience in use come to be stored independently. The storage in memory need not be limited to single lexical items, but rather includes storage of multiple words as one unit of representation. For example, *I don't know* (Bybee & Scheibman, 1999) or *no sé* 'I don't know' (Rivas & Brown, 2010), reveal reductive effects of the discourse marker compared to the lexically transparent counterpart that suggest storage of multi-word combinations as one lexical unit. Evidence from these studies support a view espousing separate lexical storage for historically related lexical items whereby effects of use are stored on the word, the combination of words, or possibly as part of the articulation plan at a more abstract level of the construction [e.g. *es decir* 'I mean' (Brown & Rivas, 2024)].

Phonological reduction is also associated with the grammaticalization of TAM markers: e.g., *I am going to visit* > *I am gonna visit*. Bybee (2010) argues that grammaticalized constructions are specific examples of old constructions whose components undergo a loss of analyzability and compositionality. Through multiple instances of repeated use, the source construction ([*going*] [*to*]) that includes a movement verb ('I am going') and a purposive clause ('in order to') ceases to be parsed as two separate units each with their own meaning contributing to an overall interpretation of the entire construction. This recurrent pathway of change gives rise to the emergence of new units (chunk [*going to*]) that may undergo phonological reduction (*gonna*). This is represented visually in Figure 1.

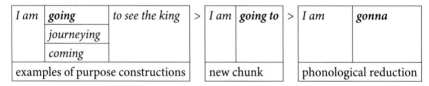

Figure 1. Sample progression of lexical item to grammaticalized form

As with the English case illustrated above, Spanish has a future construction that derives from the same source construction containing a movement verb and a purpose clause: [*voy*][*a*] > [*voy a*] + INFINITIVE. This construction may be regarded as a new chunk out of an old construction such as: *vengo* 'I come' / *voy* 'I go' / *llego* 'I arrive' / *salgo* 'I leave' + *a* 'to' + INFINITIVE. In the same way that *I am going to* reduces to *gonna*, previous studies (Lipski, 2008, p. 113, Silva-Corvalán & Enrique Arias, 2017, p. 237) suggest *voy a, vas a, va a, vamos a*, and *van a* undergo phonological reduction when they are part of the periphrastic future construction: Spanish *voy a comer* [boj-a-ko'mer] > [b(w)a-ko'mer]. Phonological reduction of the future auxiliary has not been extensively explored in a corpus-based analysis, so it is difficult to ascertain how pervasive and advanced this reduction may be.

Contexts in which *ir* is highly grammaticalized as part of the construction expressing futurity [*ir* (PRESENT) *a* + INFINITIVE] co-exist in present-day Spanish with other uses in which *ir* retains its original lexical meaning of movement (e.g., [*ir a* + ALLATIVE COMPLEMENT] which provides an opportunity for exploration. We can determine the contexts in which the construction [*ir a*] undergoes phonological reduction by comparing its duration across different construction types; more grammaticalized vs. less grammaticalized meanings. Our ultimate goal will be to determine whether the greater phonological reduction as measured by duration of the construction [*ir a*] correlates with those contexts in which the construction is used in combination with an infinitival form to express futurity. Through the analysis of synchronic variation in Spanish, we aim to empirically test the degree to which increased grammaticalization may yield decreased duration.

3. Data

In order to determine whether durational differences exist between the different uses of the [*ir a*] combination in naturalistic data, we use the ESLORA corpus (*ESLORA: Corpus para el estudio del español oral*, 2022). This corpus represents approximately 650,000 words of spoken Spanish derived from sixty hours of sociolinguistic interviews and twenty hours of casual conversation between sixty different Spanish speakers from Galicia, Spain. The conversations were recorded between 2007 and 2015. This publicly available corpus provides an orthographic transcription of the speech paired with the accompanying audio.

From this corpus we extract all the examples of first-person plural form *vamos a* 'we go, we are going to' (N=517). We choose the first-person plural form (*vamos*) because, unlike the other person-number forms (*voy* 'I go', *vas* 'you go', *va* 'she goes', *van* 'they go', *vais* 'you guys go'), *vamos* is bisyllabic, which increases the likelihood of capturing subtle differences in durations across the word. From these examples, we make certain exclusions. We do not consider in this analysis instances of *vamos a* that form part of the relatively frequent (N=238) discourse marker *vamos a ver* 'let's see' (Brenes Peña, 2008), because it has been grammaticalized to express a procedural meaning and therefore lies outside the envelope of variation we consider. An additional 121 examples are excluded due to truncation, overlap, anonymization edits, and background noise that impede the acoustic analysis of durations. These procedures yield 158 examples on which we base this project.

For each target, we also extract the pause-bounded fluent speech preceding and following the token of *vamos a*. The preceding speech context contains all words between the pause, defined as cessation of speech (>.50 sec.), up to the start of the target, and the following context is comprised of all words spoken after the target and before a following pause.

4. Methods

In order to measure target durations, we visually inspect and manually delimit each token of *vamos a* in Pratt (Boersma & Weenink, 2019). Using synchronized waveforms and spectrographic displays, we first locate the onset of the initial consonant /b/ as the start of the target word. Word-initial /b/ in Spanish is prescriptively realized as a voiced, bilabial stop [b] after pauses and nasals, and has an approximant realization in all other phonetic contexts (Navarro Tomás, 1977 [1918]). Within this tendency, however, there is a wide range of variation that is both social (Lipski, 2012) and dialectological, with pronunciations ranging from stops to outright deletions (Eddington, 2011; Carrasco et al., 2012).

For stop realizations ($N=24$) we mark the beginning of the *vamos a* token at the onset of stop closure. In cases of deleted tokens ($N=9$), in which no closure or discernible constriction is evident, the word start is established at onset of the /a/ vowel. For the majority of the tokens ($N=125$) we rely upon cues such as decreases in intensity and formant structure to mark the onset of the approximant [β]. The end of the *vamos a* targets is measured after /a/ realization. For cases in which the following word begins with /a/ ($N=32$), such as *vamos a hacer* 'we're going to do' or *vamos a Asturias* 'we're going to Asturias', target word end is set at the midpoint of the two contiguous /a/ phones.

These methods allow us to calculate a duration of all target tokens of *vamos a* in order to test whether significant differences in duration exist for the different uses of the dyad. Based upon the reading of these tokens in context, we code all targets for the meaning they express. We consider four different meanings of the form *vamos a*. Three of these meanings are conveyed by means of the construction [*vamos a* + INFINITIVE]: future ($N=64$), hortative ($N=45$) and habitual ($N=9$), each described in turn below. The other meaning, which we will call 'movement' ($N=40$), is realized through the construction [*vamos a* + ALLATIVE COMPLEMENT].

Excerpt (1) provides an example in which [*vamos a* + INFINITIVE] expresses future meaning. We classify the [*vamos a* + INFINITIVE] construction that appears in Excerpt (2) as hortative, following Gómez Torrego (1999, p. 3369), who identifies this function specifically for first person plural *vamos a*. The other meaning that [*vamos a* + INFINITIVE] conveys is habitual, exemplified in (3). In these cases, the construction indicates a habitual action (e.g., *todos los fines de semanas* 'every weekend') in the present. Finally, in (4) we provide an example of *vamos a* followed by an allative complement. In both (3) and (4), the verb *ir* maintains its lexical meaning of movement:

(1) Future: [*vamos a* + INFINITIVE]
Ahora <u>vamos a</u> coger una persona que pague autónomos
now go-PRS.1PL to hire-INF DET-F.SG person that pay-SBJV.3SG
'Now we're going to hire a person who is self-employed' SCOM_M31_038

(2) Hortative: [*vamos a* + INFINITIVE]
Yo creo que lo <u>vamos a</u> dejar aquí porque si no nos quedamos sin comer
I think-PRS.1SG that it go-PRS.1PL to leave-INF here because if no us-REFL remain-PRS.1PL without eat-INF
'Let's stop here, I think. Otherwise, we won´t have time to do lunch' SCOM_E_11

(3) Habitual: [*vamos a* + INFINITIVE]
Todos los fines de semana <u>vamos a</u> comer allí
all-M.P det-M.P end-M.P of week go-PRS.1PL to eat-INF there
'We go there to eat every weekend' SCOM_M13_008

(4) Movement: [*vamos a* + ALLATIVE COMPLEMENT]
Por ahora le gusta ir conmigo porque sabe que <u>vamos a</u> mil sitios diferentes
for now DAT-3S please-PRS.3S go-INF with-me because know-PRS.3S that go-PRS.1PL to thousand place-M.P different-P
'For now she likes to come with me because she knows that we're going to a thousand different places' SCOM_H22_026

Variable durations of words and segments in production reflect effects of multiple factors of the production context simultaneously. We seek to control the independent effects of such variables in order to ascertain whether meaning also significantly contributes to duration of targets. Therefore, we code each of the target tokens for the following linguistic factors:

Preceding pause: This control factor is included to allow us to consider potential durational differences of *vamos a* stemming from the position the construction occupies in the utterance. Tokens in utterance initial positions may be accompanied by greater articulatory prominence than tokens embedded in utterance internal positions. As such, we code each case of *vamos a* for whether it is preceded by pause ($N=25$) or not preceded by pause ($N=133$). The presence of pauses preceding the targets impeded our ability to calculate a pre-context speaking rate in syllables per second comparable to tokens in fluent discourse. We were thus unable to include pre-context speaking rate in our models without excluding the 25 tokens, which represented a significant portion of the already small data set. For this reason, pre-context speaking rate is not included in the regression models.

Post-context speaking rate: A strong correlation is found between target durations and contextual speaking rate. As speaking rates increase, target durations tend to decrease (Fosler-Lussier & Morgan, 1999; Gahl, 2008; File-Muriel & Brown, 2011; Arnon & Cohen Priva, 2013; Hualde & Prieto, 2014; Nadeu, 2014; Lohmann, 2018; Brown et. al., 2021). We include in our analysis speaking rate of all the fluent stretches of speech that appear after the targets in syllables per second. No targets of *vamos a* were followed by a pause. We measure durations of the context following the target. The post-context speaking rate is determined by the number of lexical syllables in the following context divided by the duration of the context following the target.

Predictability: Word predictabilities have been shown to constrain variant forms of words in production (Jurafsky et al., 2001; Bell et al., 2009). As predictability of forms increases, durations of words decrease, perhaps owing to speech planning faciliatory effects. For each token of *vamos a,* we code for the word that appears afterwards. Using the oral section of *Corpus del español* (Davies, 2002-), we determine frequency values for each of the following words and the string frequency of *vamos a* in combination with the following word. From these values we calculate the predictability of *vamos a* (w| w+1) from the word that follows [N *vamos a* + following word/N following word]. There were seven cases in our data that did not appear in the *Corpus del español* oral data. For these tokens, we calculate the predictability from the ESLORA corpus. Then, we take an average over the predictability of the seven tokens. The log of the predictability of these seven rare combinations is −0.127.

5. Results

The quantitative analysis of the spoken tokens of *vamos a* does not suggest an obvious durational difference across the four different construction types (future, habitual, hortative, movement) analyzed here. As is evident in Table 1, the average duration of *vamos a* targets when used with future meaning, for example, is .298 seconds, whereas the average target duration for tokens used with an allative (movement) is .309. The average target duration (0.240) across the nine tokens of *vamos a* expressing a habitual meaning is significantly lower [t(117) = −2.334, $p < .05$] than future and hortative (.298) uses. The average duration (.294) of the three constructions paired with an INFINITIVE is not significantly [t(158) = −0.840, $p > .05$] shorter than the movement tokens (.308) of *vamos a.*

Table 1. Average durations of *vamos a* target types

Construction type	N	Average duration (sec)	Standard deviation
Future	64	0.298	0.07
Habitual	9	0.240	0.07
Hortative	45	0.298	0.06
Movement	40	0.309	0.09
	158	0.297	0.08

How do these durations compare to other words spoken by these speakers? We take an average speaking rate in syllables per second from our data set based upon the previous and following target contexts. This measure excludes the target tokens. The average speaking rate of the target contexts across all speakers is 6.9 (s.d. 1.9) syllables per second, whereas the average speaking rate for the *vamos a* tokens is 10.8 (s.d. 2.9). It is apparent that regardless of the construction type, the dyad *vamos a* is spoken at a relatively fast rate of speech, perhaps reflecting the high token frequency of the combination (795.3 per million in ESLORA).

The durations for target tokens of *vamos a* discussed here, however, have not yet been considered in combination with other factors known to constrain variable durations and those discussed in Methods above. To determine whether any lack of durational difference evident in Table 1 masks a correlation with speech rate, predictability, or pause adjacency, for example, we conduct a linear mixed effect model of the data using R *(lme4)* with speaker (*N*=51) and following word (*N*=96) as random effects (R: The R Project for Statistical Computing, n.d.).

Initial data explorations including all independent factor groups and their pairwise interactions reveal a marginally significant (*p*=0.055) difference within the meaning category whereby movement tokens differ from the other construction types with longer target durations. Consequently, given our small database, we create a binary meaning category contrasting movement tokens to the [*vamos a* + INFINITIVE] construction types (conflating future, hortative, and habitual). Additionally, this model identifies another marginally significant interaction between meaning of the construction and log post context rate (*p*=0.051) which is included in subsequent models with all the independent predictors.

Table 2 reports the results of the best linear mixed effects model (determined by the AIC) predicting log of the target duration for the 158 examples in our data. We use as our dependent variable the log duration of *vamos a* tokens coded as a continuous variable. The quantitative analysis allows us to measure the independent effects of both the fixed as well as the random factors on the durations of target tokens. The estimate provides a measure of likelihood of durational difference; positive estimates suggesting greater duration, negative estimates indicating

Table 2. Linear mixed effect model predicting log durations of target *vamos a* tokens

Random effects	Variance	Std. Dev.		
Speaker (Intercept)	0.001	0.031		
Following word	0.001	0.035		
Fixed effect	**Estimate**	**Std. Error**	**Pr (>|t|)**	**Significance**
(Intercept)	−0.206	0.119	<0.1	.
Meaning: [*vamos a* + INFINITIVE]	−0.278	0.138	<0.05	*
Preceding Pause: yes	0.003	0.024	>0.1	n.s.
Predictability	−0.027	0.013	<0.05	*
Post-Context Rate	−0.451	0.152	>0.01	**
Post-Context Rate X	0.324	0.169	0.056	.
Meaning: [*vamos a* + INFINITIVE]				

Positive coefficients are associated with longer durations of *vamos a*
Number of observations: 158
Random effects N: Speaker = 51, Following Word = 96
AIC = −209.531
Signif. codes: 0 '***' 0.001 '**' 0.01 '*' 0.05 '.' 0.1 'ns' 1

decreased duration. The analysis also allows us to identify the confidence level (provided by the *p* value) of factors significantly contributing to durational difference of target tokens.

As is evident in Table 2, the duration of target tokens of *vamos a* is significantly conditioned by three factors: meaning, predictability, post-context speaking rate. Importantly, target durations are shorter when the construction type is [*vamos a* + INFINITIVE] compared to the [*vamos a* + ALLATIVE COMPLEMENT] (used to express movement). This result suggests that *vamos a* is shorter when it expresses a grammatical meaning (*e.g.* future as part of the periphrastic construction) compared to when it maintains its lexical meaning of motion. This result will be discussed in the following section.

Predictability of the word following the target tokens significantly predicts duration. As predictability of the following word increases, target durations decrease. This result is in line with previous research that demonstrates a correlation between word and segment durations and predictabilities of surrounding linguistic units (Jurafsky et al., 2001; Bell et al., 2009). Predictable words can be retrieved quickly, and faster lexical access may yield speeded productions.

Additionally, the rate of the context following the target significantly predicts the duration of *vamos a* in these data. As the speaking rate of the post-context increases, the duration of the target decreases. This result, showing that faster context rates predict shorter target durations, is to be expected given findings in previous research (referenced above). Post-context rate has a marginally significant interaction with the construction type. For both meaning types, as post-context rate increases, target durations of *vamos a* decrease. Although having a similar effect on duration, the effect of post-context rate is felt more acutely on movement tokens compared to the [*vamos a* + INFINITIVE] construction types.

Lastly, the presence or absence of a pause preceding the targets does not significantly predict durations in these data. Possibly with a more robust sample of data, a pause initial strengthening effect, identified in previous studies, might emerge.

6. Discussion

The grammatical, semantic and pragmatic changes that grammaticalization processes of tense-aspect-mood markers entail often lead to phonological reduction. The Spanish periphrastic construction [*ir* (PRESENT) *a* + INFINITIVE] is well advanced in its grammaticalization process as the preferred future marker in present-day Spanish. Although the grammatical and semantic changes it undergoes are well described, it has not been empirically demonstrated if the construction undergoes phonological reduction. The goal of this study was to specifically test whether durational differences exist in spontaneously produced tokens of the construction [*vamos a* + INFINITIVE] compared to its etymologically related counterpart [*vamos a* + ALLATIVE COMPLEMENT], in which the verb maintains its original meaning of 'motion'.

To do this, we employed the ESLORA corpus to locate all instances of *vamos a* in order to conduct acoustic analyses of *vamos a* duration in naturally occurring discourse. Using variationist methodology, we also considered linguistic factors known to constrain word durations such as contextual speech rate and word predictabilities. Our results revealed a significant difference in *vamos a* duration based upon the meaning of the construction. When *vamos a* expresses movement in combination with an allative complement, its duration is significantly longer than when *vamos a* is part of the periphrastic construction [*ir* (PRESENT) *a* + INFINITIVE]. This difference is evident when controlling for contextual factors (Table 2). This result demonstrates empirically the claim that grammaticalized constructions undergo phonological reduction.

Notwithstanding such an interpretation of these results, the findings we report may also support an alternative explanation. Regardless of the meaning that [*vamos a* + INFINITIVE] expresses (e.g., future, habitual, hortative), shorter target durations are likely. Consequently, what seems to be driving reduction is not the meaning of 'futurity' but the periphrastic construction in itself. As mentioned above, [*ir* (PRESENT) *a* + INFINITIVE] is grammaticalized in present-day Spanish as the preferred marker of future, especially in spoken language. However, this construction can express other meanings such as habitual present. Since future meaning does not behave differently from habitual (or hortative) meaning in this dataset as far as target reduction, we suggest that it is the construction [*ir* (PRESENT) *a* + INFINITIVE] that allows for the reduction of *vamos a*. This reduction is triggered by the process of auxiliarization that *vamos* undergoes when it is part of the periphrastic construction. As *vamos* becomes an auxiliary verb, the degree of unit-hood between *ir*, *a* and the infinitive increases gradually. This leads to a loss of compositionality and analyzability of the construction (Bybee, 2010), which contributes to a durational differentiation. This durational difference, potentially represented at the level of the more abstract construction, is represented visually in Figure 2. *Vamos a* is shorter when functioning as an auxiliary (on the left) compared to the duration when it is a lexical verb expressing movement towards (on the right).

[[*vamos a*] + INFINITIVE]   vs.   [[v a m o s a] + ALLATIVE COMPLEMENT]

Figure 2. Durational differences between *vamos a* construction types

The construction [*vamos a* + INFINITIVE] has a higher textual frequency than the construction in which *vamos a* is followed by an allative complement. In the ESLORA corpus, 78% (*N*=517) examples of *vamos a* occur with an infinitival form. This tendency is even more marked in a larger, perhaps more representative, spoken corpus such as the one found in *Corpus del español* (Davies, 2002–), in which 92% (*N*=3198) of the examples of *vamos a* are followed by an infinitive. Frequency is a well-known contributor to reduction in speech production. The effects of usage frequency apply not just to lexical items but also to construction types. High frequency words and constructions are likely to undergo greater phonological reduction than low frequency ones (Bybee, 2001; Phillips, 2006). The shorter duration of the periphrastic construction could emerge from this difference in frequency across construction types.

Durational differences across construction types suggest independent lexical storage (e.g., Exemplar Model of lexical representation) for the two types of *vamos a* studied here. In an exemplar model (Bybee, 2001; Pierrehumbert, 2001), the lexical representations stored in memory reflect details speakers have regarding phonetic realizations, contexts of use, and extralinguistic correlates, based on their experience with the linguistic units. The phonetic shape of the [*vamos a* + INFINITIVE] construction, with greater likelihood of reduction, becomes associated in memory with the construction itself. As speakers plan productions, the durationally reduced exemplars can be chosen as targets for use. This process has been described as a type of feedback loop (Kemmer & Barlow, 2000). In this way, the two construction types have their own paths of variation and change.

Our interpretation of the quantitative study should be couched within the understanding that they are based upon a limited sample size. Thus, although we used for our analysis 80 hours of conversational data, the next steps would be to include more data points extracted from a larger sample. Additionally, other varieties of Spanish should be considered in order to determine whether these results hold in non-contact varieties. Further, although we would not predict substantive differences, a logical next step would be to analyze all the paradigmatic forms of *ir* (*voy, vas, va, vais, van*) in order to see if they present the same phonetic tendencies or whether different person/number forms reflect varying degrees of grammaticalization. This study examined duration as a measure of difference across construction types, though other forms of reduction may prove to be relevant such as phone and syllable lenition or deletion.

7. Conclusion

The purpose of this study was to employ naturalistic data to provide a descriptive overview of the patterns of reduction in the [*ir* (PRESENT) *a* + INFINITIVE] construction in comparison to the purportedly homophonous and lexically transparent ones expressing 'movement towards' ([*ir* (PRESENT) *a* + ALLATIVE COMPLEMENT]). We extracted all forms of *vamos*, the first person plural present form of *ir* 'go,' followed by *a* in a large corpus of oral Galician Spanish (ESLORA). While statistically controlling for linguistic factors known to condition speech rates (contextual speaking rates, word predictabilities, pause adjacency), we employed a linear mixed effect model to compare speaker target rates across construction types. This study confirms faster rates of articulation across the [*vamos a*] construction when followed by an infinitival form than when followed by an allative complement. Our tentative results reveal that the phonological reduction of *vamos a* occurs regardless of the meaning it conveys (future, hortative, habitual). We suggest that shorter durations may not reflect the meaning of futurity, but rather may be associated with those constructions in which *vamos a* has undergone a process of auxiliarization as it becomes part of the infinitival periphrastic form.

References

Aaron, J. E. (2006). *Me voy a tener que ir yendo*: A corpus-based study of the grammaticization of the *ir a* + INF construction in Spanish. In E. N. Sagarra & A. J. Toribio (Eds.), *Selected Proceedings of the 9th Hispanic Linguistics Symposium* (pp. 263–272). Cascadilla Proceedings Project.

Aaron, J. E. (2010). Pushing the envelope: Looking beyond the variable context. *Language Variation and Change, 22*, 1–36.

Aaron, J. E. (2014). A certain future: Epistemicity, prediction, and assertion in Iberian Spanish future expression. *Studies in Hispanic and Lusophone Linguistics, 7*(2), 215–240.

Aponte Alequín, H., & Ortiz López, L. A. (2010). Una perspectiva pragmática del presente progresivo con valor de futuro en el español del Caribe. In E. C. Borgonovo, M. Español-Echevarría, & P. Prévost (Eds.), *Selected Proceedings of the 12th Hispanic Linguistics Symposium* (pp. 109–121). Cascadilla Proceedings Project. https://www.lingref.com/cpp/hls/12/index.html

Arnon, I., & Priva, U. C. (2013). More than words: The effect of multi-word frequency and constituency on phonetic duration. *Language and Speech, 56*(3), 349–371.

Bell, A., Brenier, J. M., Gregory, M., Girand, C., & Jurafsky, D. (2009). Predictability effects on durations of content and function words in conversational English. *Journal of Memory and Language, 60*(1), 92–111.

Blas Arroyo, B. (2008). The variable expression of future tense in Peninsular Spanish: The present (and future) of inflectional forms in the Spanish spoken in a bilingual region. *Language Variation and Change, 20*, 85–126.

Boersma, P., & Weenink, D. (2019). *Praat: Doing phonetics by computer.* http://www.praat.org/

Brenes Peña, E. (2008). Enunciación y conexión: *Vamos a ver*. In I. O. Moreno, M. C. Velarde, & R. G. Ruiz (Eds.), *Actas del XXXVII Simposio Internacional de la Sociedad Española de Lingüística (SEL)*. Universidad de Navarra, Spain. http://www.unav.es/linguis/simposiosel/actas/

Brinton, L. J., & Traugott, E. C. (2005). *Lexicalization and Language Change*. Cambridge Univ. Press.

Brown, E. L., & Rivas, J. (2024). Constructional sources of durational shortening in discourse markers. *Linguistics: An Interdisciplinary Journal of the Language Sciences, 62*.

Brown, E. L., Raymond, W. D., Brown, E. K., & File-Muriel, R. J. (2021). Lexically specific accumulation in memory of word and segment speech rate. *Corpus Linguistics and Linguistic Theory, 19*(1), 1–27.

Bybee, J. (2001). *Phonology and Language Use*. Cambridge Univ. Press.

Bybee, J. (2010). *Language, Usage and Cognition*. Cambridge Univ. Press.

Bybee, J. (2015). *Language Change*. Cambridge University Press.

Bybee, J., & Scheibman, J. (1999). The effect of usage on degree of constituency: The reduction of *don't* in English. *Linguistics, 37*(4), 575–596.

Bybee, J., File-Muriel, R., & Souza, R. N. (2016). Special reduction: A usage based approach. *Language and Cognition, 8*, 421–446.

Bybee, J., Perkins, R. D., & Pagliuca, W. (1994). *The Evolution of Grammar. Tense, Aspect, and Modality in the Languages of the World*. John Benjamins.

Carrasco, P., Hualde, J.I., & Simonet, M. (2012). Dialectal differences in Spanish voiced obstruent allophony: Costa Rican vs. Iberian Spanish. *Phonetica*, 69, 149–179.

Cipria, A. (2021). The futurate reading of the Spanish present progressive (*estar* +-ndo). In L. Baranzini and L. de Saussure (Eds.), *Aspects of Tenses, Modality, and Evidentiality* (pp. 81–99). Brill.

Company, C. & Concepción. (2006). Tiempos de formación romance II. Los futuros y condicionales. In C. Company (Ed.), *Sintaxis Histórica de la Lengua Española* (Vol. 1, pp. 349–422). Fondo de Cultura Económica.

ESLORA: Corpus para el Estudio del Español Oral. (2022). http://eslora.usc.es

Davies, M. (2002). *Corpus del Español*. http://www.corpusdelespanol.org

de Prada Pérez, A., Gómez Soler, I., & Feroce, N. (2021). Variable future-time expression in Spanish: A comparison between heritage and second language learners. *Languages*, 6(4), 206.

Eddington, D. (2011). What are the contextual phonetic variants of /β ð ɣ/ in colloquial Spanish. *Probus*, 23, 1–19.

Ernestus, M., & Smith, R. (2018). Qualitative and quantitative aspects of phonetic variation in Dutch *eigenlijk*. In F. Cangemi, M. Clayards, O. Niebuhr, B. Schuppler, & M. Zellers, (Eds.), *Rethinking Reduction* (pp. 129–163). De Gruyter Mouton.

File-Muriel, R., & Brown, E. (2011). The gradient nature of *s*-lenition in Caleño Spanish. *Language Variation and Change*, 23, 223–243.

Fleischman, S. (1982). *The Future in Thought and Language: Diachronic Evidence from Romance*. Cambridge University Press.

Fosler-Lussier, E., & Morgan, N. (1999). Effects of speaking rate and word frequency on pronunciations in conversational speech. *Speech Communications*, 29, 137–158.

Gahl, S. (2008). Time and thyme are not homophones: The effect of lemma frequency on word durations in spontaneous speech. *Language*, 84(3), 474–496.

Giordano, R. (2022). "Ir a + infinitivo" y su potencial comunicativo. *Círculo de Lingüística Aplicada a la Comunicación*, 89, 145–154.

Gómez Torrego, G. & Leonardo. (1999). Los verbos auxiliares. Las perífrasis verbales de infinitivo. In I. Bosque & V. Demonte (Eds.), *Gramática Descriptiva de la Lengua Española* (Vol. 2, pp. 3323–3389). Espasa Calpe.

Gonen, E., Livnat, Z., & Amir, N. (2015). The discourse marker *axshav* ('now') in spontaneous spoken Hebrew: Discursive and prosodic features. *Journal of Pragmatics*, 89, 69–84.

Gudmestad, A., & Geeslin, K.L. (2011). Assessing the use of multiple forms in variable contexts: The relationship between linguistic factors and future-time reference in Spanish. *Studies in Hispanic and Lusophone Linguistics*, 4, 3–34.

Gutiérrez, M. (1994). On the future of future tense in the Spanish of the Southwest. In C. Silva-Corvalán, (Ed.), *Spanish in the Four Continents: Studies in Language Contact and Bilingualism* (pp. 214–226). Georgetown University Press.

Hopper, P. (1991). On some principles of grammaticization. In E.C. Traugott and B. Heine (Eds.), *Approaches to Grammaticalization* (Vol. 1. pp. 17–35). John Benjamins.

Hopper, P., & Traugott, E.C. (2003). *Grammaticalization*. Cambridge Univ. Press.

Howe, C. (2013). *The Spanish Perfects. Pathways of Emerging Meaning*. Palgrave MacMillan.

Howe, C. (2021). Auxiliary selection in secondary grammaticalization. Evidence from the Spanish periphrastic past. In E. K. Eide & M. Fryd (Eds.), *The Perfect Volume: Papers on the Perfect* (pp. 439–460). John Benjamins.

Hualde, J. I., & Prieto, P. (2014). Lenition of intervocalic alveolar fricatives in Catalan and Spanish. *Phonetica, 71*(2), 109–127.

Jurafsky, D., Bell, A., Gregory, M., & Raymond, W. D. (2001). The effect of language model probability on pronunciation reduction. *International Conference on Acoustics, Speech, and Signal Processing (ICASSP)*.

Kemmer, S., & Barlow, M. (2000). Introduction: A usage-based conception of language. In E. M. Barlow and S. Kemmer (Eds.), *Usage-Based Models of Language* (pp. vii–1). CSLI.

Labov, W. (1994). *Principles of Linguistic Change* (Vol. 1). *Internal Factors*. Wiley-Blackwell.

Lipski, J. (2008). *Afro-Bolivian Spanish*. Iberoamericana Vervuert.

Lipski, J. (2012). Geographical and social varieties of Spanish: An overview. In J. I. Hualde, A. Olarrea, & E. O'Rourke (Eds.), *Handbook of Spanish Linguistics* (pp. 1–26). Wiley-Blackwell.

Lohmann, A. (2018). Time and thyme are NOT homophones: A closer look at Gahl's work on the lemma frequency effect including a reanalysis. *Language, 94*(2), 180–190.

Martínez Gómez, R., & Ibarra Zetter, K. (2017). Funciones y duración de *o sea*: Datos del corpus conversacional tapatío. *Anuario de Letras. Lingüística y Filología, 5*(1), 85–115.

Nadeu, M. (2014). Stress-and speech rate-induced vowel quality variation in Catalan and Spanish. *Journal of Phonetics, 46*, 1–22.

Navarro Tomás, T. (1977). *Manual de Pronunciación Española* (19th ed.). Centro Superior de Investigaciones Científicas.

Orozco, R. (2005). Distribution of future time forms in Northern Colombian Spanish. In E. D. Eddington (Ed.), *Selected Proceedings of the 7th Hispanic Linguistics Symposium* (pp. 56–65). Cascadilla Proceedings Project.

Orozco, R. (2007). The impact of linguistic constraints on the expression of futurity in the Spanish of New York Colombians. In K. Potowski & R. Cameron (Eds.), *Spanish in Contact: Educational, Social, and Linguistic Inquiries* (pp. 311–328). John Benjamins.

Orozco, R. (2018). *Spanish in Colombia and New York City. Language Contact Meets Dialectal Convergence*. John Benjamins.

Penny, R. (1991). *A History of The Spanish Language*. Cambridge Univ. Press.

Phillips, B. S. (2006). *Word Frequency and Lexical Diffusion*. Palgrave Macmillan.

Pierrehumbert, J. B. (2001). Exemplar dynamics: Word frequency, lenition and contrast. In J. Bybee and P. Hopper (Eds.), *Frequency and the Emergence of Linguistic Structure* (pp. 137–157). John Benjamins.

Plug, L. (2005). From words to actions: The phonetics of *eigenlijkin* two communicative contexts. *Phonetica, 62*(2–4), 131–145.

R: The R Project for Statistical Computing (n.d.). https://www.r-project.org/

Rivas, J., & Brown, E. L. (2010). Variable development of intersubjectivity in Spanish. In A. Sánchez and M. Almela (Eds,), *A Mosaic of Corpus Linguistics. Selected Approaches.* (pp. 61–78). Peter Lang.

Schubotz, L., Oostdijk, N., & Ernestus, M. (2015). Y'know vs. You know: What phonetic reduction can tell us about pragmatic function. In E. S. Lestrade, P. Swart, & L. Hogeweg (Eds.), *Addenda. Artikelen voor Ad Foolen* (pp. 361–380). Radboud University.

Schwenter, S., & Torres Cacoullos, R. (2008). Defaults and indeterminacy in temporal grammaticalization: The 'perfect' road to perfective. *Language Variation and Change, 20*(1), 1–39.

Sedano, M. (2006). Importancia de los datos cuantitativos en el estudio de las expresiones de futuro. *Signos, 39*(61), 283–296.

Silva-Corvalán, C., & Enrique-Arias, A. (2017). *Sociolingüística y Pragmática del Español* (2nd ed.). Georgetown University Press.

Tagliamonte, S. A. (2012). *Variationist Sociolinguistics. Change, Observation, Interpretation.* Wiley-Blackwell.

PART III

New approaches to sociolinguistic studies

CHAPTER 7

Subject pronoun expression in Colombian Spanish in Philadelphia
An interdisciplinary analysis of SPE variation and cognitive adaptation

Camila Franco
Temple University

Spanish in the United States is a testament to language change from different dialects and cultures. Subject pronoun expression (SPE) remains a showcase variable in Spanish, and we still find nuances about SPE and its distribution across different communities. Here, I describe the results of a mixed-method approach to SPE in Colombian Spanish in Philadelphia. Colombian Spanish has a differential distribution of SPE, with higher overt usage in Coastal Spanish versus lower Andean Spanish rates. There is much to see and understand about the intergenerational transitioning on SPE and the bilingual cognitive adaptation that the diaspora entails for some speakers. The interaction among cognitive, social, and linguistic variables frames bilingualism in the United States as a multifaceted language experience.

Keywords: bilingualism, Spanish in the US, unified syntax, sociolinguistics, subject pronoun expression

1. Introduction

According to the U.S. 2022 Census, the South American population in Philadelphia, Pennsylvania is 16.1% in the county and 15.4% in the city of Philadelphia, amounting to 1,567,258 inhabitants. Philadelphia has seen steady Colombian population growth, primarily around the northeastern area, where several shops and traditional Colombian restaurants have opened to cater to the expanding Hispanic community. Zip Atlas shows that around 5% of this population is of Colombian ancestry, and almost 3% resides in the same zip code in Philadelphia: 19135 or the Tacony neighborhood. In general, in the Hispanic population of Philadel-

https://doi.org/10.1075/ihll.42.07fra
© 2025 John Benjamins Publishing Company

phia, there is a sense of a well-established community of Colombian residents in the northeastern area (5th Street), with dispersed communities across the suburbs (i.e., West Chester, Media, and Bryn Mawr) and other parts of the city such as South and West Philadelphia. In this chapter, we will look at the sociolinguistic and social aspects of SPE change and the apparent effect of the diaspora in cognitive bilingual recall. To successfully analyze the diverse types of data, I used a mixed-variable statistics model, following Orozco's (2018a) recommendations on the implementation of SPE inferential statistics in variationist studies.

2. Subject pronoun expression (SPE) and unified syntax

2.1 Subject pronoun expression in Colombian Spanish

Subject pronoun expression in research behaves as a binary dependent variable where the speaker can use overt pronouns next to a morphological inflection which is called overt pronoun, unlike the using inflection called null pronoun. In *pronombrista* studies of Spanish, overt subjects tend to be less common in mainland Spanish with a prevalence of null subjects of over greater than 70%, whereas coastal Spanish has a 50–60% usage of null subjects depending on the dialectal variation, age of the population, and country. This can be determined by social changes, gender norms and generational changes as well. Additionally, across Spanish-speaking countries, there seems to be a slightly different distribution for coastal and mainland variations. Even inside the mainland, some speakers may have varying rates of SPE.

Colombian Spanish presents a particularly notable SPE variation between *costeño* Spanish and *andino* Spanish. Additionally, Colombia has *Caleño* Spanish — where voseo is present — creating a unique interaction between dialects and SPE rates. Orozco and Hurtado are two relevant authors who have described the behavior of different SPE rates in multiple iterations. For example, Orozco's (2015) study on *Barranquillero* Spanish reported closer to a 50% SPE alternation of overt and null subjects and a rate of 34% overt pronominal rate in *Barranquillero* Spanish. Orozco highlighted the significance of internal linguistic factors such as tense-mood-aspect, semantic verb type and switch reference. Hurtado and Gutiérrez-Rivas (2016) delved into the usage of *"uno"* and its functionality as a highly versatile pronoun in *Barranquillero* Spanish.

Orozco and Hurtado (2021) collaborated in their study of *Medellín* Spanish describing the behavior of internal language constraints and predictors of change in *Paisa* Spanish. Mainland Spanish behaves at a lower overt pronominal rate; however, *Paisa* Spanish exhibits a pronominal rate of 28%, which situates it as "the highest overt pronominal rate ever found in a monolingual mainland speech community." Additionally, they emphasized how verb type and discursive functions of verbs and sentences further explain and organize the behavior of SPE into a potentially cognitive-driven phenomenon.

Colombian American Spanish has made the rounds in both authors' research. Hurtado (2001) looked at SPE between Colombian residents and Colombian Americans in Miami-Dade County and found extralinguistic predictors of change in SPE mainly related to language proficiency and language attitude. Ambiguity seemed to be one of the biggest predictors of overt SPE, whereas English has an inconclusive influence on overt SPE rates. Orozco (2018a) investigated the Colombian population in NYC and described the behavior of SPEs (higher SPE in NYC) and similarities of linguistic conditioning between Colombian Spanish and United States-based Colombian Spanish with clear social variable differences, mostly noting the gender gaps and gender role reversal as well as the weight of age as predictors of change.

Colombian Spanish in the United States is then expected to behave similarly to that of Colombia in internal constraints: tense-mood-aspect of the finite verb, reflexive or nonreflexive use of the verb, specific or nonspecific reference, discourse connection between verbs, type of lexical content of the verb, clause type where the verb appears, the appearance of the verb in a set phrase, and the section of the interview where the clause is found. Semantic types of verbs should be predictors of overt SPE usage. However, there is a possibility for differential behavior in external linguistic factors (bilingual confidence and language proficiency) and sociolinguistic variables (age and gender).

These differences between populations highlight the importance of speech community identity in drawing conclusions in comparative sociolinguistic research. Colombian dialectal differences that would traditionally be non-significant or would have a low chance of interaction have the potential to become relevant when studying Spanish-speaking immigrant communities in other regions. First, coastal and mainland interactions indicate that multicultural communities with different dialectal backgrounds coexist in spaces with new social structures and values. Second, Colombian immigrants coexist with English, which, although it has been observed that it has no relevance in SPE, does affect the social values and behaviors in new settlements.

Otheguy et al. (2007) described how different dialects in the same area can undergo an apparent language accommodation. The authors also mentioned a varying null subject usage and a tendency to an overall higher overt pronoun usage observed in the increased mainlanders' overt pronoun rate and decreased coastal speakers' overt pronouns, respectively. The SPE result is an age-dependent social negotiation involving Spanish and English still conditioned by internal linguistic constraints. Barrera-Tobón and Raña-Riso (2016) also investigated NYC's variation through corpus-based sociolinguistics. Their findings suggested that English proficiency and time of exposure are two key variables that influence null subject variation, adding to the mix of potential predictors of SPE change in Colombian Spanish. These *pronombrista* studies point out how removing the geographically preserved difference between mainland and coastal dialects influences null subject variation and reminds us to look into regional origin inside bilingual communities because both aspects carry social value and can influence SPE differences.

2.2 Unified syntax and bilingual cognition

Because English influence tends to be inconclusive in *pronombrista* studies, I have incorporated the concept of unified or shared syntax that stems from the theory that there is a shared syntax across bilingual speakers' languages. In other words, both languages are readily available at any given time, which allows the bilingual speaker to read, speak, and comprehend either language. In principle, this means that a higher bilingual proficiency would allow the speaker to access syntactic information faster, without needing to translate or look for equivalences in either language. Hartsuiker et al. (2004) proved this through an experiment in which they provided speakers with L1 priming in certain verb tenses that later were shown to influence L2 verb production. English/Spanish bilinguals participated in a description task where they produced oral picture descriptions in English based on cards provided by the researchers. Through this study, the authors concluded that for Spanish sentences to prime English sentences there had to be a shared syntactic activation process that included both languages because it would be impossible for separate systems to influence each other if they were not active at the same time.

Shin (2012), Helasvuo (2004), and Declerck et al. (2020) investigated other cognitive aspects of shared syntax activation by measuring the reading and response time of bilingual subjects when prompted with either of their two languages. All researchers concluded that there must be a shared cognitive space for language because both grammars were readily accessible. To explain the phenomenon, they proposed that *the parallel model hypothesis* and *the sentence superiority hypothesis* could contribute to showing how shared syntax affects language acquisition. Both hypotheses derived from the formal approaches in bilingualism that put forward its transversal influence variably across the phonology, morphology, and syntax of one or both languages. Depending on the speakers' frequency of use in the two languages, it may be possible for bilinguals to compartmentalize their L1 and L2 to carry out different tasks. For example, some speakers described their first language to be more akin to home or familiar spaces whereas their second language helped them communicate and grow in a globalized society. The bilingual mind seems to show an interaction between the two grammars, which can cause differences in reading time, voice onset time, grammatical structure, and syntactic categories. This would mean that SPE could also be affected by the bilingual confidence and proficiency of a group of speakers.

Considering the diaspora, and the sociocultural difficulties that Latin American communities experience in the United States, this cognitive view proves helpful in representing the Latinx population because it opposes the common belief that sometimes describes bilinguals as confused, losing their language, or even not real bilinguals when they do not perform perfectly. From a sociolinguistic standpoint, one should not equate bilingualism with native proficiency as a criterion for social acceptance or social prestige. O'Rourke and Potowski (2016) conducted cross-generational studies in different Latino bilingual communities, in which speakers adapted to what their bilingual context required, forming a speech community that benefited multiple dialects according to their prestige; this meant that Mexican communities would accommodate toward Dominican or Puerto Rican groups (i.e., closer to what covert prestige demanded) to achieve a higher level of social acceptance in their bilingual groups. Adding the concept of unified syntax to commonly analyzed sociolinguistic variables might open a new outlook connecting sociolinguistic behavior with psycholinguistic behavior by allowing us to understand the bilingual mind as both cognitively and socially proficient, and to explore whether those two related behaviors influence each other or not.

3. Methodology

3.1 Data collection

I collected the data set from February 2022 to November 2022. It comprises of 30 United States-based Colombians and eight Colombian participants. All participants reported some knowledge of English and a certain level of bilingual confidence. Reports of knowledge of English included taking English classes and courses, and/or earning certificates. Colombian participants had not lived abroad for more than six months and had not travelled outside Colombia in the last six months. In total, the corpus comprises 21 hours of recorded interviews, 38 questionnaires, 38 bilingual language profiles and 38 rapid visual parallel presentation (RPVP) accuracy tests. Recordings were transcribed and annotated to account for: "*yo, tú, el, ella, ellos, ellas, ustedes, nosotros, nosotras*" and null subjects. The completed data set of the Philadelphia-based participants yielded 4,588 subjects, and the Colombia-based data set yielded 1,408 subjects. In this sample, the pronombre "uno" was not annotated, as it appeared under 50 times in the whole data set

Data were annotated in a CSV file that could be directly uploaded into the mixed effects model in Rbrul. Demographic data such as education, type of job, and sociolinguistic information such as gender and age were also annotated (see Table 1).

Table 1. Corpus annotation and coding

Verb	Subject	Null/overt	Personandnumber	Tense	Moodaspect	Lexicalcontent
tengo	O	Null	FPS	presente	indicativo	stative
llegué	O	Null	FPS	pretérito	indicativo	external
vivo	yo	Overt	FPS	presente	indicativo	stative

Spoken data were obtained through semi-structured sociolinguistic interviews in which speakers were encouraged to talk about their experiences and overall perceptions of themselves and others in the United States or Colombia, their family, work in the United States and Colombia, and other topics that facilitated the production of informal language. For RPVP, the participants took a computer-based test where they were asked to recall an L2 word (Spanish or English) contained in a sentence written in their L1 (English or Spanish). The L2 word was presented in either a grammatical or non-grammatical position. Participants in Colombia presented it virtually with the researchers' supervision, whereas Philadelphia-based participants took it in person. The bilingual linguistic profile was also part of the laboratory data and was obtained through the virtual questionnaire provided by the University of Texas, Austin (Birdsong et al., 2012). However, it was not found significant in the current study.

3.2 Reading recall test

Participants were asked to read different sentences at 200 ms (basic reading speed) and then to immediately recall a specific highlighted word that might be presented in either grammatical or non-grammatical positions. Every participant took the test by sitting in front of a computer; the sentences were presented through a grey and black interface that cycled 120 sentences in random order at 200 ms. Sentences were divided into four groups of 30: for Group 1, unified syntax sentences, with L2 words in grammatical positions; Group 2, sentences with L2 words in agrammatical positions; Group 3, L1 sentences with grammatical positions; and Group 4, L1 sentences with agrammatical positions. After 200 ms, the sentence was replaced by hash tags (#) and a dot on top of one of the words. Participants had to recall this word and type it again; the speed of recall was not part of the test (see Figure 1).

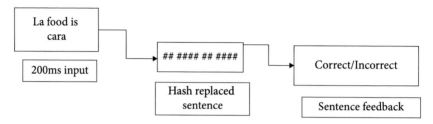

Figure 1. Reading recall procedure

4. Results

With a total of 4,588 language tokens produced by 30 participants, I had to use a model that could find clusters of variation in similar populations. I decided to use a mixed effect regression model; this model works by looking through each "cluster" (in this case, each individual participant) and testing for predictors that are replicable across the whole sample. This allows the researcher to look at the influence of regional origin, age, gender and reading recall results in relation to a binary variable of null and overt subjects.

Using the step-up and step-down tools in Rbrul, the system ran 188 iterations of the Philadelphia speakers' model until it found the most stable run (see Table 2). The predictors obtained by this process were: person and number, tense, mood-aspect, time of residency in the United States, type of social network, place of birth, and reading recall. We can see the distribution of each variable, and the percentage of null subjects used per variable.

In Table 2, logodds refers to the likelihood of the dependent variable's occurring. In this case, the variation between null and overt pronouns, values that are higher than 0, suggest that the variable favors null over overt pronouns. Zero means a neutral effect, and negative values mean that the variable would go in the opposite direction, which would favor overt pronouns over null. The n is the total number of tokens; the proportion is the stress shift for each factor level (meaning at what percentage the category shifts from null to overt) and factor weight is a probability from 0 to 1 of the exponential effect of each category in the null versus overt variation.

It is important to note that in earlier test runs of the model gender was listed as a highly significant variable; however, the distribution of participants was asymmetric, with most participants willing and able to complete the study

Table 2. Mixed effect model in Rbrul

	Change Over /(null+overt)			
Tense	Logodds	n	Proportion	Factor.weight
Perfecto	0.764	176	11%	0.682
Progresivo	0.689	5	20%	0.666
Gerundio	0.521	23	18%	0.627
Futuro	0.281	47	13%	0.57
Pretérito	−0.248	1155	24%	0.438
Presente	−0.526	2666	29%	0.371
Pluscuamperfecto	−0.528	33	28%	0.371
Imperfecto	−0.953	483	37%	0.278
Mood-aspect	Logodds	n	Proportion	Factor.weight
Imperativo	2.180	43	3%	0.898
Gerundio	0.410	105	11%	0.601
Indicativo	−0.605	4259	28%	0.353
Subjuntivo	−0.609	134	27%	0.352
Condicional	−1.376	47	43%	0.202
Person and number	Logodds	n	Proportion	Factor.weight
First Person Plural	0.873	322	11%	0.705
Third Person Plural	0.483	479	15%	0.618
Third Person Singular	0.192	1007	17%	0.548
First Person Singular	−0.631	2573	35%	0.347
Second Person Singular	−0.917	207	39%	0.286
Place of birth	Logodds	n	Proportion	Factor.weight
Santander	0.737	968	29%	0.676
Bogotá	0.162	750	23%	0.54
Valle	0.136	1008	30%	0.534
Antioquia	−0.428	1226	30%	0.395
Huila	−0.607	636	22%	0.353
Social networks	Logodds	n	Proportion	Factor.weight
Mostly American	0.221	1509	28%	0.555
Mostly Latina	0.196	289	39%	0.549
Mixed	−0.417	2790	26%	0.397

Table 2. *(continued)*

	Change Over /(null+overt)			
Time Of residency	Logodds	n	Proportion	Factor.weight
GroupB 5–10 years	−0.88	580	48%	0.293
GroupA 1–4 years	0.25	1992	27%	0.562
Group C 10+ years	0.63	2016	25%	0.652
Reading recall	**Logodds**	**n**	**Proportion**	**Factor.weight**
41to60	0.409	1509	31%	0.601
61to80	0.222	289	23%	0.555
20to40	−0.631	2790	46%	0.347

being women (20 women and 10 men). This caused the model to drop gender as a significant variable because the SPE behavior of most women behaved similarly, and the model could not determine a stable significance. The gender variable is reported in Section 4.2 and later discussed in Section 5. Age did not appear as a significant variable in this data set.

4.1 Linguistic predictors of SPE

Tense, mood-aspect, and person and number were found to be highly significant ($p < 0.001$). This agrees with *pronombrista* literature. Table 2 shows the behavior of tense with *imperfecto* having 37% usage of overt pronoun versus the 11–29% usage in other variables. This agrees with observed behavior in Colombian Spanish (Orozco & Hurtado, 2021). Following other studies, I separated mood-aspect to account for other categories inside the mixed effect cluster. The conditional mood shows an exceptional tendency to overt pronouns with 43% of occurrences being overt pronouns. It is notable as well that most of the sentences used by participants were in the *indicativo* where I found 28% overt pronoun usage, which is still higher than average for mainland SPE rates, and similar to what Orozco & Hurtado found in *Paisa* Spanish.

Because the semi-structured interviews inquired about the personal experiences and thoughts of each participant, it is not a surprise to see a higher usage of singular grammatical persons, particularly "yo" and "tú", which showed only 35% and 39% of overt subject usage, respectively. This agrees with other studies and shows that Colombian Spanish in Philadelphia is behaving similarly to its Colombian counterparts and even other Spanish-speaking communities (Limerick, 2019; Lastra & Martín Butrageño, 2015; Flores-Ferrán, 2002).

4.2 Sociolinguistic predictors of SPE

In this study, I consider place of birth and language acquisition, social networks (as in speech community), gender, and time of residency, as sociolinguistics variables. The place of birth and language acquisition provide the speaker with a language prestige perception as well as cultural knowledge. Social networks in an immigration context should be considered strong predictors of change since they provide speakers with sociolinguistic information about the area they resided in (Milroy & Milroy, 1992).

Not surprisingly, one of the lowest percentages of overt subject usage is 23% by *Bogotanos*, followed by another *andino* region, Huila. A high number of this sample was from either Valle or Antioquia, presenting both *Valluno* and *Paisa* Spanish. In this case, both have 30% overt pronoun usage, and still agree with previous studies on these dialects' SPE rates, although that is still higher than in Colombia.

For social networks, I asked participants to describe their social circles according to the number of American Anglo Saxons, non-Latinos, and Latino people who comprised their social group. There were three categories: mostly American, mostly Latino and mixed. Mixed and mostly American groups preserved original Colombian SPE, whereas mixed social networks seemed to tend to higher usage of overt pronouns.

In Table 3, we can see the distribution of overt and null subjects according to gender. It is possible to notice why the model dropped the variable, because the significance of gender was incredibly high ($p = 2.79^{-6}$) and could throw other predictors off. It is important to mention that this distribution seems to be conservative, although we do notice a 27% of overt pronoun usage in women, while men stay at 22%. This agrees with Orozco's (2018b) findings on women leading linguistic innovation in the US. However, a more balanced sample should produce more interesting data and potential trends.

Table 3. Gender and subject pronouns

	Null	Overt	Null%	Overt%	Total
Female	2961	1122	72.5%	27.5%	4083
Male	392	113	78%	22%	505
Total	3353	1235	73%	27%	4588

Time of residency in the United States also resulted significantly in the model. In this data set, participants were coded in three groups according to the time they had resided in the United States: Group A, 1–4 years; Group B, 5–10 years; and, Group C, 10+ years. Surprisingly, Group B has one of the highest percentages of overt pronoun usage with 48% overt subject pronouns, Group A follows with 27%, and finally Group C returns to a more traditional or standard overt pronoun distribution with 25% overt subject pronouns. This finding agrees with Otheguy and Zentella's (2012), Limerick's (2019) and Orozco's (2018b) observations on dialectal leveling over time of residency as well as the formation of a speech community that levels SPE to its more commonly found distribution.

4.3 Cognitive predictors of SPE

I used the RPVP test to determine the accuracy with which participants could recall and correctly type the missing word in a four-word sentence. Instead of testing the reading speed, this test measures the participant's ability to access their syntactic knowledge to answer with a correct assertion of what type of word could fill the blank, independent of the language this word is presented in. Participants who are considered highly proficient would score around 60–70% in this test, with the possibility of scoring higher because there is no buffered time between languages. Lower results suggest that the participant struggles to access the syntactic inventory, and therefore they cannot complete the task successfully. A result of 40% or less would suggest that the participant has less knowledge of their L2 and cannot recall most of the words because most of the processing time is spent on understanding the sentence.

In this study, I found that scores from 20–40% recall have 46% usage of SPE, scores in the 40 to 60% range have 31%, and the highest recall bracket of 60 to 80% presents with 23% SPE. This suggests that a better recall capacity, and more accurate syntax processing would result in preserving the standard SPE rate. Because this analysis considers the results of all the corpus, we can confidently assert that participants with high unified syntax behave similarly to other communities of Spanish in the United States, and participants with lower scores see an increase on their overt pronoun usage suggesting that inter-dialectal contact with Spanish is more determinant of higher overt SPE rates.

5. Discussion

In this study, I have reported the results of a mixed effect regression model with 4,588 tokens of SPE in Philadelphia Colombian Spanish. Through this model the independent variables of person and number, tense, mood-aspect, time of residency in the United States, type of social network, place of birth, and reading recall present a description of the SPE rate in Philadelphia. It is highly promising to find significant similarities with Orozco and Hurtado's studies. Colombian communities in Philadelphia are exhibiting the behavior of other well-established and long-standing Spanish-speaking communities such as the Dominican and Puerto Rican communities in NYC in the United States.

The significance and standard SPE rates for grammatical personal, and number and tense-mood-aspect situate this study within the *pronombrista* literature, allowing results to contribute to the growing body of literature on Spanish in the United States. It is particularly encouraging to find that the *Condicional* and *Imperfecto* have the highest occurrence of overt subjects whereas other tenses see a standard distribution from other studies (Hurtado, 2005). In this data set, semantic verb type, priming and switch reference were coded but not considered significant by the model. This could be due to the nature of the interviews that looked for a more anecdotical type of discourse. More research is needed in these cognitive areas of language to completely assert the cognitive influence of verbs in SPE.

Regarding sociolinguistic variables, gender and age have always been present and relevant in *pronombrista* studies. However, this corpus did not report a significance in age, and dropped gender as a predictor variable due to data imbalance. The corpus had participants from 21–45 years of age, so it is possible that the continuum was not diverse enough to generate significance. A recoding of the data into age groups rather than keeping age as a continuous variable may yield significance and could improve the understanding of the age variable in the data set.

The relevance of social circles and social networks as well as the time of residency are very promising, especially because of their predicting capacities for a newer population such as new immigrant groups and heritage speakers. These factors could possibly contribute to defining and understanding the social processes that contribute to the formation of a speech community more accurately. It is necessary to look into the actual content of the sociolinguistic interviews, to look into behaviors, thoughts, and notions from speakers (Showstack, 2018) that could further explain why each type of social circle has varying SPE rates. It is interesting to see how mostly Latino social networks tend to influence a lower null SPE usage. It would be necessary to look at this variable with a bit more attention, especially asking participants to provide a description of the national origin of their social circle because it could further explain SPE variation rates.

It is also recommended that we look further into the social and political environment that Group B (5–10 years in the United States) experienced when immigrating. This group had already settled in the area before the COVID pandemic and saw a change in the presidential election of 2016; these groups experienced changes in politics and probably in legislation in Philadelphia, as well as hitting the pandemic years while residing in the United States. There could be a relationship between the SPE rate differences and the feeling of insecurity, unrest, or unfamiliarity with the US context. This data is available as transcribed interviews and will be considered in future investigations.

As expected, the place of birth plays a key role as a Colombian SPE predictor. It is notable to mention the amount of data that came from *Valluno* Spanish, especially because it tends to be a harder-to- study variable due to its localization and closeness to *Costeño* Spanish. It is also worth noting that *Paisa* Spanish in Philadelphia shows a similar SPE distribution to what Orozco and Hurtado found in Medellin. This further supports the need of more studies that consider interactions between Colombian dialects because some might be more prone to SPE variation than others.

On the topic of cognitive variation, the implementation of RPVP testing proved to be a highly promising and inexpensive way of incorporating cognitive testing into sociolinguistic research. On one hand, this accuracy test showed that proficient bilinguals were more capable of separating language systems and thus they exhibit behavior that agrees with other Spanish in the U.S. communities. On the other, it shows that less accuracy in recall is related to higher overt pronouns. It begs the question of what could cause these differences in SPE rates. Could it be possible that these results are related to a process of adaptation that the Philadelphia population is experiencing where each participant is navigating different stages of intralinguistic variability (Torres Caucollos & Travis, 2015)? If so, does this mean that the processes of dialectal leveling and speech community formation are dependent on Spanish-speakers' being sufficiently proficient in both languages? Or is this related to social exposure and the interaction between social circles and the national origin of different Spanish speakers?

6. Conclusions

This paper successfully contributes to Spanish in the US literature, especially in *pronombrista* information of the Philadelphia area. The incorporation of cognitive experimental testing proved enriching to the *pronombrista* analysis, mostly confirming that there must be an accurate knowledge of syntax for syntax to vary according to traditional behaviors, and that a lot of variation can happen in intermediate stages of syntactic integration. The present study suggests a strong relationship among linguistic constraints, sociolinguistic variables, reading recall tests, and social experiences as observed in the following aspects:

1. Grammatical person, number, tense-mood-aspect were found to be significant predictors of null SPE usage. This is congruent with other *pronombrista*

studies and situates the population of Colombian Spanish speakers in Philadelphia in line with other communities in the United States.
2. Time of residency, social networks and place of birth were significant in this study. This articulates two important things about the Colombian immigrant community:
   a. Colombian immigrants tend to preserve their original SPE rates, or if they change, they change according to the rules of the U.S. Spanish speech communities.
   b. The amount of time spent in the United States influences SPE rates, and more time of residency reflects leveling behaviors observed in NYC and Southeastern communities.
   c. The divergent behavior of Group B in this data set must be further analyzed because social and political contexts could further explain these SPE changes.
3. Gender and age variables have the potential to be significant in the Philadelphia population: more participants are needed to obtain diverse ages as well as more male participants in the corpus.
4. RPVP testing can contribute to and explain certain aspects of SPE variation. In particular, it shows that English contact is still not conclusive for SPE variation, while supporting the claim that Spanish behaves independently as a language in the United States.

In summary, SPE variation in the Colombian Philadelphia community reflects a complex interaction of social, linguistic, and cognitive variables. It supports what other researchers have found so far: that Spanish in the United States is not a mix, but rather an intergenerational variation that results from multiple dialects and different relationships among communities (Bessett & Carvalho, 2021). This, connected to what other researchers have found about Spanish in the United States, shows that SPE contributes to the growing knowledge on bilingual systems in the United States.

Additionally, these results suggest that implementing reading recall in sociolinguistic data interpretation seems promising. Interdisciplinary research challenges the practice of studying language from one perspective, proving research against reductionism, and engaging in conversations about the immigrant experience.

References

Barrera-Tobón, C., & Raña-Riso, R. (2016). A corpus-based sociolinguistic study of contact-induced changes in subject placement in the Spanish of New York City bilinguals. In S. Sessarego & F. Tejedo-Herrero (Eds.), *Spanish language and sociolinguistic analysis* (pp. 323–342). John Benjamin Publishing Company.

Bessett, Ryan M., & Carvalho, A. M. (2021). The structure of US Spanish. In S. M. Beaudrie & S. Loza (Eds.), *Heritage language teaching: Critical language awareness perspectives for research and pedagogy* (pp. 44–62). Routledge.

Birdsong, D., Gertken, L. M., & Amengual, M. *Bilingual language profile: An easy-to-use instrument to assess bilingualism*. COERLL, University of Texas at Austn. Web. 20 Jan. 2012. https://sites.la.utexas.edu/bilingual/

Declerck, M., Wen, Y., Snell, J., Meade, G., & Grainger, J. (2020). Unified syntax in the bilingual mind. *Psychonomic Bulletin and Review 27*(1), 149–154.

Flores-Ferrán, N. (2002). *Subject personal pronouns in Spanish narratives of Puerto Ricans in New York City: A sociolinguistic perspective*. Lincom Europa.

Hartsuiker, R. J., Pickering, M. J., & Veltkamp, E. (2004). Is syntax separate or shared between languages? Cross-linguistic syntactic priming in Spanish-English bilinguals. *Psychological Science 15*(6), 409–414.

Helasvuo, M. (2004). Shared syntax: The grammar of co-constructions. *Journal of Pragmatics 36*(8), 1315–1336.

Hurtado, L. M. (2001). La variable expresión del sujeto en el español de los colombianos y colombo- americanos residentes en el condado de Miami-Dade [Doctoral dissertation]. University of Florida.

Hurtado, L. M. (2005). El uso de tú, usted y uno en el español de los colombianos y colombo-americanos. In L. Ortiz-López & M. Lacorte (Eds.), *Contactos y contextos lingüísticos: El español en los Estados Unidos y en contacto con otras lenguas* (pp. 185–200). Iberoamericana / Vervuert.

Hurtado, L. M., & Gutiérrez-Rivas, C. (2016). La versatilidad del pronombre uno para expresar posicionamiento frente a lo enunciado en el español de Barranquilla (Colombia). *Forma y Función 29*(1), 37–60.

Lastra, Y., & Martín Butragueño, P. (2015). Subject pronoun expression in oral Mexican Spanish. In A. M. Carvalho, R. Orozco, & N. L. Shin (Eds.), *Subject pronoun expression in Spanish: A cross-dialectal perspective* (pp. 39–58). Georgetown University Press.

Limerick, P. P. (2019). The discursive distribution of subject pronouns in Spanish spoken in Georgia: A weakening of pragmatic constraints? *Studies in Hispanic and Lusophone Linguistics 12*(1), 97–126.

Milroy, L., & Milroy, J. (1992). Social network and social class: Toward an integrated sociolinguistic model. *Language in Society*, 21(1), 1–26.

O'Rourke, E., & Potowski, K. (2016). Phonetic accommodation in a situation of Spanish dialect contact: Coda /s/ and /r̄/ in Chicago. *Studies in Hispanic and Lusophone Linguistics 9*(2), 355–399.

Orozco, R. (2015). Pronominal variation in Colombian Costeño Spanish. In A. M. Carvalho, R. Orozco, & N. L. Shin (Eds.), *Subject pronoun expression in Spanish: A cross-dialectal perspective* (pp. 17–37). Georgetown University Press.

Orozco, R. (2018a). *Spanish in Colombia and New York City: Language contact meets dialectal convergence*. John Benjamins.

Orozco, R. (2018b). El castellano colombiano en la ciudad de Nueva York: Uso variable de sujetos pronominales. *Studies in Hispanic and Lusophone Linguistics 11*(1), 89–129.

Orozco, R., & Hurtado, L. M. (2021). A variationist study of subject pronoun expression in Medellín, Colombia. *Languages 6*(1), 5.

Otheguy, R., Zentella, A. C., & Livert, D. (2007). Language and dialect contact in Spanish in New York: Toward the formation of a speech community. *Language 83*(4), 770–802.

Otheguy, R., & Zentella, A. C. (2012). *Spanish in New York: Language contact, dialectal leveling, and structural continuity*. Oxford University Press.

Shin, J. A., & Christianson, K. (2012). Structural priming and second language learning. *Language Learning, 62*(3).

Showstack, R. (2018). Spanish and identity among Latin@s in the U.S. In K. Potowski (Ed.), *The Routledge Handbook of Spanish as a Heritage Language* (pp. 96–106). Routledge.

Torres Cacoullos, R., & Travis, C. E. (2015). Foundations for the study of subject pronoun expression in Spanish in contact with English: Assessing interlinguistic (dis)similarity via intralinguistic variability. In A. M. Carvalho, R. Orozco, & N. L. Shin (Eds.), *Subject pronoun expression in Spanish: A cross-dialectal perspective* (pp. 81–100). Georgetown University Press.

CHAPTER 8

Ideologies of linguistic authority and the role of language choice in *El procés* trial

Marina Cárcamo
Seattle University

This study analyzes the ideologies of linguistic authority of the members of the 2016–2017 Catalan government and social representatives judged at *El procés* trial. It explores their general language ideologies, whether their views on linguistic authority are traditional or post-naturalistic concerning Catalan and Spanish,[1] and the relevance of language choice in this politically loaded trial. The analysis reveals a prevalence of post-naturalistic conceptualizations of linguistic authority. Catalan is ideologized as a language of expression and identity, associated with post-naturalistic anonymity. Spanish is linked to anonymity for public communication but is also considered authentic by some Catalans. Language is central to the trial and the political conflict, with one of the defendants even citing it as a key factor for the Catalan independence movement.

Keywords: language ideologies, linguistic authority, legal context, Catalonia, Spain

1. Introduction

Catalonia and Spain have had a tense political relationship throughout the current Spanish democracy, mainly since the mid-2000s (Holesch & Jordana, 2021). The catalytic moment occurred in September 2012 when 1.5 million people rallied in Barcelona, bringing Catalan national identity to the global stage, advocating for the *right to decide* on Catalonia's sovereignty. The subsequent year saw an even larger gathering as people formed the *Via Catalana*, a 480-kilometer demonstration, known as the *Catalan Way to Independence*, drawing international media attention. A diverse coalition, representing center-right to progressive left parties in the Catalan Parliament, united to advocate for an independence referendum

---

1. In this paper, *Spanish* is a synonym to *Castilian*.

in 2014 (Minder, 2013). Despite the Spanish government's opposition, a nonbinding citizens' consultation in 2014 saw 2.3 million voters, with 90% supporting statehood and 80% favoring outright independence (Generalitat de Catalunya, 2014; Ríos, 2014). This movement, sparked in 2010, responded to the Spanish Constitutional Court's limitations on the Catalan Statute of Autonomy. The rapid transformation of possibilities and challenges faced by Catalonia reflected global economic effects and a deep-rooted pride in culture and language (Woolard, 2016).

On October 1, 2017, the Catalan government (Generalitat) held a referendum on whether the region should declare independence. The results were 90% in favor of independence, although only 42% of the Catalan population turned out to vote (Baquero, 2017). On October 27, 2017, the pro-independence parties in the Catalan Parliament declared Catalonia independent, after all the members who opposed independence walked out in protest (Pérez, 2017). The Spanish government ruled the referendum illegal under articles 92, 167.3 and 168.3 of the Spanish Constitution of 1978 (Constitución Española, 1978), and international organizations including the European Union, United Nations, North Atlantic Treaty Organization, and Organization for Economic Cooperation and Development did not recognize Catalonian independence (Eitb.eus, 2017). By contrast, a 2018 poll by the Centre d'Estudis d'Opinió (2018, p. 50) revealed that 68.4% of Catalans believed Catalonia had the right to hold a self-determination referendum.

In response to the independence movement, the then-president of Spain, Mariano Rajoy, dissolved the Catalan Parliament, terminated the appointments of all Catalan government officials, and called for elections in Catalonia in December 2017 (Pérez, 2017). Following that, the Spanish National Court (Audiencia Nacional) issued an order for the detention pending trial of the vice-president, seven former ministers from the Catalan government, as well as the presidents of two pro-independence organizations, Assemblea Nacional Catalana and Òmnium Cultural (Carpio, 2017). Another former minister, Santi Vila, was able to avoid detention on bail of 50,000 euros. Additionally, the former president of the Catalan devolved Parliament Carme Forcadell was later sent to prison by the Supreme Court (Rincón, 2018). The former president of Catalonia Carles Puigdemont and four former ministers (Toni Comín, Clara Posantí, Meritxell Serret, and Lluís Puig) fled the country and all of them except Meritxell Serret (who returned to Catalonia in 2021) still live in exile. The defendants faced a joint trial in Madrid in February 2019, following over a year in pre-trial detention. The trial was formally identified as *Causa especial 20907/2017* but was commonly referred to as *El procés*[2] by Spanish media. The primary defendants were ex-Vice-President Oriol Junqueras; ex-Ministers Joaquim Forn, Jordi Turull, Raül Romeva, Josep Rull, Dolors

---

2. *El procés* also refers to the constituent process of independence in Catalonia.

Bassa, Meritxell Borrás, and Santi Vila, Carles Mundó; ex-president of the Catalan Parliament Carme Forcadell; Jordi Sànchez, president of Assemblea Nacional Catalana; and Jordi Cuixart, president of Òmnium Cultural (Recuero, 2019).[3]

Although all the defendants are fluent in both Catalan and Spanish, the lawyers of Junqueras, Romeva, Sànchez, Rull, Turull, Cuixart, and Forcadell requested that the defendants speak in Catalan at the trial with simultaneous interpretation into Spanish (Solé Altimira, 2019; Plataforma per la Llengua, 2020). Simultaneous interpretation requires specific and expensive equipment, including having everyone present wear headphones. The presiding judge, Manuel Marchena, rejected using simultaneous interpretation, on the basis that it would restrict the principle of a public trial, since the audience outside the courtroom would not understand the proceedings (El Confidencial, 2019). Instead, he offered consecutive interpretation, where the interpreter takes notes while a speaker is talking, then translates a lengthy segment of speech when there is a pause. These defendants rejected this procedure on the basis that it would "go against the orality principle" (Josep Rull, February 20, 2019); that is, the ability to present their arguments without interruption. Instead, the defendants decided to speak in Spanish and express their opinions and claims regarding their inability to use Catalan in the courtroom. In practice, however, their testimony contained frequent code-switches into Catalan and translations from Catalan to Spanish of exhibits presented at the trial. In fact, Cuixart and Turull had to translate into Spanish the exhibits that the prosecution presented in Catalan, which also had ideological implications.

This study analyzes the ideologies of linguistic authority of the defendants in *El procés*, a trial that represented a microcosm of the political conflict between Catalonia and Spain. Nevertheless, this study specifically concentrates on the testimonies of the defendants, who serve as political and social representatives of pro-independence ideologies in Catalonia. The ultimate goal of this research is to analyze and comprehend the prevailing language ideologies within the pro-independence segment of the Catalan population. While these defendants stand as representatives and community members of this population in Catalonia, it is crucial to recognize that their testimonies are meticulously crafted presentations consciously chosen and rehearsed as part of their defense preparation. However, these testimonies are assumed to be crafted based on their political and language ideologies, serving as a significant argument in their defense. In fact, given that most of these defendants had not had the chance to make public state-

---

3. Except from Cuixart, all of them belonged to two different nationalist political parties: ERC (left-wing; Junqueras, Romeva, Bassa, Forcadell, and Mundó) and former CiU/current Junts (center right-wing; Forn, Rull, Turull, Vila, Borràs, and Sànchez).

ments about their detention during the pre-trial period of over a year, the trial provided them with an opportunity to publicly address their voters and the pro-vote/independence-supporting Catalan populations.

This investigation opens by identifying the general language ideology themes included in the defendants' claims and opinions in their testimonies, then turns to whether these ideologies align with traditional or post-naturalistic views of the linguistic authority of Catalan and Spanish (see Woolard, 2016). Finally, it seeks to understand the relevance of language choice and usage in this politically loaded trial.

2. Language ideologies and linguistic authority

In this study, I follow Irvine's definition of language ideologies as "conceptualizations about languages, speakers, and discursive practices … that are pervaded with political and moral interests and are shaped in a cultural setting" (Irvine, 2012, p.1). Even though language ideologies may refer to language in general, specific languages, specific language varieties, or specific ways of using language (Fuller & Leeman, 2020), I examine only those language ideologies that express the speaker's attitude toward *specific languages*, which usually are influenced by nationalism (Eckert, 1983; Handler, 1988; Sonntag & Pool, 1987; Woolard & Schieffelin, 1994). These types of ideologies are referred to as *ideologies of linguistic authority* by Woolard (2005; 2016), which I will explain below. Both explicit discursive forms and implicit ideologies are addressed in this study.

2.1 Language ideologies and nationalism

Nationalism, as defined by Gellner (1993), is the political ideology that holds that "the national state, identified with a national culture and committed to its protection, is the natural political unit" (p. 422). In the 20th century, two types of nationalism were defined: civic (or political) nationalism and ethnic (or cultural) nationalism, based on Meinecke's notions of Staatsnation (state-nation) and Kulturnational (cultural nation) respectively (Karolewski & Suszycki, 2011; Gat & Yakobson, 2013; Trautsch, 2019). The legitimacy of a nation in civic nationalism is built upon the participation of the citizens (shared political principles), while in ethnic nationalism (or ethnonationalism) it comes from the identity (culture or ethnicity) of the people (Geeraerts, 2008; Woolard, 2016). In civic nationalism, all citizens (regardless of race, color, creed, gender, language, or ethnicity) who subscribe to the nation are part of the state (Trautsch, 2019). In ethnic nationalism, language together with culture is the identity or essence (*Volksgeist*) of the nation and the symbol of nationhood (May, 2012). Blommaert (1999) and May (2012) concur that a language is not only a component of culture, but also a political fact in many ethnic and ethnonationalist movements, as is the case with some pro-independence movements in Catalonia.

Within the framework of minority or minoritized[4] language rights, which encompasses the entitlement of minority/minoritized languages to exist in spaces dominated by majority or common languages (May, 2012), Sonntag and Pool (1987) highlighted a notable paradox. They pointed out that ethnic nationalist language ideologies, which may involve rejecting language diversity and linking language competence to loyalty to the nation, often originate from movements advocating for minority languages. Woolard and Schieffelin (1994) argued that hegemonic nationalist ideologies and ethnic nationalist ideologies from minoritized cultures and languages share significant similarities.

In Catalonia, an ongoing shift from ethnic nationalism to civic nationalism has taken place since the beginning of the 21st century, due to the influence of post-national globalization and the high presence of immigrants (both from Southern Spain and other countries). According to Woolard (2016), many Catalanists have aimed to recruit Spanish-speaking and immigrant-descent citizens for the right-to-vote (referendum) movement, and the Catalan society has been "refashioning the ties between language and identity in Catalonia" (Woolard, 2016, p. 6).

2.2 Nationalistic language ideologies in Catalonia

In Catalonia, ideas and ideologies related to nationalism and minority/minoritized language rights are expressed through two primary bounded terms: *llengua pròpia* and *normalització lingüística* (Süselbeck, 2008). According to Branchadell (1997) and Süselbeck (2008), *llengua pròpia* has different meanings, depending on the context of its use, meaning either "one's own language" and "proper language." This term is what Bakhtin (1987) called an intertext, that is, a word or term that alludes to the particular text where it was first used. The first use of *llengua pròpia* in the sense of (Catalans') own language first appeared in the Statute of Autonomy of Catalonia (Estatut d'autonomia de Catalunya, 1979). Subsequently, in 1995, Jordi Pujol, the first president of Catalonia after Franco's dictatorship, referenced

---

4. A *minority* language is one spoken by a small speech community (less than 50 percent in a given nation-state) or that sometimes does not hold official status (Grenoble & Singerman, 2014), whereas a *minoritized* language is a minority language that has historically and actively been minimized in a region or a nation, as a result of a lack of protection by public policies and language planning (Groff, 2017; Nevins, 2022).

both meanings of the term in a speech titled *What does language represent for Catalonia?*[5] (Pujol, 1995). He described the concept of one's own language as "something that belongs to a person or a thing and defines the identity of that person or that thing" and that of proper language as "something that is authentic as opposed to something that is borrowed" (Süselbeck, 2008, p.13). Süselbeck (2008) points out that the way Pujol used Catalan's "own language" is a clear expression of the one language, one nation ideology. This ideology refers to the attitude that only a single language (one's own language) should be spoken in a nation. Branchadell (1997) further associated *llengua pròpia* with the notion of Catalan having its origins in Catalonia, as the "historic language" of that region (Marí, 1995).

Related to concept of one's own or original language, Geeraerts (2008) discussed how individuals choose to speak their *own* language when they want to express their identity or their culture. For these speakers, their language is part of their identity. While Geeraerts delves into the role of language as a means to articulate personal identity (*language as medium of expression*), *own language* denotes a community-based and ethnonationalist identity, where language (specifically, Catalan) is a symbol of nationhood.

For many Catalans, Spanish is merely the official language of the Spanish state, and they do not view it as their *llengua pròpia* (Branchadell, 1997; Sinner & Wieland, 2008; Colino, 2009; May, 2012). On the other hand, a survey on language use carried out by the Generalitat de Catalunya (2018) reported that Spanish was the language of identity for 46.6% of the Catalan population, while 36.3% ascribed this status to Catalan. Only 6.9% of the population embraced a bilingual Catalan-Spanish identity, and 9.7% cited other languages or combinations of languages as their own language. This is one of the reasons why authors like Caminal (2007), Branchadell (2010), and Riera Gil (2013) state that Catalan cannot be referred to as *llengua pròpia*. Since the beginning of the 21st century, political actors tended to replace the term *llengua pròpia* by *llengua comuna* (common language), a parallel shift to the turn from ethnic to civic nationalism with major political implications. Riera Gil (2013) explains that the concept *llengua comuna* is imported from Quebec and emerged in texts like the *Pacte nacional per la immigració*[6] (Generalitat de Catalunya, 2008), the manifesto *El català, llengua comuna* (Plataforma per la Llengua, 2008), and the Llei 10/2010, a welcome law for immigrants and returnees in Catalonia. Although there is not a clear definition for *llengua comuna*, the concept represents an inclusive term and an element of social cohesion for all Catalans (including descendants of Spanish and international migrants).

---

5. All translations from Catalan and Spanish to English are mine.
6. National pact for immigration.

Nonetheless, the Statute of Autonomy of Catalonia (Estatut d'autonomia de Catalunya), as updated in 2006, designates Catalan as the language of government institutions, of the education system (except from the Spanish, English, and other foreign language classes), and of mass media. According to Sinner and Wieland (2008), many Catalans believe that the Statute of Autonomy of Catalonia (2016 [2006]) should promote the use of Catalan in Catalonia, just as the Spanish constitution promotes the use of Spanish in Spain. This language policy is referred to *normalització lingüística* (linguistic normalization). In theory, *normalització lingüística* aims at promoting de jure and de facto status of Catalan, that is, making Catalan more prevalent in institutional and public spaces in Catalonia in order that the Catalan society recovers a *normal* linguistic situation (similar to pre-Franco era) (Heller, 2007; Süselbeck, 2008; Woolard, 2016; Generalitat de Catalunya, 2017). Linguistic normalization was first implemented in Catalonia by the Law of Linguistic Normalization in Catalonia in 1983 (Llei de Normalització Lingüística a Catalunya, 1983), and it has been regulated by the Consortium for Linguistic Standardization/Normalization since 1989 (Generalitat de Catalunya, 2017). Nonetheless, authors like Rees (1996) and Süselbeck (2008) asserted that the real goal was not balanced bilingualism (which could be utopic) but language shift from Spanish to Catalan to create a feeling of Catalan nationalism and transform Catalonia into a homogenous and unique nation. In this sense, Süselbeck (2008) insists that *normalització lingüística* connects advocacy for minoritized linguistic rights to reclaiming a homogeneous Catalan nation. According to Süselbeck's (2008) results, Catalan, the authentic language of a minoritized culture, becomes a national and common language to be used in public spaces, such as schools, universities, institutions, etc.

Eckert (1983) explored this issue as a fundamental paradox: When claiming independence or autonomy, a region is required (1) "to be large and diverse enough to comprise a viable economic unit"; and (2) to have a shared heritage that justifies "the unification of the region and its separateness from the larger political unit it is part of" (p. 289). In order to establish the cultural, historical, and linguistic commonality needed for both (1) and (2), the region must suppress subregional diversity. In relation to languages and nationalism, minority/minoritized languages spoken in those regions (*ethnic* or authentic voices) become *civic* or anonymous voices that need to remove its indexicalities, such as class or gender (Atkinson, 2018, p. 779). Consequently, Eckert (1983) states that this process is no different than oppression by the majority state, which likewise requires the submersion of local diversity. This authenticity versus anonymity dichotomy was proposed and refined by Woolard and Schieffelin (1994), and Woolard (2005; 2016) over many years. Beginning in 2001, Gal and Woolard referred to these ideologies toward specific languages (among others) as *ideologies of linguistic authority*.

2.3 Ideologies of linguistic authority

As previously mentioned, authenticity and anonymity are two ideologies of linguistic authority that co-constitute each other (Woolard, 2016). Based on sociolinguistic naturalism, linguistic authenticity recognizes that a language is rooted in a territory, is valued for its relationship to a particular community, and is an essential expression of that community. It follows, then, that minoritized languages, which tend to be local languages spoken in minoritized communities, are typically associated with the ideology of authenticity. From the perspective of authenticity, speaking in one's own language is linked to sincerity and represents the most reliable means to access the *truth* (Woolard, 2016, p. 30). On the other hand, linguistic anonymity is based on the ideals of rational communicative exchanges, in which the majority of the population invests in a language with political authority (Woolard, 2016, p. 25). Languages grounded on the anonymity ideology are viewed as public, and as voices from nowhere, implying that they cannot be attributed to a specific speech community, as their social origins are erased ideologically (Irvine & Gal, 2000). The anonymity ideology is usually associated with the hegemonic languages, the common languages, or the linguas francas. This idea of the common language has also been referred to as the intercultural language (Von Gleich, 2008), a language of communication between cultures and nations.

According to Woolard (2005), "hegemonic languages ... rest their authority on a conception of anonymity" (p. 10). Traditionally, Catalan nationalist politicians have ideologized Catalan as an authentic and minoritized/minority language (the *own language* and original voice of Catalonia) and Spanish as an anonymous language in Catalonia, never recognized as Catalonia's *own language* but as the language of others. Presently, as Soler (2012) and Woolard (2016) found in their studies, Catalan is no longer ideologized as an authentic minority language, since it is widely spoken in all public spheres in Catalonia (up to 30% of Catalonia's population speak it as their first language; Woolard, 2016) and has acquired overt social prestige.

Meanwhile, Branchadell advocated for abandoning the authenticity-anonymity debate and adopting instead a post-naturalistic (or post-nationalist) perspective, in which the "one-to-one nation-language correspondence is no longer taken for granted" (2012, p. 8). Upon returning to Catalonia in 2007 to explore how the same participants conceptualized anonymity and authenticity two decades later, Woolard (2016) identified emerging post-naturalistic ideological frameworks. This time, she observed that most of their perspectives transcended this binary logic, aligning with Branchadell's argument. These perspectives reflected forms of rooted cosmopolitanism, emphasizing the internationalization of regional identities, including those with immigrant descent. The participants leaned towards a post-naturalistic understanding of authenticity as a dynamic project, constructed throughout one's life, rather than as an inherent origin tied to one's mother tongue (Woolard, 2016, p. 300). The majority of speakers who aligned with these ideologies framed their experiences in the so-called biographical chronotope (Bakhtin, 1981), because they interpreted their "linguistic growth in apolitical terms of individual growth" (Woolard, 2016, p. 286). Others kept their ideologies and experiences within the socio-historical chronotope, as unchanging subjects whose language ideologies are based on their political ideologies in a transformed time-place.

All the aforementioned concepts have been relevant in the multilingual landscape of Spain in the post-Franco era, as the Spanish constitution adopted in 1978 recognized Catalan, Galician, and Basque as co-official languages with Spanish in their respective provinces. May (2012) reminded us that it is important for all languages that form and maintain a particular national identity to be considered in the public sphere. Nevertheless, the plurilingual recognition and status did not exist all over Spain, but only in the bilingual regions, which Boix-Fuster (2008) said is "insufficient" (p. 281). Recently in September 2023, the Spanish Congress implemented an amendment to Article 6 of the Congress Rules, permitting the use of languages officially recognized in autonomous communities as outlined in the Constitution and corresponding Statute of Autonomy (Congreso de los Diputados, 2023). The scenario in the Spanish Congress contrasts sharply with the situation in judicial settings, exemplified by the *El procés* trial in 2019, where despite the defendants being bilingual citizens, the Supreme Court, one of the main legal institutions of Spain, disregarded their linguistic diversity (Ortega, 2019). In fact, according to Ortega (2019), court officials did not even attempt to correctly pronounce the defendants' last names.

While linguistic diversity is recognized as a cultural heritage deserving protection in Spain (Article 3.3, Article 20 from the Spanish Constitution, 1978), the Constitutional Court has not translated this acknowledgment into legal consequences. Spain ratified the European Charter for Regional and Minority Languages in 2001, committing to protect minority languages across various domains, yet implementation varies. The responsibility for promoting minority languages is predominantly delegated to the Autonomous Communities (Morales-Gálvez & Cetrà, 2022). According to the Spanish Ministry of Territorial Policy and Public Function (2021), Article 231 of the Spanish Organic Law on the Judiciary (LOPJ) recognizes the right to choose the language(s) in legal proceedings, ensuring effective legal protection under Article 24 of the Spanish Constitution. However, a key requirement is that none of the parties objects to the selected language, fearing a lack of proficiency might compromise due process and partially violate Article 9 of the European Charter for Regional and Minority Languages. Therefore, the responsibility for assessing potential denial of due process (and consequently, the denial of linguistic rights) lies with the judicial authority.

In summary, the field of language ideologies in Catalonia focuses on ideologies toward specific languages, particularly influenced by nationalism. Woolard and Gal (2001) coined the term *ideologies of linguistic authority* to encapsulate these ideologies towards specific languages. Woolard's investigation into ideologies of linguistic authority among Catalan high-school students identified two primary categories: authenticity and anonymity. The authenticity ideology acknowledges a language's connection to a specific territory and community, while the anonymity ideology is grounded in rational communicative ideals, where the majority invests in a language with political authority. Another prominent language ideology examined in Catalonia is the concept of "one nation, one language," founded on the notion that each nation is defined by a singular language and vice versa.

In Catalonia, nationalistic language ideologies have been discussed through three pivotal terms in their language ideological narrative: *own language* (emphasizing Catalan as the essence and symbol of nationhood), *common language* (positioning Catalan as an inclusive element fostering social cohesion), and *linguistic normalization* (reflecting efforts to elevate Catalan to genuine co-official status and enhance its presence in institutional settings).

The discussion on nationalism delved into civic nationalism (centered on shared political principles) and ethnic nationalism (rooted in cultural identity), investigating their impacts on language identity and ideologies. Catalonia has undergone a transformation from ethnic to civic nationalism in recent times, a shift attributed to the influences of post-national globalization and immigration. This transition from ethnic to civic nationalism in Catalonia has also brought about a transformation in ideologies of linguistic authority, characterized by the emergence of post-naturalistic frameworks.

Concluding the theoretical framework, attention turned to Spain's multilingual landscape and the hurdles facing plurilingualism in the trial. This highlighted disparities and issues associated with linguistic diversity and the rights of minoritized languages. The preceding discussion unveiled the intricate connections between language ideologies, linguistic authority, political discourses, and nationalism within the context of Catalonia.

Based on the language ideology topics discussed above, my first research objective is to examine the predominant language ideology topics evident in the defendants' testimonies. Subsequently, utilizing Woolard's linguistic authority model as a framework, my secondary research goal is to investigate the ideologies of linguistic authority, specifically authenticity and/or anonymity, that appear to be present as the defendants express their views on Spanish and Catalan. Finally, considering that in Catalonia, language has been a significant social symbol and a longstanding political issue (Woolard, 2016), I aim to explore the significance of language choice and language use in the context of this trial.

3. Methodology

The corpus of analysis comprises the testimonies and closing arguments of the 12 defendants in the *procés* trial. I watched and listened to the videos of these testimonies (publicly available on YouTube) and extracted segments where language usage in the trial and language-related matters were discussed. Notably, these discussions were present in the speeches of all defendants except for 2 individuals (Mundó and Vila). Most of these segments were present in the opening remarks of their testimonies, where they expressed their dissatisfaction with being unable to use Catalan in their statements. Only a handful of segments were extracted from the defendants' concluding arguments, specifically (9), (13), (16), (25), and (26), and the only segments where the defendants respond to questions (essentially reviewing exhibits) are (20), (21), and (22). In the analysis section, I will provide context to these responses by incorporating their corresponding questions. I manually transcribed these specific segments, which amounted to approximately 7 hours of speech. It's noteworthy that all texts were in Spanish, except for those explicitly presented in Catalan.

The analytical approach employed involves a qualitative thematic analysis, drawing inspiration from Clarke and Braun's methodology (2021), and a discourse analysis framework following Woolard (2016). Thematic analysis, as defined by Clarke and Braun (2021) "involve systematic processes of data coding to develop themes, which are the ultimate analytic purpose" (p. 47). The flexibility of thematic analysis allowed for an inductive approach, enabling the development of an analysis that captured both the explicit themes and underlying ideologies. This approach provided descriptive as well as interpretative insights into the data. To address research aims (1) and (2), I identified segments within the corpus that addressed topics related to language ideologies and linguistic authority. Subsequently, I coded these segments (texts) into semantic labels (reflecting explicit or surface meaning) and latent labels (reflecting implicit or conceptual meaning). Utilizing the bounded terms and concepts from the theoretical framework and recognizing consistent meanings across the dataset, I established *candidate themes* for each language (Catalan and Spanish) through descriptive coding. These candidate themes were then consolidated into the *final themes* (see "Final themes" in Tables 1 and 2).

Chapter 8. Ideologies of linguistic authority and the role of language choice in *El procés* trial

Table 1. Candidate and final themes surrounding Catalan from data analysis

Candidate themes	Final themes
– *Own language*	– *Own language*
– *Native language*	– *Language as a medium of expression*
– *Language as a medium of expression*	– *Minoritized/minority language*
– *Cultural expression*	– *Linguistic normalization*
– *Minoritized language*	– *Common language*
– *Minority language*	
– *Lawful language*	
– *Linguistic normalization*	
– *Common language*	
– *Intercultural language*	

Table 2. Candidate and final themes surrounding Spanish from data analysis

Candidate themes	Final themes
– *Common language*	– *Common language*
– *Intercultural language*	– *Own language*
– *Koiné*	
– *Own language*	
– *Native language*	

Drawing from the conceptual framework of language ideologies and ideologies of linguistic authority, I applied a discourse analysis methodology to uncover the implicit ideologies that underlie the themes discussed in connection with the sociopolitical context (see "General ideologies" and "Ideologies of linguistic authority" on Table 3).

Table 3. General ideologies and ideologies of linguistic authority surrounding Catalan and Spanish retrieved from the analysis corpus

General ideologies	Ideologies of linguistic authority
– One nation, one language	– Authenticity (both traditional and post-naturalistic conceptualization)
	– Anonymity (both traditional and post-naturalistic conceptualization)

To explore discussions on the significance of language choice in the trial (research aim 3), I also employed a thematic analysis methodology. First, I pinpointed texts addressing the bilingual proficiency of court members and the issue of plurilingualism in Spain. Following the identification of candidate themes from these texts (see "Candidate themes" on Table 4), I conducted an interpretation to discern patterned meanings and ultimately derived the final themes (see "Final themes" on Table 4).

Table 4. Candidate and final themes of the relevance of linguistic diversity and language rights in the trial retrieved from the corpus analysis

Candidate themes	Final themes
– *Nationalism/Catalanism*	– Linguistic incompetence and intelligibility between Catalan and Spanish
– *The historical authority of Spain as an oppressive entity*	
– *Disagreement with the Supreme court of Spain in relation with the language use in the trial and the consequences of the decision for Catalonia and Spain*	– Plurilingualism as a feature of the Spanish state
– *Relevance of this trial for Catalonia and Spain*	– Relevance of this trial for Catalonia and Spain

Finally, to enhance the robustness of the thematic analysis in this study, I conducted an interrater reliability test. I enlisted a language ideologies researcher (rater 2) to perform a parallel analysis, providing her with the corpus, contextual information, literature on the bounded terms, and the framework of ideologies of linguistic authority. She conducted a thematic analysis for each excerpt, offering concise justifications for her analysis. For each excerpt, I scrutinized both analyses, assessing the level of agreement between my analysis and hers using a scale from 0 to 1, as illustrated in Table 5. A score of 0 denoted no agreement, 0.5 denoted partial agreement (acknowledging shared themes with the potential for one rater introducing an additional theme not considered by the other), and a score of 1 signified perfect agreement.

Table 5. Scale of agreement with values and explanations for inter-rater reliability test

Level of agreement	Value	Explanation
None	0	Different theme(s) per excerpt.
Partial	0.5	Some shared themes exist between Rater 1 and Rater 2, with the possibility that Rater 1 might introduce an extra theme not covered by Rater 2, or vice versa.
Perfect	1	Same number of themes and same theme(s) per excerpt.

Subsequently, I calculated the percentage agreement. The test results reveal a 91.38% level of agreement among the raters, suggesting that there was no complete disagreement in any excerpt, with only three instances of partial disagreement (excerpts [4], [13], and [22]). To rectify the 8.62% of misrepresented data, I (rater 1) deliberated on the three excerpts exhibiting partial agreement with rater 2. I revised the analysis for these three excerpts by integrating the criteria of both researchers. In the absence of agreement, I would have sought the input of a third rater.

4. Analysis

This analysis is divided into two parts: the first part unveils complementary and conflicting bounded terms and underlying ideologies of linguistic authority surrounding Catalan and Spanish; and the second part analyzes discussions of language choice and usage in trial as explained below. The original texts in Spanish and Catalan are shown on the left side and their correspondent translations into English, on the right side.

4.1 Themes and ideologies surrounding Catalan

Beginning with the ideologies that relate to Catalan, the main language-related themes discussed are *own language; language as a medium of expression; minoritized/minority language; linguistic normalization;* and *common language*.

4.1.1 *Own language*

As previously discussed, *own language* is a bounded term found in Catalan language policy texts that has a nationalistic connotation and is based on sociolinguistic naturalism. It specifically denotes Catalan as the language representing Catalonia's identity and national character. One text in the corpus exemplified the own language theme. In (1), it seems that Rull purposefully uses *own language* to identify Catalan as not only their first language, but also their historic language in the highly politicized context of the trial.

(1) "Son razones de naturaleza fáctica. Para mí, el derecho a poder utilizar la **lengua propia**, y la **lengua materna**, es un *derecho fundamental*. A través del mecanismo de traducción consecutiva, creo que se vulnera este derecho."

"These are reasons of a factual nature. For me, being able to use **one's own language,** and the **mother tongue,** is a *fundamental right*. Through the mechanism of consecutive translation, I believe that this right is violated."

(Josep Rull, February 20, 2019)

In this passage, the use of *own language* (associated with the nation of Catalonia) contrasts with the use of *mother tongue*, which is less politically charged than the former. *Mother tongue* refers to Catalan as a means of expressing personal identity. Thus, in this section, Rull strategically employs both terms to articulate his identity as a citizen of Catalonia as a nation-state and as an individual for whom Catalan is an integral part of his identity. Hence, it appears that there are two distinct types of authenticity ideologies at play: ethnonationalistic authenticity concerning Rull's own language and personal authenticity linked to the mother tongue.

Example (1) also contains the minority language rights theme (the italicized words). In this instance, Rull advocates for his right to use their mother tongue during the trial, emphasizing the entitlement of Catalan as a minoritized language to exist in this judicial setting traditionally dominated by Spanish (as a majority language). Given that the defendants meticulously crafted their testimonies and the trial was widely televised, it appears intentional that they raise the issue of minority language rights, illustrating to the audience that their linguistic rights are dismissed in the trial (within the Spanish state), similar to the political rights they advocate for: the right to a self-determination referendum and the right to adhere to the results of that referendum.

4.1.2 *Language as a medium of expression*

While *own language* referred to Catalan as a symbol of nationhood and nationalist identity, the theme *language as a medium of expression* represents language as freedom and expression of personal identity. Eight different excerpts delve into this theme, predominantly underscoring the significance of employing their mother tongue during the trial and how doing so enhances their ability to express themselves with eloquence and be more authentic.

In (2), Junqueras reflects on the relevance of language choice in this trial in order to fully express himself, and in (3), he mentions that consecutive interpretation does not help with communication, if they speak in their *mother tongue*.

(2) "Querría traer a colación una intervención … del día de ayer, en que reflexionaba sobre la importancia de **la lengua materna** y de los matices, … me hago mía esa intervención"

"I would like to bring up a statement… from yesterday, in which they reflected on the importance of the **mother tongue** and nuances… I make that intervention my own."

(Oriol Junqueras, February 14, 2019)

(3) "La traducción consecutiva...no facilita, que podamos eh... hablar cada uno en **nuestra lengua materna**"

"Consecutive translation ... doesn't make it easier, for everyone to, uh ... speak in **our mother tongue**."
(Oriol Junqueras, February 14, 2019)

These texts containing the mother tongue concept suggest the presence of the authenticity ideology when discussing Catalan. However, Junqueras does not directly refer to community-based authenticity or territorial language rights per se, resembling the authenticity identified by Woolard in Barcelona during the 80s. Instead, his focus is on highlighting the individual's authenticity and the right to express oneself authentically in their mother tongue. Considering their roles as political representatives and defendants in a widely broadcasted context, this form of authenticity could somehow index community-based authenticity: as representatives of Catalan speakers (and community members), they lack the right to use their mother tongue in Spanish state institutions beyond the bilingual autonomous communities where Catalan holds co-official status. If this interpretation holds, the ideology of authenticity would transition from a community-based perspective to an individual context within members of that speech community.

Excerpts (4), (5), (6) and (7) express similar feelings about how important, natural, and positive it is for the defendants to express their arguments and identity in Catalan:

(4) "Con la decisión que ha tomado el tribunal, básicamente hacen imposible el ejercicio pleno de ... **poderme expresarme en plenitud**."

"With the decision that the court has made, they basically make it impossible ... to **fully express myself**."
(Josep Rull, February 20, 2019)

(5) "Quiero expresar **la dificultad añadida** que representa para **mi fluidez y mi expresión** [hablar en español]".

"I want to express **the added difficulty** that it represents **for my fluency and my expression** [speaking in Spanish]."
(Joaquim Forn, February 14, 2019)

(6) "No porque desconozca la lengua española, sino porque ... con ella puedo ofrecer no solo **a mi persona una mayor tranquilidad** sino también a este tribunal una **mayor naturalidad en la defensa de mis planteamientos**."

"Not because I do not know Spanish, but because ... I can offer not only **greater peace of mind to myself**, but also to this court a **greater naturalness in the defense of my proposals**."
(Jordi Sànchez, February 21, 2019)

(7) "Me expreso en las dos lenguas bien, pero tengo **más facilidad, más fluidez hablando en catalán**."

"I express myself well in both languages, but I have **more facility, more fluency speaking Catalan**." (Joaquim Forn, February 14, 2019)

In (5), (6), and (7), Rull, Sànchez, and Forn discuss their preference for using Catalan, the language that they speak more fluently and *naturally*, despite their bilingual skills, suggesting that self-expression in one's native language is essential for them. In (8), Junqueras also addresses the importance of self-expression in his mother tongue and even expresses insecurity when speaking in Spanish:

(8) "Estoy convencido que todos ustedes me querrán entender mejor incluso de lo que **yo sea capaz de explicarme**, ... espero que ... **no haya ninguna dificultad. Y también, si la hubiese,** ... debe ser interpretada en el sentido general, ... Estoy convencido de que, si así es, no habrá ninguna duda sobre nuestra inocencia."

"I am convinced that all of you will want to understand me even better than **I am able to explain myself**, ... I hope that ... there will be no difficulty. And also, **if there were [any difficulty]**, ... it must be interpreted in the general sense, ... I am convinced that, if so, there will be no doubt about our innocence."
(Oriol Junqueras, February 14, 2019)

In fact, Junqueras asks the audience to make an effort to try to understand him, since he is not as confident speaking in Spanish as in Catalan. Here, Junqueras insinuates that he does not feel on an equal footing with the prosecution, because the fact that he could not use his native language in trial places an added burden on him while trying to defend himself.

Finally, in the following extract from his closing argument, Rull, who explained that Catalan was his language of expression in (1) and (4), cannot avoid speaking in Catalan when he talks about his family, one of the most personal and intimate parts of his life (in bold):

(9) "Y han sufrido, *a la meva dona, la Meritxell, que ha de tirar endavant dos nens petits, a la meva mare, la Mariona, que pateix molt i que no entens, no entens gens que carall está passant aqui i que estem fent, als meus germans,* al resto de mi familia, a mis amigos que siempre están, siempre están."

"And they have suffered, **to my wife, Meritxell, who has to raise two small children, to my mother, Mariona, who suffers a lot and doesn't understand, she doesn't understand at all what the hell is going on here and what we are doing, to my brothers**, to the rest of my family, to my friends who are always there, always there." (Josep Rull, June 12, 2019)

Based on the authentic standpoint that associates speaking in one's own language to sincerity and intimacy (Woolard, 2016), it appears that, by speaking in his mother tongue (Catalan) when addressing a personal subject, Rull is intentionally or unintentionally putting into practice his ideology of authenticity associated with Catalan.

These texts seem to specifically underscore the individual's right or necessity to express themselves in their mother tongue, aligning with the observations made concerning the concept of *mother tongue*. The concept of mother tongue here is associated with naturalism, acknowledging the first language as the immediate and unmediated reality of speakers, surpassing human will and, consequently, being deemed more authentic. Hence, the ideology of authenticity appears to be evident in these segments, with a specific emphasis on the individual form of authenticity discussed earlier. While this individual or personal authenticity differs from community-based authenticity as understood by Woolard (2016), it is crucial to note that these defendants usually act as representatives of certain segments of the Catalan population, as we will see in excerpt (25), where Romeva says that they are representing more than 2 million people (voters in the referendum). As discussed previously, the defendants' testimonies are carefully constructed to defend themselves not just as individual defendants in a standard trial but as judged representatives of political ideas and specific population groups. In fact, Cuixart goes so far as to declare that his primary concern in the trial is not personal freedom but rather to expose the limited freedoms and rights of Catalan citizens who advocate for the right to vote (elDiario.es, February 26, 2019). Furthermore, the defendants consistently identify themselves as political prisoners, representing numerous Catalans who endorse the referendum, and characterize the trial as a political trial.

4.1.3 *Minoritized/minority language*

This theme includes the idea that Catalan (a minoritized language in Spain) is as valid as Spanish for use in a variety of contexts, particularly legal and institutional contexts. This theme was present in four distinct excerpts.

The terms *minority* and *minoritized* were evident in excerpts (10) and (11), each highlighting similar ideologies from different approaches. In (10), Forcadell explains that Catalan is a minoritized language lacking the status of a valid language. Because this language is not institutionalized in the Spanish state, Catalan speakers, particularly the defendants in this trial, face a situation of injustice and marginalization.

(10) "La realidad es que el catalán siempre acaba siendo **una lengua minorizada**, y eso hace que los hablantes muchas veces sintamos que *nuestros derechos lingüísticos son vulnerados.*"

"The reality is that Catalan always ends up being **a minoritized language**, and that often makes us speakers feel that *our linguistic rights are violated.*"
(Carme Forcadell, February 26, 2019)

In contrast, in (11), Rull portrays Catalan not as a minority language, but as a common and widely spoken language. Rull further suggests that Spanish society views Catalan as a problem or a threat.

(11) "Con demasiada frecuencia, tengo la sensación, … que aún se ve la lengua catalana, por cierto, **no una lengua minoritaria, la décima lengua más hablada de la Unión Europea**, … como una amenaza o como un problema."

"Too often, I have the feeling … that we still see the Catalan language, [which] by the way, [is] **not a minority language, [but] the tenth most widely spoken language in the European Union**, … as a problem or a threat."
(Josep Rull, February 20, 2019)

Because a minoritized language is one that has historically and actively faced marginalization within a region or nation due to a lack of protection from public policies and language planning (Groff, 2017; Nevins, 2022), it appears that both (10) and (11) posit Catalan as a minoritized language rather than a minority language (defined as a language spoken by a small speech community, usually less than 50 percent in a given nation-state, and sometimes lacking official status). Forcadell, affiliated with ERC (a left-wing party), emphasizes the idea that the language rights of Catalan citizens are being withheld, while Rull (affiliated with the former CiU/current Junts, a right-wing party) focuses on the notion that Catalan, despite its widespread use, lacks support in Spain, framing it as a threat for Spanish (the most spoken language in Spain). In (10), Forcadell seems to evoke the authenticity ideology by employing the possessive *our* in "*our* linguistic rights" to characterize the status of Catalan in Spain. However, she explicitly refers to the rights of Catalan speakers rather than all speakers in Catalonia. In this excerpt, it appears that she is invoking a personal form of authenticity, likely representing many Catalan speakers who perceive their language as minoritized. Additionally, Forcadell challenges the one nation, one language ideology, asserting that Catalan should be a language spoken in Spain alongside Spanish. In (11), the ideology of post-naturalistic anonymity (grounded in rooted cosmopolitanism) appears to be evident. While Rull discusses Catalan as one of the most spoken languages in the European Union and celebrates this fact, he emphasizes that it is also his mother tongue — a fundamental expression of himself, as previously discussed in excerpt (1). It is noteworthy that in (1), Rull seems to invoke the traditional authenticity ideology by using the concept of own language. The defendant Rull may be expressing different ideologies (traditional authenticity and postnaturalist anonymity). This divergence could be attributed to the judicial context. Although Rull meticulously crafted his statements, incorporating a more inclusive view of Catalan, alternative ideologies might surface during moments of hesitation or heightened emotions, particularly when he addresses Catalan as his language of expression.

Although excerpt (12) and (13) do not explicitly employ the terms *minority* or *minoritized*, they address language rights concerning Catalan or the status of Catalan as a minoritized language in these passages.

(12) "Considero que **mi derecho** no está en poderme expresar respecto a mis sentimientos en esta sala, sino **para defenderme en igualdad de armas,** ante una acusación que me pide injustamente 17 años de prisión. Y creo que, **como ciudadano de un estado que tiene reconocida en una parte la lengua catalana,** tengo **el mismo derecho que cualquier otro ciudadano de este estado**, en poder utilizar *mi lengua materna*, que es la lengua catalana."

"I consider that **my right** is not only to be able to express myself regarding my feelings in this room, but to **defend myself with equality of arms** against an accusation that unjustly demands 17 years of imprisonment. And I think that **as a citizen of a state that has recognized the Catalan language** in part of the state, I have the **same right as any other citizen of this state,** to be able to use *my mother tongue*, which is Catalan."

(Jordi Sànchez, February 21, 2019)

In excerpt (12), Sànchez underscores the disadvantage he encounters as a citizen of the Spanish state, given that his right to use his mother tongue is denied during the trial. By asserting that Catalan, despite its co-official status in specific Spanish regions, cannot be spoken in the trial, Sànchez implies that Catalan is a minoritized language within the Spanish state, and that minoritized language rights are being withheld. In this instance, Sànchez explicitly addresses his personal right to (authentic) expression in his mother tongue, reflecting his individual authenticity.

Finally, in (13), Borràs references a poem in Catalan to illustrate the marginalized or minoritized status of Catalan in Spain in her closing argument:

(13) "Creo que es ilustrativo el poema de Joan Maragall ..., su "Oda a Espanya", que da su visión de la realidad catalana con España. Este poema empieza con una demanda, una súplica, *Escolta Espanya, la veu de un fill que et parla en llengua no castellana*", y acaba después de no sentirse escuchado con un desencuentro *"Adéu, Espanya"*.

"I think that Joan Maragall's poem is illustrative..., his "Oda a Espanya", which gives his vision of the Catalan reality with Spain. This poem begins with a demand, a plea, **"Listen, Spain, to the voice of a son who speaks to you in a non-Castilian language"** and after not feeling heard ends with a disagreement **"Goodbye, Spain"**

(Meritxell Borràs, June 12, 2019)

In this poem, the author portrays himself as a son of Spain who speaks Catalan, a non-Spanish language. Borràs points out that the Spanish state appears to overlook Catalan, not recognizing it as a language for many citizens of the state, such as Joan Maragall (the poem's author) and herself. Consequently, these speakers feel compelled to distance themselves from Spain. Maragall viewed Catalan as a minoritized (and therefore, marginalized) language in Spain, a perspective shared by Borràs. Additionally, Borràs seems to view Catalan as a crucial language for expressing identity among many Catalan citizens, including herself. Therefore, the personal authenticity ideology is apparent in this excerpt. Simultaneously, Borràs seems to suggest that Spain adheres to one nation, one language ideology, where Spanish is considered the sole language of the country by its citizens. Furthermore, with this quote, she addresses the significant role language plays in the political conflict, emphasizing how Spain's disregard for Catalan language and identity leaves many Catalan citizens feeling marginalized and desiring to disassociate from the Spanish state.

4.1.4 *Linguistic normalization*

Linguistic normalization (the process of language shift from Spanish to Catalan as the main language of Catalonia, or the process of stable bilingualism for both Spanish and Catalan as co-official languages) was mentioned in two excerpts. In (14), Romeva directly expresses his desire for the normalization and institutionalization of Catalan in both Catalonia and Spain.

(14) "Me sumo a la reclamación y al deseo de **normalidad de utilizar la lengua catalana**. Lamento que no lo podamos hacer como habíamos pedido."

"I share the demand and the desire for **normality in using the Catalan language**. I regret we weren't allowed to do it as we had requested."

(Raül Romeva, February 19, 2019)

In excerpt (15), Rull discusses the linguistic worth of Catalan as a means of human expression that should be shared and spread, in Catalonia and even outside it, which is an implementation of linguistic normalization.

(15) "Ojalá algún día se viese **la lengua catalana**, por parte de determinados entornos, **como una riqueza**, con voluntad de **ser compartida**."

"I hope one day certain groups will see **the Catalan language as wealth**, with the will to **be shared**."
(Josep Rull, February 20, 2019)

These excerpts address the policy of linguistic normalization in Catalonia and beyond Catalonia (in the Spanish state), which constitutes a post-national approach of normalization, focusing more on the recognition of plurilingualism in the Spanish state. In fact, it seems that these segments illustrate a transcendence or overcoming of the concept of normalization (as rooted in sociolinguistic naturalism). They illustrate common features of civic nationalism, such as inclusiveness and a willingness for Catalan to be shared beyond ethnicity or national origin. Specifically, in (15), ideologies of rooted cosmopolitanism, that is, post-naturalistic anonymity seem to be invoked. Catalan is conceived as an intercultural language, cultural richness with its own identity, but with the willingness to be shared.

4.1.5 *Common language*

The theme *common language* (*llengua comuna*) or lingua franca revolves around Catalan serving as an inclusive element that fosters social cohesion in Catalonia. This theme appears in excerpt (16), where Cuixart explains the role of Catalan as a lingua franca in the education system and in the Catalan society in his closing argument.

(16) "[Cataluña es] un país de inmigrantes donde sus ciudadanos decidieron hace más de 40 años que **la lengua catalana sería la lengua vehicular en las escuelas,** para así lograr que todo el mundo tuviera la igualdad de oportunidades, y que nadie tuviera que renunciar a su *lengua de origen*. Y prueba de esto es que hoy en Cataluña se pueden hablar más de 300 lenguas, y que **el catalán sigue siendo una lengua de cohesión social**."

"[Catalonia is] a country of immigrants where its citizens decided more than 40 years ago that **the Catalan language would be the lingua franca** in schools, in order to achieve equal opportunities for everyone and so that no one would have to give up their *original language*. And proof of this is that today in Catalonia, more than 300 languages can be spoken, and **Catalan continues to be a language of social cohesion**."
(Jordi Cuixart, February 26, 2019)

During the era of Franco's dictatorship, Catalan faced restrictions and was relegated to private spheres, being marginalized and minoritized. Although Catalan began to be integrated into the education system in the late 70s, it was not until 1998 that it definitively established itself as the primary language in schools (Departament d'Ensenyament – Generalitat de Catalunya, 2015). By becoming the lingua franca in education, according to Cuixart's explanation, Catalan not only became the language of origin for many Catalan citizens but also a shared language providing equal opportunities for all citizens, regardless of whether they speak Catalan as their mother tongue or come from different linguistic backgrounds as immigrants. In (16), Cuixart asserts that the promotion of Catalan serves as an inclusive and unifying factor in Catalan society, fostering social cohesion and mutual understanding, irrespective of the diverse linguistic backgrounds of its speakers. Cuixart's inclusive perspective aligns with the ideology of post-naturalistic anonymity. In this perspective, the public and general adoption of Catalan is viewed through the lens of rooted cosmopolitanism, emphasizing the promotion of regional identity and language within diverse communities, including international, Spanish-speaking, and immigrant-descendant populations. This perspective underscores the role of Catalan in promoting unity and pluralism within Catalonia.

4.2 Themes and ideologies surrounding Spanish

In terms of the ideologies and language-related themes associated with Spanish, I found two main types: *common language*, and *own language*.

4.2.1 *Common language*

This theme is associated with the notions of lingua franca and intercultural language and considers Spanish as an institutionalized or shared language that is spoken all over Spain and is the means of communication in Spanish institutions. In excerpt (17) below, Junqueras identifies Spanish as the language that all Spanish citizens speak, so he can use it to communicate with them.

(17) "Para mí **es un placer, hablar en castellano, porque me da la oportunidad** además de **dirigirme al conjunto de la ciudadanía española**, después de un año y medio de, de silencio forzado."

"For me **it is a pleasure to speak in Castilian, because it gives me the additional opportunity** to **address all Spanish citizens**, after a year and a half of forced silence."

(Oriol Junqueras, February 14, 2019)

In this excerpt, Junqueras emphasizes that he wants to communicate with the Spanish people in their language, aiming to provide them with a clearer understanding of the facts surrounding his case. This text highlights how relevant languages are in this politicized trial. In (18), Romeva does not explicitly label Spanish as the common language of Spain, but he recognizes the need to communicate in Spanish during the trial and deploys his bilingualism to communicate with all parties in this context:

(18) "Pero en todo caso también me sumo al hecho de que no tengo ningún inconveniente en hacerlo [testificar] en castellano."

"But in any case, I also agree with the fact that **I have no problem doing it [testifying] in Spanish**."
(Raül Romeva, February 19, 2019)

In this excerpt, Romeva does not encounter any difficulty speaking the other language (as opposed to his own language), because it is the language spoken by the majority of the audience. The traditional ideology of anonymity envelops Spanish in these excerpts, viewing it primarily as for communicating with Spanish citizens, even though Junqueras and Romeva do not encounter any issues using it in that particular context.

4.2.2 *Own language*

The following utterance recognizes Spanish as the language of identity for many Catalans and as a language of Catalonia:

(19) "Yo quiero sumarme a la protesta de mis compañeros, por el hecho de que no haya traducción simultánea al catalán… De todas formas, … no tengo absolutamente ningún problema en hablar en español, porque **el español es también una lengua de Cataluña** y, además, es **la lengua materna de muchos catalanes y catalanas**."

"I want to join the protest of my colleagues due to the fact that there is no simultaneous translation into Catalan … In any case, … I have absolutely no problem speaking Spanish, because **Spanish is also a language of Catalonia** and, furthermore, it is **the mother tongue of many Catalans**."
(Carme Forcadell, February 26, 2019)

Forcadell takes the bilingualism of Catalans as a given and asserts that Spanish is the original language and mother tongue for many of them. In doing so, she rejects the one nation, one language ideology, emphasizing that both Spanish and Catalan are languages of Catalonia. In elucidating that both Catalan and Spanish are languages of Catalonia, Forcadell is disavowing a traditional authenticity ideology associated with either Catalan or Spanish. Consequently, her earlier assertions in (10) regarding language rights appear to be indeed rooted in individual rights to mother tongue and individual authenticity, rather than community/nation rights or community-based authenticity.

Certainly, Forcadell's overall stance on the authenticity ideology seems to stem from a post-naturalistic viewpoint. She emphasizes that Catalans (residents of Catalonia) may regard Spanish as both their mother tongue and language of identity (as highlighted by Branchadell, 1997; Sinner & Wieland, 2008; Colino, 2009; May, 2012). As a result, Spanish is recognized as a language of Catalonia, which may symbolize Catalan culture and identity. Therefore, she acknowledges Catalan authenticity as an *ongoing project* where Spanish can be integrated, rather than perceiving it as a rigid, essentialist, and exclusive identity.

In summary, the key themes prevalent in the defendants' testimonies regarding Catalan encompass *own language, language as a medium of expression, minority language rights, linguistic normalization*, and *common language*. The theme of *own language* signifies ethnonationalist and community-driven authenticity, while language as a medium of expression refers to Catalan as a manifestation of personal identity and individual authenticity. Only Rull in (1) explicitly discusses Catalan as the *own language*, representing the traditional ideology of authenticity. In eight distinct excerpts, Junqueras, Rull, Forn, and Sànchez delve into Catalan as a language of personal authenticity and an essential expression of their identities. While this type of authenticity is labeled *individual*, it is argued that these defendants, who often function as political representatives in this context, may also index community-based authenticity, as evident in references to the mother tongue in (2) and (3): "la lengua maternal" (*the* mother tongue) and "nuestra lengua maternal" (*our* mother tongue).

In relation to minority language rights, Forcadell emphasizes that Catalan consistently faces minoritization, with the language rights of Catalan speakers often being violated (excerpt [10]). In (11), Rull contends that Catalan is not a minority language but one of the most spoken in the European Union. Simultaneously, he asserted in (1) that Catalan is a language intrinsically linked to identity. This excerpt (11) showcases the ideology of post-naturalistic anonymity. Sànchez and Borràs (excerpts [12] and [13]) also discuss language rights, concluding that Catalan is still minoritized by the Spanish state. Both excerpts align with the ideology of personal authenticity. Sànchez asserts his right to speak his mother tongue, and Borràs implies that the Catalan language is so integral to the identity of many Catalans that Spain's neglect of it leaves numerous Catalan citizens feeling marginalized and inclined to disassociate from the Spanish state.

Regarding linguistic normalization, Romeva and Rull advocate for the expansion of Catalan beyond Catalonia to the Spanish state, maintaining its distinct identity. Particularly in (15), the post-naturalist ideology of anonymity is invoked, describing an inclusive and pluralistic normalization process that seems to overcome the traditional concept of *normalization* (as based on sociolinguistic naturalism). Finally, in excerpt (16), Cuixart perceives Catalan as a common language whose widespread use among various speaker types (Catalan-descendent, immigrant-descendent, more Spanish-speaking, etc.) will foster social cohesion. In this excerpt, Cuixart demonstrates an ideology of post-naturalistic anonymity surrounding Catalan.

In the case of Spanish, it is regarded as both a common language in Spain (not in Catalonia) and as the mother tongue or own language of some Catalans. On the one hand, Junqueras and Romeva view it as a common language for communication with Spanish citizens. While these defendants use it without hesitation during the trial, they do not identify it as a language rooted in Catalonia or consider it a language of personal expression. Instead, they view it as an intercultural language for communication with Spanish citizens. Thus, these defendants portray Spanish as an anonymous language for them, signifying the presence of the ideology of anonymity in these segments. On the other hand, Forcadell expands on the notion that Spanish serves as the mother tongue for many Catalans, acknowledging Catalonia as a bilingual nation and rejecting the one nation, one language ideology. In general, Forcadell's position on the Catalan authenticity ideology seems to emanate from a post-naturalistic perspective, wherein both Catalan and Spanish may signify Catalan identity.

The subsequent section of the analysis addresses the third research objective concerning the relevance of Catalan usage and language choice in trial, as well as plurilingualism in Spain.

4.3 Relevance of language choice and usage in trial

There are specific texts in relation to: the lack of linguistic competency among the judge and lawyers conducting the trial proceedings [excerpts (20), (21), and (22)], plurilingualism in the Spanish state and during the trial [excerpts (23), and (24)], and the importance of the trial for Catalonia and Spain politics [excerpts (25) and (26)].

4.3.1 *Linguistic incompetence and intelligibility between Catalan and Spanish*

In the following extracts, the defendants complain about court officials' lack of linguistic competence of the court, which forces them into the role of translator. Specifically, the following segments are retrieved from discussions with the prosecutors while reviewing exhibits presented in Catalan.

(20) "Les hago la traducción … al castellano y todo. Sí, este era uno de los motivos por los que pedíamos estar juzgados, **en un juzgado que fuera competente lingüísticamente** …, porque el problema ahora está en que yo tengo que hacer de traductor, cuando **si el juzgado fuera competente lingüísticamente, … no tendría que hacer yo ahora de traductor**"

"I'll do the translation … into Castilian and everything. Yes, this was one of the reasons why we asked to be judged, **in a court that was linguistically competent** …, because the problem now is that I have to act as a translator, when **if the court were linguistically competent, …, I would not have to act as a translator now**."
(Jordi Cuixart, February 26, 2019)

(21) "No pensaba que yo haría de traductor del [sic] **castellano de usted, del catalán**"

"I didn't think that I would be **a translator of** [sic] **Spanish from Catalan for you**."
(Jordi Turull, February 19, 2019)

On the one hand, Cuixart and Turull ([20] and [21]) criticize that the court did not use translation services or simultaneous interpretation, and they had to provide language services for the prosecution. On the other hand, in extract (22), Cuixart asserts that Spanish speakers should easily understand Catalan if they choose to do so. He implies that the court and the prosecutors are making no effort to understand Catalan, even though it is a cognate language of Spanish (therefore, it is intelligible for Spanish speakers) and most of the documents presented as exhibits are written in Catalan, one of the languages of Spain. This extract raises the possibility that the linguistic conflict is also political, or vice versa, that the political conflict is also linguistic.

(22) "Cuando yo digo *cul a terra i resistència pacífica* no hay mucho margen de duda. *Cul a terra*, que es "culo en el suelo", **que esto lo entiende todo el mundo**, y resistencia pacífica, **que también se entiende**."

"When I say *cul a terra i resistència pacífica* there is not much room for doubt. *Cul a terra*, which is 'ass on the ground,' **which anyone can understand**, and peaceful resistance, **which is also generally understood**."
(Jordi Cuixart, February 26, 2019)

4.3.2 *Plurilingualism as a feature of the Spanish state*

Excerpt (23) supports the idea that all the languages, nations, and cultures of Spain should be recognized, not just in specific regions but all over Spain. Sànchez effectively scolds court officials for setting a negative example for Spain, which ought to be a pluricultural and plurilingual state.

(23) "Lamento que ... el Tribunal Supremo haya perdido una oportunidad también para hacer pedagogía de **lo que debería ser un estado pluricultural, plurinacional** y reconocimiento de una diversidad."

"I regret ... that the Supreme Court has missed an opportunity also to teach **what a pluricultural, plurinational state should be,** and the recognition of diversity."
(Jordi Sànchez, February 21, 2019)

In (24), Sànchez argues that a widespread and actual recognition of the plurilingualism of Spain would have helped resolve the conflict, and perhaps prevented the need for a trial. He highlights the relevance of using his mother tongue, Catalan, to the political conflict and to the lack of understanding between the Spanish government and Catalonia.

(24) "Y probablemente, ... si tuviéramos **una actitud distinta de las instituciones del estado** [reconocimiento del plurilingüismo], respecto a cuestiones como la que ahora estoy comentando [el uso del catalán en este juicio], **probablemente, hoy este juicio no tendría sentido, porque no habríamos llegado a la situación donde hemos llegado**"

"And probably, ... if there were **a different attitude from state institutions** [recognition of plurilingualism] regarding issues like the one I am now commenting on [use of Catalan during the trial], **today this trial would probably not make sense, because we would not have reached the situation we have arrived at.**"
(Jordi Sànchez, February 21, 2019)

4.4 Relevance of this trial for Catalonia and Spain

Finally, excerpts (25) and (26), retrieved from the closing arguments of Romeva and Cuixart respectively, confirm that the defendants represent a broader spectrum of the Catalan society (in [25], the 2 million people that voted in the referendum), and that this trial is a microcosm that could serve to address the Catalan and Spanish societies as a whole.

(25) "En este banquillo, no estamos sentadas solo 12 personas, **están sentadas más de 2 millones de personas que se sienten a través de nuestras personas concernidas**"

"Not only 12 people are sitting on this dock, **there are more than 2 million concerned people sitting here with us.**"
(Raül Romeva, June 12, 2019)

(26) "No estamos de acuerdo con la cárcel [sentencia], pero ... hemos detectado que **es un altavoz que nos permite denunciar de manera más, más contundente la vulneración de derechos fundamentales** y la falta de democracia que estamos sufriendo *los ciudadanos del estado español*"

"We do not agree with the prison [sentence], but... we have detected that **it is a loudspeaker that allows us to denounce in a more forceful way the violation of fundamental rights** and the lack of democracy that we, *the citizens of the Spanish state, are suffering.*"

(Jordi Cuixart, February 26, 2019)

In (26), Cuixart explains in his closing argument that the trial verdict serves as a public platform to expose the political misconduct perpetrated by the Spanish government, particularly in light of the injuries suffered by numerous voters on October 1, 2017, and the perceived absence of democracy within the Spanish state. In this context, it is logical to infer that the term *citizens of the Spanish state* pertains to the defendants in the trial, all of whom are citizens of Catalonia and representatives of many Catalans. Notably, Cuixart labels these Catalans as *citizens of the Spanish state* instead of simply Spanish or Catalan citizens. This choice of terminology suggests that, despite their pro-independence stance for Catalonia, they still fall under the jurisdiction of the Spanish state. It underscores the idea that their fundamental rights as citizens of the Spanish state are being disregarded, including their linguistic rights in the trial.

5. Discussion

In this study, I aimed to address three main research aims. My first research objective was to analyze the prevailing language ideology themes evident in the defendants' testimonies in this nationally relevant trial. The predominant themes in the defendants' testimonies regarding Catalan include *own language, language as a means of expression, minority/minoritized language rights, linguistic normalization*, and *common language*. Only Josep Rull referred to Catalan as the *own language* of Catalonia, suggesting an essentialist and traditional language-nation-identity perspective (excerpt [1]). In contrast, most of the defendants portray Catalan as their *mother tongue* and a personal and essential *medium of expression or identity* that allows them to communicate more *naturally* and effectively (excerpts [2–8]). Notably, Catalan was used to discuss intimate and personal topics, as evidenced in excerpt (9). Furthermore, Forcadell, Rull, Sànchez, and Borràs conceive Catalan as *a minoritized language* in Spain (that is, a historically and actively minimized language), and claim their linguistic right to speak this language in the Spanish state (excerpts [10]–[13]). Rull adds that Catalan is not, in fact, a minority language because it is one of the most spoken in the European Union. However, Spain does not seem to recognize the significance of this language.

Catalan is also regarded as a *common language* (excerpt [16]), a vernacular meant to be *normalized* (excerpt [14]) and disseminated throughout Catalonia among speakers of diverse linguistic backgrounds (including international, Spanish-speaking, and immigrant-descendant populations), and beyond the region to the Spanish state. In this sense, excerpts (14)–(16) illustrate a transcendence or overcoming of the concept of normalization (as rooted in sociolinguistic naturalism) and common features of civic nationalism, such as inclusiveness and a willingness for Catalan to be shared beyond ethnicity or national origin. These excerpts align with the revision suggested by Caminal (2007), Branchadell (2010) and Riera Gil (2013) for Catalan, advocating for its portrayal as a *llengua comuna* with an inclusive 21st-century perspective, rather than as a *llengua pròpia*. The only theme that may suggest the one nation, one language ideology is *own language*, although this ideology is not explicitly articulated in excerpt (1).

In relation to Spanish, Junqueras and Romeva conceive it as the *common language* used to communicate with other populations in Spain. While these defendants use it without hesitation during the trial, they do not identify it as a language rooted in Catalonia or consider it a language of personal expression. On the contrary, Forcadell believes that many Catalans recognize it as their own language, or more accurately, their native language, as evident in excerpt (19). This perspective aligns with the findings from the survey on language use in Catalonia reported by the Generalitat de Catalunya in 2018. Furthermore, Forcadell acknowledges Catalonia as a bilingual nation, and consequently, rejects the one nation, one language ideology.

Second, I aimed to explore the ideologies of linguistic authority, focusing on authenticity and/or anonymity, as they manifest in the defendants' expressions regarding Spanish and Catalan. On the one hand, some traditional conceptualizations of linguistic authority emerge, but they are not prevalent among these Catalan speakers. Catalan is only ideologized as authentic (as a symbol of nationhood) in one segment, while Spanish is conceived as an anonymous language in two excerpts ([17]–[18]) by Junqueras and Romeva. In these testimonies, there is a distinct form of authenticity ideology at play: individual authenticity. This type of ideology is linked to the idea of personal expression and an individual's essential self, not directly tied to nationalism (refer to excerpts [2]–[8] and [12] and [13]), and it is associated with the claims of these defendants to speak their mother tongue in this trial.

On the other hand, post-naturalistic conceptualizations of linguistic authority are slightly more prevalent than traditional ideologies. The ideology of post-nationalist anonymity, based on rooted cosmopolitanism, becomes apparent in relation to Catalan. Catalan is envisioned as a *common language* in Catalonia, accommodating speakers from diverse backgrounds. Furthermore, it is widely spoken at the European level, and aspires to establish a presence in the Spanish state (refer to excerpts [11], [14]–[16]). The post-naturalist authenticity ideology seems to be referenced in excerpt (10), where Forcadell recognizes Catalan authenticity as an ongoing project that allows for the integration of the Spanish language. This stands in contrast to perceiving it as a rigid, essentialist, and exclusive culture or identity. In this excerpt, Forcadell ideologizes Spanish as authentic for some portion of the Catalan population, transcending sociolinguistic naturalism.

Since the analysis centers around politicians and representatives who support Catalan nationalism and represent pro-independence voters [excerpt (25)], ideologies framed in a socio-historical chronotope were expected. However, these traditional ideologies are rare in these testimonies. Instead, post-naturalistic ideologies, primarily related to rooted cosmopolitanism, are more prominent. The presence of these post-naturalistic ideologies likely results from the shift from ethnic nationalism to civic nationalism in Catalonia over the past few years, a turn observed by Woolard in her study of high-school students in Barcelona. However, it is important to note that while Woolard identified a complete shift in her sample, the findings of the present study cannot be compared with Woolard's 2016 results, given the focus on a sample of high-school students in Barcelona, a place with a higher number of Spanish speakers in Catalonia, whose ideologies were framed within a biographic chronotope.

Nevertheless, as discussed earlier, these ideologies can also be interpreted as a legal strategy employed by the defendants to present a more inclusive and reasonable approach to language and Catalanism, aiming for better understanding by the Spanish Supreme Court. In these excerpts, at least, the defendants appear to be cautious in avoiding the invocation of the traditional language-nation-identity model.

Finally, I delved into the significance of language choice and language use within the context of this trial, and the results show that they play an important role for several reasons. First, the conflict over language choice created a situation where defendants repeatedly invoked issues of language in their testimonies. Second, the defendants cast being able to speak their native language (or mother tongue) as a fundamental right which, in their view, the court members deny. They compare this linguistic right to the rights they are advocating for during the trial — namely, the right to hold a referendum on the independence of Catalonia and to implement the results of the voting. Third, the conflict about modes of interpretation is also symbolic of the dynamic between Spanish institutions and Catalan institutions. In other words, language usage is directly intertwined with political conflict. On the one hand, the Spanish Supreme Court opted for consecutive interpretation and declined to provide simultaneous interpretation, citing the need to distribute headphones for the audience, a rationale that seemed insufficient. On the other hand, the defendants (representing a previous government of Catalonia and pro-independence Catalan parties) deliberately eschewed consecutive interpretation, leveraging the language issue (along with other *hot-button* issues) to support their case and sometimes to delegitimize the trial. Hence, language choice was strategically for political ends even before the trial commenced, which supports the notion that languages serve political facts, a concept discussed by Blommaert (1999) and May (2012).

Finally, plurilingualism is understood as an advantageous linguistic situation in the trial and in Spain more broadly. In fact, these Catalan speakers believe that a true recognition of plurilingualism in Spain would improve the political conflict between Spain and Catalonia, which aligns with the perspectives of Boix-Fuster (2008); Branchadell (2012); Vilarrubias and Claudio de Ramón (2014, 2019); and Ortega (2019).

6. Conclusion

To the best of my knowledge, this is the first study to analyze language ideologies and the role of language choice in the *El procés* trial, a nationally (and even internationally) significant proceeding for Catalonia and for Spain. By combining scholarly literature on language ideologies with the historic-political texts in Catalonia, it thoroughly investigates ideologies of linguistic authority, nationalism, and the role of language in the context of this trial. Although the defendants chose to speak in Spanish in trial, the findings show that Catalan was regarded as the mother tongue and language of expression of these defendants, while Spanish was generally ideologized as the *other* language primarily used for communication purposes. However, the new conceptualizations of linguistic authority in Catalonia are more present than the traditional conceptualizations (authenticity associated to Catalan and anonymity associated to Spanish), aligning with Woolard's (2016) findings among grown-up high-school students in Barcelona. Although these findings could be attributed to the shift from ethnic nationalism to civic nationalism in 21st-century Catalonia, they may also be shaped by the legal, political, and high-profile context. The frequent invocations to these language ideologies and language-related topics support the premise that language plays an important role in this micro setting that partially mirrors the political dynamics between Catalonia and Spain.

Overall, this study contributes to the current knowledge of ideologies of linguistic authority in relation to nationalism and minoritized language rights in Catalonia and Spain. Additionally, it uncovers the relevance of plurilingualism to the political situation in Spain. Although this research focuses on the defendants' testimonies, future studies could expand on this work by examining the entire trial, including statements of witnesses, attorneys, and others, to test if the different political stances influence their language ideologies. Another avenue of investigation would be to investigate how these ideologies were represented in the Catalan, Spanish, and international media. Finally, future studies could analyze these ideologies in relation to language identity, language contact, and the language forms used (similarly to Moosmüller (1989) and Blas Arroyo (2020)'s research).

References

Atkinson, D. (2018). On anonymity and authenticity: Catalan and Spanish in an independent Catalonia: Linguistic authority and officiality. *Language in Society*, 47(5), 1–23.

Bakhtin, M.M. (1981). *The dialogic imagination* (C. Emerson & M. Holquist, Trans.). University of Texas Press.

Bakhtin, M.M. (1987). *Speech genres and other late essays* (V.W. McGee, Trans.). University of Texas Press.

Baquero, C.C. (2017, October 2). Un 90% de 'síes' con 2,2 millones de votos y una participación del 42%, según el Govern. *El País*. https://elpais.com/ccaa/2017/10/02/catalunya/1506898063_586836.html

Blas Arroyo, J.L. (2020). "Madrit nos roba" Contacto de lenguas, variación e ideología en el discurso político catalán. *Spanish in Context* 17(1), 30–57.

Blommaert, J. (1999). *Language ideological debates*. Mouton de Gruyter.

Boix-Fuster, E. (2008). 25 años de la Constitución Española. Las ideologías lingüísticas en la configuración del Estado español. In K. Süselbeck, U. Mühlschlegel, & P. Masson (Eds.), *Lengua, Nación e Identidad: La Regulación del Plurilingüismo en España y América Latina*. Iberoamericana Vervuert.

Branchadell, A. (1997). *Liberalisme i normalització lingüística*. Empúries.

Branchadell, A. (2010). Més enllà del català. Els reptes lingüístics de Catalunya. *La Catalunya plural*. Fundació CatDem.

Branchadell, A. (2012). One Nation, One (Common) Language? Language and Nationalism in 21st Century Catalonia. *RECODE – Responding to Complex Diversity in Europe and Canada Working Papers Series*.

Caminal, M. (2007). La reforma dels estatuts i la llengua catalana. *Revista de Llengua i Dret 47*. Generalitat de Catalunya.

Carpio, J.A. (2017, November 2). La juez decreta prisión sin fianza para Junqueras y otros siete exconsellers imputados de rebelión y sedición. *Radio Televisión Española.* http://www.rtve.es/noticias/20171102/junqueras-otros-siete-exconsellers-condenados-prision-sin-fianza/1631922.shtml

Centre d'Estudis d'Opinió (2018, July 20). *Baròmetre d'Opinió Política. 2a onada 2018.* Generalitat de Catalunya. http://upceo.ceo.gencat.cat/wsceop/6748/Taules%20estad%C3%ADstiques%20-901.pdf

Clarke, V., & Braun, V. (2021). *Thematic analysis: A practical guide.* SAGE.

Colino, C. (2009). Constitutional change without constitutional reform: Spanish federalism and the revision of Catalonia's Statute of Autonomy. *Publius: The Journal of Federalism 39*(2), 262–288.

Congreso de los Diputados (2023). *XV Legislatura. Proposición de reforma del Reglamento del Congreso. Proposición de reforma del Reglamento del Congreso de los Diputados. (410/000001).* https://www.congreso.es/es/busqueda-de-iniciativas?p_p_id=iniciativas&p_p_lifecycle=0&p_p_state=normal&p_p_mode=view&_iniciativas_mode=mostrarDetalle&_iniciativas_legislatura=XV&_iniciativas_id=410%2F000001

Constitución Española (1978). https://www.boe.es/buscar/pdf/1978/BOE-A-1978-31229-consolidado.pdf

Departament d'Ensenyament — Generalitat de Catalunya (2015). *La llengua a l'escola catalana. Un model d'èxit.* https://educacio.gencat.cat/ca/departament/publicacions/monografies/llengua-escola-catalana/

Eckert, P. (1983). The paradox of national language movements. *Journal of Multilingual and Multicultural Development 4*(4), 289–300.

Eitb.eus (2017, October 27). La comunidad internacional no apoya la independencia catalana. https://www.eitb.eus/es/noticias/politica/detalle/5173911/la-comunidad-internacional-no-apoya-independencia-cataluna/

El Confidencial (2019, February 14). *Marchena rechaza que haya traducción simultánea del catalán en el juicio al 'procés'.* https://www.elconfidencial.com/espana/cataluna/2019-02-14/traduccion-catalan-juicio-supremo-proces-marchena_1824930/

elDiario.es (2019, February 26). *Jordi Cuixart declara en el juicio al procés (26/02/2019, mañana).* YouTube. https://www.youtube.com/watch?v=tBKH2Bgqnpk&t=6153s

Estatut d'autonomia de Catalunya (1979). https://web.gencat.cat/ca/generalitat/estatut/estatut1979/

Estatut d'autonomia de Catalunya (2016 [2006]). https://www.parlament.cat/document/cataleg/48089.pdf

Fuller, J., & Leeman, J. (2020). Language ideologies. In J. Fuller & J. Leeman (Eds.), *Speaking Spanish in the US: The Sociopolitics of Language* (pp. 63–90). Bristol, Blue Ridge Summit: Multilingual Matters. https://doi-org.ezproxy4.library.arizona.edu/10.21832/9781788928298-006

Gal, S., & Woolard, K. (2001). *Languages and publics: The making of authority.* Routledge.

Gat, A., & Yakobson, A. (2013). Introduction: Is nationalism recent and superficial? In A. Gat & A. Yakobson (Eds.), *Nations: The Long History and Deep Roots of Political Ethnicity and Nationalism* (pp. 1–26). Cambridge University Press.

Geeraerts, D. (2008). The logic of language models: Rationalist and romantic ideologies and their avatars. In K. Süselbeck, U. Mühlschlegel, & P. Masson (Eds.), *Lengua, Nación e Identidad: La Regulación del Plurilingüismo en España y América Latina*. Iberoamericana Vervuert.

Gellner, E. (1993). Nationalism. In W. Outhwaite & T. Bottomore (Eds.), *Blackwell Dictionary of Twentieth-Century Social Thought* (pp. 409–11). Basil Blackwell.

Generalitat de Catalunya (2008). *Pacte nacional per a la immigració*. https://llengua.gencat.cat/web/.content/documents/acolliment/arxius/09_to_pactenacionalimmigracio.pdf

Generalitat de Catalunya (2014). *9N 2014: Tu hi participes, tu hi decideixes*. http://www.participa2014.cat/resultats/dades/ca/escr-tot.html

Generalitat de Catalunya (2017). *Consorci per a la Normalització Lingüística*. https://llengua.gencat.cat/ca/direccio_general_politica_linguistica/02_organismes_vinculats/06_consorci_per_a_la_normalitzacio_linguistica/

Generalitat de Catalunya (2018). *Enquesta d'Usos Lingüístics de la Població*. https://llengua.gencat.cat/web/.content/documents/dadesestudis/altres/arxius/dossier-eulp-2018.pdf

Grenoble, L., & Singerman, A. R. (2014). Minority Languages. *Oxford Bibliographies*. https://www.oxfordbibliographies.com/display/document/obo-9780199772810/obo-9780199772810-0176.xml.

Groff, C. (2017). Language and language-in-education planning in multilingual India: a minoritized language perspective. *Language Policy* 16(2), 135–164.

Handler, R. (1988). *Nationalism and the politics of culture in Quebec*. University of Wisconsin Press.

Heller, M. (2007). *Bilingualism: A social approach*. Palgrave MacMillan.

Holesch, A., & Jordana, J. (2021). The politics of unilateral secession in the European Union: The case of Catalonia. *Territory, Politics, Governance* 11(6), 1–20.

Irvine, J. (2012). Language ideologies. In *Oxford Bibliographies*. Oxford University Press. https://www.oxfordbibliographies.com/view/document/obo-9780199766567/obo-9780199766567-0012.xml#.

Irvine, J. T., & Gal, S. (2000). Language ideology and linguistic differentiation. In P. Kroskrity (Ed.), *Regimes of Language* (pp. 35–84). School for American Research.

Karolewski, I. P., & Suszycki, A. M. (2011). *The nation and nationalism in Europe: An introduction*. Edinburgh University Press.

Llei 10/2010, del 7 de maig, d'acollida de les persones immigrades i de les retornades a Catalunya (2010). https://portaljuridic.gencat.cat/eli/es-ct/l/2010/05/07/10

Llei de Normalització Lingüística a Catalunya (1983). https://llengua.gencat.cat/web/.content/documents/legislacio/llei_de_politica_linguistica/arxius/lleinl83.pdf

Marí, I. (1995). Algunes distincions objectives essencials per l'aplicació igualitària dels drets lingüístics. *Drets lingüístics i drets culturals a les regions d'Europa. Actes del Simposi Internacional: Girona, 23'25 d'abril de 1992*, 42–51. Barcelona: Generalitat de Catalunya, Departament de Cultura. https://www.gencat.cat/llengua/documentacio/articles/DOT5Sim_Simposi_Inter_Drets_Ling/DOT5Sim_Cmar.pdf

May, S. (2012). *Language and minority rights: ethnicity, nationalism and the politics of language*. Routledge.

Minder, R. (2013, December 13). Catalonia clashes with Madrid over independence vote. *The New York Times*. http://www.nytimes.com/2013/12/13/world/europe/catalonia-madrid.html

Moosmüller, S. (1989). Phonological variation in parliamentary discussions. In Wodak, R. (Ed.), *Language, power and ideology: Studies in political discourse*, pp. 165–181. John Benjamins Publishing Company.

Morales-Gálvez, S., & Cetrà, D. (2022). Regulating language: Territoriality and personality in plurinational Spain. *Ethnicities* 22(2), 253–273.

Nevins, A. (2022). *When minoritized languages change linguistic theory*. Cambridge: Cambridge University Press.

Ortega, R. (2019, February 27). Orgull de catalanades. *El País*. https://cat.elpais.com/cat/2019/02/27/cultura/1551262905_047633.html

Pérez, D. (2017, October 27). El Parlament declara la independencia de Cataluña. Eitb.eus – Euskal Irrati Telebista. https://www.eitb.eus/es/noticias/politica/detalle/5173461/el-parlament-declara-independencia-cataluna-27-octubre-2017/

Plataforma per la Llengua (2008). *El català, llengua comuna*. Barcelona: Plataforma per la Llengua. http://www.plataforma-llengua.cat/doc/manifest_santjordi08.pdf

Plataforma per la Llengua (2020). El judici *dEl procés* (sense drets lingüistics?). *La Corbella 34*, 6–9. https://issuu.com/plataformaperlallengua/docs/plataforma_per_la_llengua_corbella-34-web

Pujol, J. (1995). *Què representa la llengua a Catalunya?* Generalitat de Catalunya.

Recuero, M. (2019, February 12). Claves del juicio al procés de Cataluña, un proceso histórico para la España constitucional. *El Mundo*. https://www.elmundo.es/espana/2019/02/11/5c608ccafc6c83134c8b4682.html

Rees, E. L. (1996). Spain's linguistic normalization laws: The Catalan controversy. *Hispania* 79(2), 313–321.

Riera Gil, E. (2013). Sobre el concepte polític de llengua comuna: una aproximació teòrica i comparada. *Revista de Llengua i Dret 60*, 91–110.

Rincón, R. (2018, March 25). El juez envía a prisión sin fianza a Turull, Rull, Forcadell, Romeva y Bassa. *El País*. https://elpais.com/politica/2018/03/23/actualidad/1521803813_204955.html

Ríos, P. (2014, November 9). El 81% de persones voten sí a la independència de Catalunya. *El País*. http://cat.elpais.com/cat/2014/11/09/catalunya/1415542400_466311.html

Sinner, C., & Wieland, K. (2008). El catalán hablado y problemas de la normalización de la lengua catalan: Avances y obstáculos en la normalización. In K. Süselbeck, U. Mühlschlegel, & P. Masson (Eds.), *Lengua, Nación e Identidad: La Regulación del Plurilingüismo en España y América Latina* (pp. 131–164). Iberoamericana Vervuert.

Solé Altimira, O. (2019, January 16). El uso del catalán en el juicio al 'procés' divide a las defensas. *elDiario.es*. https://www.eldiario.es/catalunya/politica/catalan-juicio-proces-divide-defensas_1_1744648.html

Soler, J. (2012). The anonymity of Catalan and the authenticity of Estonian: Two paths for the development of medium-sized languages. *International Journal of Bilingual Education and Bilingualism* 16(2), 153–163.

Sonntag, S. K., & Pool, J. (1987). Linguistic denial and linguistic self-denial: American ideologies of language. *Language Problems & Language Planning* 11(1), 46–65.

Spanish Ministry of Territorial Policy and Public Function (2021). *Information document on the implementation of the recommendations for immediate action based on the 5th monitoring cycle*. European Charter for Regional or Minority Languages. https://rm.coe.int/spainiria5-en-pdf/1680a15366

Süselbeck, K. (2008). "Lengua, nación e identidad en el discurso de la política lingüística de Cataluña". In K. Süselbeck, U. Mühlschlegel, & P. Masson (Eds.), *Lengua, Nación e Identidad: La Regulación del Plurilingüismo en España y América Latina*. Iberoamericana Vervuert.

Trautsch, J. M. (2019). Introduction: A global approach to civic nationalisms. In J. M. Trautsch (Ed.), *Civic Nationalisms in Global Perspective* (pp. 1–29). Routledge.

Vilarrubias, M., & Claudio de Ramón, J. (2014, November 26). Todas las lenguas de España. *El País*. https://elpais.com/elpais/2014/11/26/opinion/1417024274_514424.html

Vilarrubias, M., & Claudio de Ramón, J. (2019, May 6). Derechos para todos: razones por una ley de lenguas oficiales. *Agenda Pública El País*. http://agendapublica.elpais.com/derechos-para-todos-razones-para-una-ley-de-lenguas-oficiales

Von Gleich, E. (2008). Conflictos de ideologías lingüísticas en sistemas educativos: tres décadas (1975'2005) de observación y análisis en los países andinos Bolivia, Ecuador y Perú. In K. Süselbeck, U. Mühlschlegel, & P. Masson (Eds.), *Lengua, Nación e Identidad: La Regulación del Plurilingüismo en España y América Latina*. Iberoamericana Vervuert.

Woolard, K. (2005). Language and identity choice in Catalonia: The interplay of contrasting ideologies of linguistic authority. *UC San Diego: Institute for International, Comparative, and Area Studies*. https://escholarship.org/uc/item/47n938cp

Woolard, K. (2016). *Singular and plural: Ideologies of linguistic authority in 21st century Catalonia*. Oxford University Press.

Woolard, K., & Schieffelin, B. B. (1994). Language ideology. *Annual Review of Anthropology 23*, 55–82. Annual Reviews Inc.

CHAPTER 9

A sociolinguistic analysis of a deep learning based classification model of South American *voseo* in X posts

Falcon Restrepo-Ramos
University of Nebraska at Kearney

Here, I present the implementation of a dialectal classification system that uses *voseo* in X (formerly Twitter) posts to identify speakers of Colombian (*Paisa* and *Caleño*) and Argentine (Buenos Aires and La Plata) Spanish. Two datasets of over 18,000 posts were collected from recent X posts according to the geolocalization of the tweet. The data was used to train and evaluate a transformer-based machine learning classifier of South American *voseo*. Results show that the system is able to identify the *voseo* region with a high degree of accuracy (0.84 F1 and 0.88 AUC ROC — Area Under the Receiving Operating Characteristic Curve). A sociolinguistics analysis of each dataset gave further insights on the accuracy of the classifier, the status of *voseo*, and the discourse function of *voseo* and other second-person singular forms of address (2PS), particularly in the context of Colombian *voseo*. An examination of the lexical, syntactical, and grammatical properties of Colombian and Argentine *voseo* also offered more detailed information on the properties not considered by the model. The natural language processing (NLP) methods presented here aim to pave the way for innovative approaches with high potential in Spanish sociolinguistics research.

Keywords: regional and national *voseo*, machine learning classification, lexical sophistication, syntactic complexity, computational sociolinguistics

1. Introduction

The study of the variable use of second person singular forms of address (2PS) in Latin American Spanish is a topic of traditional interest in the field of Hispanic sociolinguistics (Flores-Ferrán, 2007; Moyna & Rivera-Mills, 2016; Restrepo-Ramos & Denbaum-Restrepo, 2022). Speakers of *Paisa* Spanish and *Caleño* Spanish, two of the most representative dialectal varieties of Colombian Spanish, use a tripartite system of 2PS, where *voseo* (i.e., pronominal, and verbal forms of *vos*) is used as the colloquial form of address (Michnowicz & Quintana Sarria, 2020). In addition, *voseo* is a staple of Argentine Spanish and is currently accepted country wide as part of the Argentine linguistic norm (García Negroni & Ramírez Gelbes, 2020). Currently, text classification is one of the most common tasks in machine learning and natural language processing (NLP), and there is an increasing interest in introducing NLP technologies in sociolinguistic research (Nguyen et al., 2016). Adding state-of-the-art text artificial intelligence (AI) and NLP approaches to the identification of dialectal features in Latin American varieties is a promising area of inquiry and might provide novel applications in the sociolinguistics field.

This work reports on the deployment of a machine learning (ML) model developed to classify South American *voseo* dialects (i.e., Colombia and Argentina) in X posts. I used a state-of-the-art transformer-based model of Spanish pretrained on contextual embeddings from Google's BERT (Bidirectional Encoder Representations from Transformers) (Cañete et al., 2020). In addition, I examine the sociolinguistic properties and linguistic complexity associated with both Spanish dialects with the aim of providing insights into the features (not) used by the classification algorithm. For this additional analysis, I followed a natural language processing approach to extract indices of lexical sophistication, examine the function of each 2PS, obtain measures of syntactic complexity, and verbal TAM (tense, aspect, and mood) of each South American dialect.

The choice of these two South American dialects was not random. Colombia is located in the northernmost tip of South America and includes an array of regional dialects influenced by the geographical distribution of its speakers, either residing in the highlands, the coastlines, or the plains (Díaz-Collazos, 2015). From these regional varieties, the Spanish spoken in the highlands of the Province of Antioquia in the Western side of the Andean Mountain range and the Colombian variety of the Province of Valle del Cauca are two of the most noticeable, because they possess a range of dialectal markers, namely a tripartite system of second person singular forms of address (2PS), including *tú, usted*, and *vos* (Denbaum-Restrepo, 2023). For this study, X posts were collected from the capitals of these provinces, Medellín (Antioquia) and Cali (Valle del Cauca). In contrast, Argentina is located in the southern cone of South America and uses a nationally recognized *voseo*. From the dialects of this vast country, the *Porteño* variety is one of the most prominent (Española, 2005). The region where *Porteño* is spoken encompasses the areas of the capital of the country, Buenos Aires, La Plata, among other municipalities. Given the extreme opposite geographical distances across South America (~4,950 km or 3075 miles) and the status of *voseo* in their own territory, obtaining X data from these two areas will serve for comparing South American *voseo* from divergent regions and examining the sociolinguistic features employed by a ML classification algorithm.

This study is important because it adds relevant and innovative research on the study of second person singular forms of address in two well-known Hispanic countries, where *voseo* is a regional dialectal marker (i.e., Colombia) (Denbaum-Restrepo, 2023) and Argentina, where it has national recognition (Pešková, 2011). Moreover, the importance of this study also lies on its interdisciplinary methods used for creating a machine learning model from X data capable of classifying two *voseo* regions with a high degree of accuracy and its crossroads with Spanish sociolinguistics research. This paper aims to establish future interdisciplinary work on artificial intelligence and sociolinguistics that delves into new and existing phenomena in Hispanic dialects.

The research questions posed for this study are the following: (1) What degree of accuracy can be obtained with a ML model trained to classify South American *voseo* on X posts? (2) What sociolinguistic features are relevant (or not relevant) for the ML model that help in the classification of Colombian and Argentinian *voseo*? I expect to find sociolinguistic contextual markers proper of each dialect, such as the differential status of *voseo*, colloquial discourse, and grammatical-syntactical properties related to the specific function and use of *voseo*. This paper is organized according to the following sections. First, I will synthetize previous literature on the differences between Colombian and Argentinian *voseo*, the use of dialectal markers in social media, and the role of artificial intelligence in sociolinguistic research. Next, I will detail the methodology employed to collect and analyze the X data. Subsequently, I will present the results of the ML model and the evaluation of the sociolinguistic features of both South American dialects. Finally, I will discuss the main findings of this work related to previous literature and their contribution to the field of Spanish sociolinguistics.

1.1 The current situation of Colombian and Argentinian *voseo*

In many Hispanic American varieties there is a tripartite system of 2PS, which includes the pronominal forms and the verbal conjugations of *tú, usted*, and *vos*, known as *tuteo, ustedeo*, and *voseo*, respectively. Due to historical reasons (Díaz-Collazos, 2015), *voseo* in Colombia has become widespread at the provincial level. Precisely, the regional varieties of Colombian Spanish spoken in Medellín and Cali use *voseo* as a mark of regional identity for the locals, while excluding speakers of other *non-voseante* regions (Denbaum-Restrepo, 2021; Jang, 2013). On the one hand, the case of the Spanish spoken in Medellín and Cali involves a regional situation where *voseo* is used as a mark of prestige and cultural identity (Michnowicz & Quintana Sarria, 2020; Millán, 2014; Restrepo-Ramos, 2021;

Weyers, 2018). Medellín has been considered the *voseo* capital of Colombia and is also known as the epicenter of *Paisa* Spanish, the ethnonym used to denote speakers of this area of Colombia (Weyers, 2018), while *voseo* in *Cali* or *Caleño* Spanish is considered the default intimate 2PS, increasingly accepted over other 2PS (Michnowicz & Quintana Sarria, 2020; Millán, 2014). As such, *voseo* in both *Paisa* and *Caleño* varieties enjoy greater local prestige and widespread oral usage across speakers and even in public written signage (Restrepo-Ramos, 2022; Weyers, 2016). Therefore, in this paper, I will refer to the *Paisa* and *Caleño* varieties as Colombian Spanish. Although there are documented usage and sociolinguistic factors that differentiate both varieties, the analysis of differences between these two regional dialects lies outside of the scope of this research. This is due because *Paisa* and *Caleño* Spanish belong to the same Colombian dataset that will be analyzed against *Porteño* Spanish.

On the other hand, *voseo* is a staple of Argentinian Spanish and currently nationally accepted as the linguistic norm (García Negroni & Ramírez Gelbes, 2020). Fontanella de Weinberg (1970) highlights that in the beginning of the 20th century *usted* was widely used among young people and couples in the Buenos Aires region, but 70 years later *vos* was adopted in the vast majority of interactions. Precisely, there was a great expansion of *vos* in the literature and media during the 1960s that made *tú* practically vanish from public life (Carricaburo, 1997). García Negroni & Ramírez Gelbes (2020) argue that the current use of *vos* has increased at the expense of *usted* and *tú*, the latter being almost non-existent in the Spanish of Argentina, except when addressing a foreigner to convey social distance to a lower extent than *usted*. The same authors showed that the proportional use of *vos* during the 1960's was similar to those of the other two forms of address. However, by 2015 the frequency of use of *vos* increased exponentially, reflecting a match between the descriptive usage and the prescriptive norm established by the Academia Argentina de Letras. Currently, Argentinian *voseo* occurs with all kinds of interlocutors across every age group and social stratum. The most well-known version of Argentinian Spanish is the one spoken around the Río de la Plata, which encompasses the Buenos Aires region and La Plata, and is known as *Porteño*.

When comparing the *voseo* paradigm in both Hispanic dialects, it is clear that both conjugations in Colombian (Paisa and Caleño) and Argentine (Buenos Aires and la Plata) Spanish are the same. These dialects use the subject pronoun form of *vos*, which can be omitted according to discursive factors (Pešková, 2011), and the verbal morphology with final stress (e.g., (vos) + *comés* '(you) + eat'); a prepositional form which is identical to the subject pronoun (e.g., *para vos* 'for you'); and, finally, they share the same object pronoun as *tuteo* (*te veo* '(I) see you-*vos/tú*).

I will now review the current state of *voseo* in social media and X. This will provide us with information about the use and acceptance of this 2PS across social media platforms.

1.2 *Voseo* and social media

As *voseo* enjoys great acceptance and frequency of use in the dialects under study, social media has been a venue of analysis for its occurrence across *voseo* users. In a study on the usage of *voseo* by Hondurans and Salvadorians in the US, Martinez Barahona (2020) found that *voseo* allowed these X users to keep solidarity with each other. However, it was also found that *voseo* was suppressed to achieve recognition from outside groups, such as Mexicans, prompting the use of *tú* and other linguistic features used in the larger Latino community. These results resonate with studies on *voseo* production with Salvadorian speakers in the US. For instance, Hernández (2002) also found that Salvadorians in Houston, Texas, tend to diminish their *voseo* and transitive *andar* 'walk, go, and go around' production patterns during sociolinguistic interviews with Mexican speakers. The degree of accommodation is constrained by the age of arrival of 14 years of age or less and, thus, length of contact, as contrasted with speakers that arrived when they were older than 14 years of age by the time of arrival. An additional work of dialectal accommodation with Salvadorians speakers in Texas showed similar trends with other variables, such as /s/ reduction, whose production was modified to resemble Mexican linguistic patterns (Aaron & Hernández, 2007).

In another study on language attitudes on X users, Bani (2023) also found that *voseo* is a dialectal trait of regional distinctiveness appealing to in-group identity in most users. In addition, this phenomenon also created social stigma and legitimacy issues with *voseo* in messages of social media compared to oral production, as other users argued. The analysis of the responses of the language academies, including the Real Academia Española and the Academia Argentina de Letras, recognizes *voseo* as an integral part of several Pan Hispanic dialects. However, this social validation failed to include *voseo* in social media platforms. It is worth noting that Bani's study analyzed X messages without taking into account the geographical area of the post, which limits a more fine-grained examination of the dialect of the users. Particularly and as seen previously, Central American speakers tend to include *tuteo* at the expense of *voseo* in contexts where they are addressing Spanish speakers from other *non-voseante* areas, while users from Argentina keep *voseo* at higher frequencies across all age groups and interlocutors (Aaron & Hernández, 2007; García Negroni & Ramírez Gelbes, 2020; Hernández, 2002; Sinner, 2010; Sorenson, 2016).

Voseo in digital discourse has also been analyzed in Facebook biography sections (Cautín-Epifani & Valenzuela, 2018). In this case, it was found that Chilean verbal *voseo* was employed at significantly higher rates in younger generations compared to the older group. Despite this, overall mean values show *tuteo* being preferred across the board, particularly among women. When contrasted between genders, women chose verbal *voseo* at higher rates than men, although the difference is not statistically significant. Whether younger individuals maintain the usage of *voseo* later in life, which might signal a linguistic change, is to be seen in future work. According to these findings, it is likely that *voseo* is now being constrained by sociolinguistic factors, such as age and sex in oral Chilean Spanish.

Bland and Morgan (2020) conducted a novel study documenting the number of *voseo* users and their morphological and attitudinal patterns in a corpus of over 32 million geocoded tweets. Researchers used specific query words, including the pronoun *vos*, and *voseo* verbal morphology of five highly frequent verbs (e.g., *ser* 'to be', *pensar* 'to think', *poder* 'to be able to/can', *contar* 'to tell/count', and *volver* 'to return'). They found that *voseo* is widespread in the River Plate basin and Central America, which corresponds to countries where this 2PS is nationally stable. Lower rates of *voseo* in northern South America (e.g., Colombia) also show patterns consistent with regional *voseo*. Additionally, rates of explicit pronoun usage and verbal morphology were also obtained. Results show that the River Plate basin had the highest number of pronouns and indicative verbal conjugations of *voseo*, followed by Central America. In contrast, there was a higher rate of subjunctive forms in Central America, but some of the lowest in Argentina, which support previous observations that subjunctive *voseo* is stigmatized or pragmatically restricted in this country (Fontanella de Weinberg, 1979; Johnson, 2016; Lipski, 1994). Rates for the affirmative imperative conjugation were consistently similar between Central America and the River Plate basin. This research presents a feasible approach to obtaining and analyzing X data using computational methods. In the following review of literature, I will discuss the benefits of using artificial intelligence approaches in sociolinguistic research.

1.3 New computational approaches to Sociolinguistics

Recently, there has been a growing interest in studying the social dimension of language using new and sophisticated computational methods. Known as the emerging field of 'computational sociolinguistics,' innovative research using large-scale data-driven approaches has been produced thanks to the advent of large language models and the exponential increase of available computing power. Previously, work in this field encompassed research in computational linguistics that touched on sociolinguistic topics, language variation being a byproduct or a secondary objective (Nguyen et al., 2016). Currently, there is a trend to incorporate language use across social factors in NLP systems, which has improved programs for word prediction (Stoop & Van den Bosch, 2014), sentiment analysis (Volkova & Bachrach, 2016), syntactic parsers and taggers (Hovy & Søgaard, 2015), and bilingual corpora (Sun et al., 2019). One of the most recent leaps in NLP and artificial intelligence involves the creation of BERT or Bidirectional Encoder Representations from Transformers (Devlin et al., 2018). Inspired by the Cloze task, in which a learner needs to infer the most appropriate word in a given context, BERT is a large language model trained to predict a random subset of masked tokens from the original vocabulary based on its left and right context, hence the Bidirectional designation. The benefit of using this novel approach involves a greater understanding accuracy at the sentence level, outperforming previous models trained using a unidirectional pattern. This fine-tuned pretrained model approach has been adapted to achieve optimal performance for multiple topic-specific tasks, such as in health records for disease prediction (Rasmy et al., 2021), and has been trained to serve other languages, such as Spanish (Cañete et al., 2020).

The product of this endeavor encompasses an array of natural language generative (NLG) systems, including ChatGPT (Radford et al., 2018). Precisely, work on computational sociolinguistics has used these new artificial intelligence approaches, such as large language models or LLMs, to investigate linguistic phenomena on the internet. Dant et al. (2022) investigated the sentiment patterns of Yelp reviews of a subgroup of users. After training a generative model, that is, a model capable of generating text based on the data trained on, such as in the GPT (Generative Pre-Trained Transformer) series, they found that the model was able to create synthetic reviews that resemble accurately the sentiment conveyed by the original users. The researchers used 1.8 million reviews of American restaurants to effectively create a model that learned the lexical patterns and linguistic characteristics of different star ratings in Yelp. Although the GPT model produces credible linguistic patterns mostly aligned to the sentiment context, the model also produced informational errors in the description of the generated text, such as attributing the discovery of a bird to the wrong person. These concerns also put into evidence the need to check the information presented by this type of technology.

Other research has focused on individual differences in sociolinguistic variation. Focusing on the *that's + adjective* pattern in the British National Corpus 2014 of over 11 million words, Schmid et al. (2021) retrieved grammatical and semantic information automatically using a tailor-made Python script. Results showed that the most frequent sequences included adjectives *right, good,* and *true*, respectively. In addition, older individuals preferred the epistemic semantic class of adjectives while choosing the adjective *right* in higher frequency and disfavoring the adjective *true*. The effect of *all right* was higher in males as compared to the sequence *nice*. A higher social class and education levels also showed a tendency to choose *right* over other adjectives. These findings suggest that the sequence *that's right* has become a pragmatic, conventionalized expression that has lost its epistemic value of agreement to become a discourse marker on par with *alright, fine,* and *okay*. Data-driven approaches in sociolinguistics have increasingly become more sophisticated to study a greater number of factors in language variation. Hovy and Johannsen (2016) developed a program that allowed researchers with little to no knowledge of programming languages to explore large quantities of data across multiple sociolinguistic factors. In a case study to showcase the capabilities of the program, the authors looked into the spelling variation of *definitely* and *definitaly* in a large-scale corpus of British English websites. Search results across gender and age failed to capture the variation overlapped between social factors. However, the program allowed the ratio of occurrences to be plotted in a map of the British Isles demonstrating a regional trend in the Midlands towards the *definately* variant. These results suggest that a new phonological feature conditioned by a dialectal innovation was very likely.

This review of innovative work in sociolinguistics has shown a brief glimpse of previous work that has tapped into the potential of using computational methods in sociolinguistics research. In particular, pretrained LLMs have allowed for the creation of programs for the identification of the sentiment of users, and for our purposes, it will be employed in the dialectal identification of *voseo* in X posts. Moreover, I use NLP methods to automatically extract sociolinguistic features of language use associated with *voseo* utterances. I will provide details of the methodology in the next section.

2. Methodology

Data for this work was obtained from X posts from users across determined geographical areas in Colombia and Argentina. The Tweepy module (Roesslein, 2020) in the Python distribution was used to obtain access to X servers[1] and send queries. Search words included only the pronoun *vos*. Retweets were filtered out. Similar to previous work (Bland & Morgan, 2020), the inclusion of the pronominal form of *vos* was done to be certain that the tweet contained traces of *voseo*. The query was restricted to Spanish and geographically delimited according to the geographic coordinates of the downtown areas of Medellín and Cali in Colombia, and Buenos Aires, La Plata, and General Rodriguez in Argentina. Every query

---

1. Note: previous enrollment as a developer is required by X

was geofenced[2] 10 miles around the geographic coordinates to avoid repetition of tweets as much as possible. Additionally, any duplicate tweets were removed based on the Tweet ID. Tweets were acquired across two timelines: Colombian tweets were accessed in May 2022 during presidential elections, and Argentinian posts were obtained in March 2023. Collecting the data across two points in time was done to capture topic variations and maximize lexical differences between the two dialects. The final dataset contained 8,334 Tweets from Argentina and 10,217 posts[3] from Colombia ($N=18,551$). Dataset for this work can be accessed via the author's Hugging Face repository.

Next, the dataset was pre-processed, and every tweet was cleaned of emojis, hashtags, mentions and URLs. Then, the cleaned dataset was normalized, and punctuation marks were removed. Stop words[4] were not filtered out as a preliminary iteration of the model showed higher accuracy by including Spanish grammatical parts of speech. The effect of stop words in the model is due to the type of NLP task (i.e., text classification) and the fact that X posts are shortened natively to 140 characters. It seems that the shorter the n-gram sequence, the more need to keep stop words for the model to be more accurate. Finally, the rows in the final version of the dataset were randomly shuffled and the complete dataset was divided 75% for training ($n=13,905$ posts), 15% for development[5] during training ($n=2,781$ posts), and 10% for testing the best trained model ($n=1,865$ posts). The split datasets were converted into binary files for easier manipulation and submitted for the training algorithm. The model was trained on a single label with 0 for Colombia and 1 for else (i.e., Argentina).

An auto-generated configuration file containing all the default settings parameters for training a transformer-based single-label text categorization model was produced using Spacy *config* functionality (Honnibal et al., 2020). The GPU-enabled (Graphics Processing Unit) algorithm included the default settings and hyperparameters, namely a batch size of 128 samples before every training iteration, and an initial learning rate of 5^{e-5} with 20,000 total steps (i.e., the speed at which the model learns from the datasets). Additionally, the Spanish version of the pretrained transformer-based language model of BERT (Cañete et al., 2020) was

---

2. Geofencing: the geographical delimitation of a post. Geofencing avoids collecting posts published by X users outside the delimited geographical area.

3. Both Tweets and posts are treated as synonyms in this paper, and they refer to the same type of publication made available in X.

4. Stop words are a list of widely used words in any given language that don't provide enough lexical information for NLP purposes. Examples of stop words are 'a', 'are', 'which', 'in', 'at'.

5. A separate subset of the data is used to evaluate the model during the training phase while filtering the best performing model.

used to train the *voseo* classification model. The model was automatically stopped at 27 training epochs to avoid overfitting.

Once the best transformer-based text classification model was achieved the dataset was analyzed to explain the results of its application. The sociolinguistic analysis consisted of a lexical examination of tweets containing traces of *voseo* in Colombia and Argentina. This lexical profile allowed the extraction of the most frequent words and phrases associated with each dialect. Based on this first analysis, I conducted an examination of the status of *voseo* and other 2PS, along with the function and use of each 2PS in both datasets. Finally, a syntactical- grammatical analysis ensued.

In order to process all these data, I used several NLP components to obtain indices of lexical sophistication, syntactic complexity, and grammatical usage. For the lexical analysis, both dialectal datasets were normalized and filtered out of stop words. I used the NLTK module (Loper & Bird, 2002) to obtain the most frequent single lexical items (unigrams), and bigram and trigram sequences. For each list, the type-token ratio was measured and reported. Likewise, I contrasted the frequency of the unigrams in each *voseo* dataset with a reference corpus of Spanish movie subtitles (Cuetos et al., 2012), which contains the frequency per million of words of each token as representative of the Spanish language. It is assumed that the lower the frequency per million words, the more sophisticated or uncommon vocabulary used was.

Subsequently, I extracted indices of syntactic complexity at the sentence level. First, the Argentinian and Colombian datasets were parsed individually, which allows for tagging the part of speech of each word and dividing the syntactic units of each sentence in the datasets. I used the AnCora pretrained Spanish model (Recasens & Martí, 2010) from the Universal Dependency Project Treebank (Nivre et al., 2016) to train a Spanish parser on UDPipe, a tool that performs tokenization, PoS tagging, lemmatization, and dependency parsing on CoNLL-U format files (Straka & Straková, 2017). The CoNLL format contains parsed sentences or sentences divided syntactically according to binary arcs that represent dependencies of each token in a sentence in terms of a head and a dependent. The trained UDPipe Spanish model reached a high F1 score of 98.28% and was used to create a treebank of tagged and parsed sentences in CoNLL format from the *voseo* datasets. With the CoNLL-based tagged and parsed treebanks of Colombian and Argentinian *voseo*, I used a Python script to extract indices of syntactic complexity, such as the mean frequency of verbs, auxiliary verbs, conjunctions (coordination), relative and adverbial clauses, overall number of clauses, T-Units (i.e., sentences without sentential coordination), and words. All these measurements were obtained at the sentence level.

Finally, the same *voseo* treebank parsed with UDPipe was used to obtain the grammatical features of both *voseo* datasets. Again, a new Python script was used to automatically examine two types of measurements: the overall number of lexical items (e.g., verbs, nouns, adverbs, and verbs) and the tense, aspect, and mood of verbal structures. All these analyses will provide a comprehensive picture of the sociolinguistic differences (and similarities) in *voseo* usage in X in Argentina and Colombia captured by the machine learning model. Results are shown in the following section.

3. Results

The analysis of the data involved two steps. First, a transformer-based machine learning classifier was trained and evaluated on two *voseo* datasets of tweets from Colombian and Argentinian Spanish. Finally, I examined the sociolinguistic differences between both Spanish dialects that help in explaining the results of the machine learning model. This analysis involves the extraction of the lexical features of Colombian and Argentine *voseo* to measure indices of lexical, syntactical, and grammatical complexity of each post. Moreover, it will show the status of *voseo* along with the speech act functions of all 2PS in both settings. Here, I show the results of both analyses.

3.1 Machine learning model

Results show the best model reaching a 83.71 F1 score (the combined precision and recall scores) and 2.43 *textcat* loss or the loss of accuracy of the model. Subsequently, the model was evaluated obtaining a macro F score (e.g., the mean F1 score per label) of 81.88. Precision and recall metrics for the Colombia and Argentina labels are similar, which suggests that the model is able to correctly identify most relevant classes in both datasets. In the precision metric, the ML algorithm is evaluated according to the proportion of correct positive identifications over true and false positives. In this case, the precision score hovers in the first 80% of accurate positive identifications, which means that the model makes correct predictions over 80% of the time. For recall, the proportion of how good the model was in identifying actual positives over true positives and false negatives is measured. Recall metrics for both measurements are similar for both dialects. The overall model performance is measured by the F-score, which includes both precision and recall metrics. The combined F1-score also shows that the model can capture the differences between *voseo* dialects with a high accuracy level. The ROC (Receiver Operating Characteristic) also demonstrates the performance of the classification in the AUC or Area Under the Curve. This measurement shows that the model is able to establish correct predictions 88% of the time for both datasets in different classification thresholds. This model is publicly available for deployment in the HuggingFace repository (https://huggingface.co/FalconRR/es_pipeline) of the author. Table 1 shows the results of the evaluation of the classification model per label.

Table 1. Summary table of F score and area under the ROC curve (ROC AUC) of the classification model

Textcat	F Score (per label)			ROC AUC
	Precision	Recall	F Score	
Col	82.35	83.28	82.81	0.88
Arg	81.46	80.45	80.95	0.88

Now, as a highly accurate machine learning model has been produced, it is important to examine the sociolinguistic differences and similarities between X datasets that will help explain the results of the classification model. The following subsection of the results aims to delve into the sociolinguistic features of *voseo* in Argentina and Colombia.

3.2 Sociolinguistic analysis: Status of 2PS

In order to establish the status of *voseo* compared to other 2PS, I measured the occurrence of *tuteo* and *ustedeo* in both datasets. In this analysis, I measure the density of *tuteo* and *ustedeo* forms in X posts with *voseo* content. Traces of 2PS forms other than *voseo* were obtained according to the explicit use of pronominal forms (i.e., tú/ti, usted) and conjugation of highly frequent verbs with morphological differences, namely *ser* 'to be' (eres/es), *tener* 'to have' (tienes/tiene), *sentir* 'to feel' (sientes/siente), *pedir* 'to ask for' (pides/pide), *decir* 'to say' (dices/dice), *venir* 'to come' (vienes/viene), *oir* 'to hear' (oyes/oye), *querer* 'to want' (queres/quieres), and *seguir* 'to follow' (sigues/sigue). This analysis will display the status of the other 2PS in the context of *voseo*. Table 2 shows the number and relative frequency of *tuteo* and *ustedeo* in the datasets.

Results in Table 2 indicate that *tuteo* and *ustedeo* appear more often around *voseo* contexts in the Colombian dataset compared to Argentinian Spanish. Moreover, *tuteo* and *ustedeo* are highly marginal around *voseo* with only 16 counts in the entire Argentina dataset ($N=8,334$). Instances of other 2PS forms in the same discourse of *voseo* are known as cases of polymorphism, a phenomenon methodically studied recently (Denbaum-Restrepo, 2023). These results show that *tuteo*

Table 2. Count and relative frequency of *tú* and *usted* instances in Argentina and Colombia

	Tú (Relative frequency)	*Usted* (Relative frequency)
Col	279 (0.027)	226 (0.022)
Arg	10 (0.001)	6 (0.0007)

and *ustedeo* are basically non-existent in the Argentinian dataset, while posts in Colombia used these forms in the context of *voseo* to a comparatively greater extent. Now, we turn to the lexical features of both datasets.

3.3 Sociolinguistic analysis: Lexical features

Table 3 shows the most frequent lexicon and phrases associated with *voseo* in Colombian Spanish. For this analysis, frequent unigrams, bigrams, and trigrams were measured along with their corresponding type-token ratio (TTR).

Table 3. (Left) Five most frequent unigrams, (center) 5 most frequent bigrams, and (right) most frequent trigrams in the Colombian dataset, including computed TTR for each lexicon list

Token	Freq.	Rel. freq.	Bigram	Freq.	Rel. freq.	Trigram	Freq.	Rel. freq.
vos	7441	0.074	vos sos	803	0.0080	vos si sos	50	0.00071
sos	2944	0.029	sos vos	297	0.0029	jua jua jua	35	0.00050
si	1528	0.015	vos si	234	0.0023	si vos sos	28	0.00040
tenes/tenés	1381	0.013	si vos	200	0.0020	tenes toda razón	17	0.0002
q	622	0.006	si sos	152	0.0015	vos sos mas	15	0.00021
TTR		18348/99452=0.18	TTR		77381/99451=0.77	TTR		64540/69772=0.92

The frequency profile displayed in Table 3 shows that the pronominal form *vos* is the most common across word lists. This is expected as *vos* was used as the default query search. *Vos* was used most combined with *ser* 'to be' and its verbal conjugation (e.g., *vos sos* 'you are', *sos vos* 'are you', *si vos sos* 'if you are', *vos sos más* 'you are more'). In addition, the conjunction *si* 'if' appears highly correlated with *vos*. In most cases, this phrasal combination was used to show contempt and to insult someone, rather than to explain a conditional situation (e.g., [pero] *si vos sos [una rata acomoda...]* '[but] if you are a mouching rat with a paycheck...'). The next most common verbal conjugation in this dataset is the verb *tener* 'to have'. This verb is employed in fixed phrases as in *tenés toda [la] razón* '[you] are completely right'. In terms of the type-token ratio or TTR, results show repeated usage of single-lexical items (i.e., 0.18), but also some bigrams seem to have become lexicalized. The larger score in TTR suggests that there are higher number of sequences of words used in chunks in this dialect (0.77), particularly in phrases that combine *si* and *sos*. Also, some three-word phrases tend to appear highly frequent, but not to the same frequency as in bigrams.

Finally, the analysis of lexical sophistication shows a mean frequency of 30.87 per million words as compared to the reference corpus of Spanish subtitles. In other words, speakers of this variety employ words that would appear on average 31 times per every million words in the Spanish language.

Next, the lexicon from tweets produced by speakers of Buenos Aires and surrounding municipalities was examined. Results of the analysis are shown in Table 4.

Table 4. (Left) Five most frequent unigrams, (center) 5 most frequent bigrams, and (right) most frequent trigrams in the Argentinian dataset, including computed TTR for each lexicon list

Token	Freq.	Rel. freq.	Bigram	Freq.	Rel. freq.	Trigram	Freq.	Rel. freq.
vos	8674	0.107	vos sos	634	0.0078	vos sos pelotudo	24	0.00029
sos	1386	0.017	sos vos	290	0.0035	vos sos parte	24	0.00029
si	1236	0.015	si vos	252	0.0031	si vos sos	20	0.00024
q	1105	0.013	vos si	158	0.0019	vos vas a correr	17	0.00021
vas	355	0.004	vos sabes	114	0.0014	gracias igualmente vos	14	0.00017
TTR	16068/80897=0.2		TTR	63594/80896=0.78		TTR	77626/80667=0.96	

Similar to the Colombian dataset, *vos* was the most frequent word, along with its verbal conjugation *sos* 'to be'. In addition, conditional marker *si* 'if', the abbreviation of relative pronoun/question word *q(ue)* 'that/what', and the second-person singular form *vas* '(you) go' made the topmost frequent lexicon. Again, bigrams and trigrams are composed of several *si-vos-sos* sequences, which are used for derogatory language, as in *si vos sos un pelotudo* '[...]if you are dumbass' or in emphatic *sí* 'yes' as in *vos sí que sos vivo* 'you are really a smart Alec'. The inclusion of verbs such as *saber* 'to know' and *correr* 'to run' are used in fixed offensive expressions, such as *vos vas a correr en culo* 'you will be running naked'. It is worth noting that some of the most common bigrams and trigrams consisted of *vos vos* sequences, which were omitted for this analysis. This was due to the repeated use of *vos* at the end of a Tweet and at the beginning of a new one in the new cells of the Excel dataset. According to Leech (1999), a vocative in initial position is used for grabbing the attention of the interlocutor (e.g., *vos sos la alegría de mi corazón* 'you are the happiness of my heart'), while in final sentential position, vocatives maintain and reinforce the social relationships. This final function is seen in the pronominal form of *vos* in both datasets (e.g., *confía en vos* 'trust in yourself'). Although *vos* might not be considered a vocative in this dataset, it is used as a dialectal marker to appeal to the local identity of the interlocutors (Restrepo-Ramos, 2021).

Likewise, an examination of lexical sophistication was performed in this dataset. Results show a mean frequency of 35.17 per every million of words, a very little difference compared to the Colombian dataset.

3.4 Sociolinguistic analysis: Emotions and (Im)polite speech acts

Given the suggestive nature of the language found in the analysis of lexical features in both datasets, this subsection of the results focuses on the examination of the register and speech acts associated with each post. Based on Table 2, a proportionally balanced sample of each 2PS form ($n=1010$) were obtained from the Colombian dataset and coded according to whether an emoticon was present, and the impolite speech act expressed in the text. Figure 1 shows the relative frequency of impolite speech acts and register according to the use of an emoticon in Colombian posts.

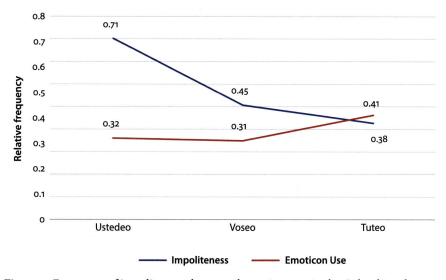

Figure 1. Frequency of impolite speech acts and emoticon use in the Colombian dataset

As displayed in Figure 1, there is a higher frequency of impolite speech acts with *usted* forms, while *voseo* and *tuteo* are used in similar proportions to express impoliteness. Overall, X users prefer *ustedeo* to express criticism, negative remarks, and rude language. In contrast, the presence of an emoticon in the post was found to be highly associated with *tuteo*, along with the lowest frequency of impolite speech. In sum, the more informal register expressed with an emoticon, the more polite the post tends to be and uttered using *tuteo*. The intermediate status of *voseo* also reveals that this form is used with a different function than *tuteo* in Colombian Spanish. Precisely, Tables 5 shows the phrases and emoticons frequently used with each 2PS in impolite posts.

Table 5. Most frequent bigrams, trigrams, and emoticons used in impolite contexts of *tuteo* in the Colombian dataset

Bigrams	Freq.	Trigram	Freq.	Emoticons	Freq.
jajaja jajaja	8	jajaja jajaja jajaja	6	💩	21
solo gusta	6	vos sos completo	4	💩	4
vives pendiente	4	quinterocalle jajajajajajaja ahora	3	😅	4
vos sos	4	teatrero payaso supera	3	🤡	3
sos completo	4	tan poca cosa	3	🙋	3
quiere decir	4	solo gusta llamar	3	💛	2
si sos	3	atención sos teatrero	3	🙈	2
gustavo petro	3	jajjaja si ves	3	🙀	1
sos vos	3	gusta ofender personas	3	🙊	1
vos partido	3	dices uribestia uribista	3	😡	1

Table 5 shows that impolite expressions with *tuteo* consist of phrases, language, and emoticons that denote mockery and criticism. In total, there were 1591 tokens analyzed in this subset. No foul words were used. Rather comparisons such as *uribestia* (i.e., a derogatory term denoting affiliation to a past president) or *teatrero* 'show maker' and criticism to the then mayor of Medellín, *quinterocalle*, make up for most of the function of impolite posts with *tuteo*. Here emoticons are composed of laughing faces, pile of poo, clown face, see-no-evil monkey, among others. Another case in point is the use of the pinching hand emoticon along with insulting expressions such as *tan poca cosa* 'such little thing' to minimize the comment made by another user. Now, let's turn to the results for impolite speech with *voseo* in Table 6.

Chapter 9. A deep learning based classification model of South American *voseo*　219

Table 6. Most frequent bigrams, trigrams, and emoticons used in impolite contexts of *voseo* in the Colombian dataset

Bigrams	Freq.	Trigram	Freq.	Emoticons	Freq.
vos sos	29	vos sos hpta	4	🤣	36
bobo hpta	8	bobo hpta vos	4	🤡	17
sos vos	6	vos sos tremendo	3	🤬	10
igual vos	6	vos sos tan	3	🥇	8
hijo puta	5	gente estúpida vos	3	😭	8
vos crees	5	sapo hpta revés	2	😏	4
hijueputa vos	5	hpta revés sos	2	💩	4
sos hpta	4	imbécil todavía falta	2	❤️	2
si vos	4	falta respeto ve	2	🟡	2
hijueputa malparido	4	manera expresarse sabe	2	👨	2

Here, we can notice that the language has a dramatic insulting tone. X users expressed verbal abuse using insulting words and abbreviations such as *hijueputa/hpta* 'motherfucker/mofo' along with *bobo* 'stupid' or *sapo* 'snitch'. Emoticons are also consistent with this type of language with frequent symbols of contempt and rudeness, including 🤣, 🤡, and 🤬. In total, there were 2626 tokens analyzed in this subset. Finally, the *ustedeo* data is displayed in Table 7.

Table 7. Most frequent bigrams, trigrams, and emoticons used in impolite contexts of *ustedeo* in the Colombian dataset

Bigrams	Freq.	Trigram	Freq.	Emoticons	Freq.
si usted	9	quintero robaste votos	4	💩	8
vale verga	6	tengalo seguro si	4	🤡	5
sos mentiroso	4	nadie votado usted	4	🤣	5
quintero robaste	4	pobre bobo hijueputa	4	🖕	4
comer mierda	4	usted plomo sangre	2	🤮	4
miedo usted	4	muertes cínico hijueputa	2	🖕	2
vos mequetrefe	4	hijueputa palabras bien	2	🐑	2
pobre bobo	4	manteco morrongo hpta	2	😄	1
bobo hijueputa	4	exasesor tarado gordo	2	😠	1
da vergüenza	3	sueñe tarado mentecato	2		

Similarly to Table 6, Table 7 shows foul language with derogative words and expressions. Notable phrases include *vale verga* 'you are worth shit', *pobre bobo hijueputa* 'you poor stupid motherfucker', and *manteco morrongo hpta* 'you low-life lazy motherfucker'. Emoticons are equivalent in nature to the *voseo* traces, including 💩, 😹, 🤪, and 🐀. There were 3021 analyzed in this subset. In sum, there is an increasing frequency and level of impoliteness speech according to the type of 2PS form used in X posts. Namely, posts with traces of *tuteo* display milder language than *voseo* and *ustedeo*, accordingly.

In the Argentinian dataset, a subset of impolite posts was extracted comparable to the previous analysis of impolite speech done with Colombian Spanish. However, only posts with *voseo* were analyzed here due to the highly marginal status of *tuteo* and *ustedeo* in Argentina. From 860 posts (10,152 tokens) 43% (*n* = 371) contained impolite speech and 20% (*n* = 176) used emoticons. Table 8 shows the most frequent expressions and emoticons found in the context of impolite speech.

Table 8. Most frequent bigrams, trigrams, and emoticons used in impolite contexts of *voseo* in the Argentinian dataset

Bigrams	Freq.	Trigram	Freq.	Emoticons	Freq.
vas a correr	18	vos vas a correr	15	😂	30
correr culo	7	vas a correr culo	4	😹	9
mil puta	5	hijo puta vos	3	😭	9
hijo puta	7	gobierno kiciidiota berni	3	💩	9
pelotuda mierda	4	vos tenés idea	3	😈	8
das asco	3	vos sos cagon	2	❤️	7
rata sos	3	q boluda vos	2	🐒	7
pelotudo sos	3	vos feo mierda	2	😍	7
cerra culo	3	sos oportunista orto	2	🤪	6
sos sorete	3	hijo mil puta	2	💧	4

Table 8 displays colloquial expressions of improper language, such as *vas a correr [en] culo* 'you will be running naked', *pelotudo/a [de] mierda* 'fucking asshole', *sos [un] oportunista [del] orto* 'you are a fucking opportunistic', and *vos sos cagón* 'you are a pussy'. Similar to the Colombian dataset, the most frequent emoticon used with impolite speech is the 'face with tears of joy' emoticon in posts such as "[…] *vos desde que naciste porque sos un bobo* 😂" '[…] since you were born because you are a dumbass 😂'. Insults in impolite speech work as a way to express mockery, name-calling, and plain offensive language between X users.

Frequently, the use of emoticons add salt to the injury to either make fun of other users or to describe them visually (e.g., 🙊, 💩, 🐄).

3.5 Syntactic and grammatical features

The analysis of syntactic features was also conducted for both main datasets. Table 9 shows the mean frequency of the syntactic predictors for Colombian and Argentinian Tweets, namely verbs, words, auxiliary verbs, different types of clauses, T-units, and coordinating conjunctions. All these features were measured at the sentence level.

Table 9. Syntactic predictors at the sentence level for the Colombian (left) and Argentinian (right) dataset

Colombia		Argentina	
Measure	Mean frequency	Measure	Mean frequency
Words	17.5	Words	20.4
Overall Clauses	2.93	Overall Clauses	3.35
Verbs	2.25	Verbs	2.76
T-Units	1.98	T-Units	2.21
Coordination	0.77	Coordination	0.88
Auxiliary Verbs	0.61	Adverbial Clauses	0.71
Adverbial Clauses	0.58	Auxiliary Verbs	0.68
Relative Clauses	0.38	Relative Clauses	0.43

Table 9 shows the measures of syntactic complexity in the tweets from Colombia and Argentina. Overall, Argentinian tweets tend to be longer in terms of average number of words and T-Units per sentence. Moreover, there are more verbal constructions and embeddedness in the same dataset. This is seen in the mean frequency of verbs and clauses. An inspection of both datasets show that Argentinian tweets include content about the local soccer league, while Colombian Tweeter users tend to discuss the political situation of the country, as general presidential elections were held in June 2022. The syntactical properties of both datasets help in explaining the results of the machine learning classifier.

With regards to the analysis of grammatical indices of complexity, Figure 2 shows a breakdown of different parts of speech used in both datasets. There were in total 214,844 words in the Colombian dataset and 170,396 words in the Argentinian dataset.

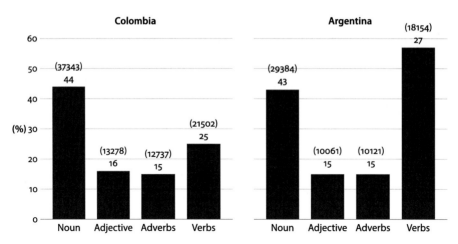

Figure 2. Breakdown of different parts of speech used in Colombia and Argentina

X users in both datasets tend to use similar proportions of nouns, verbs, adverbs, and adjectives. In terms of the tense, aspect, and mood of verbs in both sets of tweets, there are noticeable similarities.

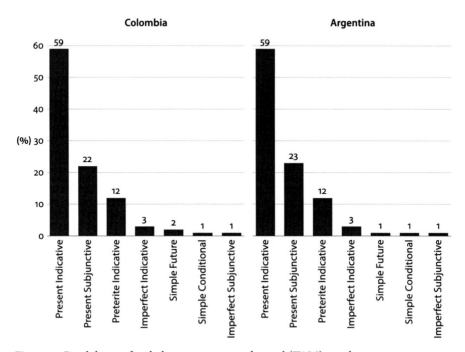

Figure 3. Breakdown of verbal tense, aspect, and mood (TAM) per dataset

Precisely, the proportions of TAM usage are almost identical, which suggests that Tweets with *voseo* content are expressed with consistent verbal conjugations despite geographical and dialectal distance. In sum, both varieties are very similar in their overall verb tense/aspect/mood distribution, which seems to be practically orthogonal to tense. The results on the syntactic and grammatical complexity show that many indicators have little effect on the features considered by the machine learning algorithm and the accuracy level reached by the classifier. Rather, results suggest that contextualized sociolinguistic information allowed the model to achieve a high degree of accuracy. I will discuss the sociolinguistic implications of these findings in light of these analyses in the following discussion and conclusion section.

4. Discussion and conclusion

In this paper, I have reported on the development and deployment of a machine learning classification model of South American *voseo* in X posts trained on a transformer-based fine-tuned model of Spanish BERT. Additionally, I conducted a sociolinguistic analysis of the two *voseo* datasets to offer insights into the language features of the regional *voseo* of *Paisa* and *Caleño* Spanish, and the national stable *voseo* spoken in the Rio de la Plata, Argentina. Results show the production of a highly accurate, domain-specific dialectal classification model that reached an ROC AOC of 0.88. This first finding responds directly to the first research question posed for this research.

Of special interest is the sociolinguistic analysis of both datasets. I first established the status of *voseo* in both settings. In Colombia, there were traces of *tuteo* and *ustedeo* in the domain of *voseo*, having its space in a small number of posts. The use of alternating 2PS forms to address the same interlocutor in the same speech segment is known as polymorphism, a phenomenon recently systematically addressed in the Hispanic Linguistics literature (Restrepo-Ramos & Denbaum-Restrepo, 2022). In contrast, no use of *tuteo* and *ustedeo* was documented in Argentina, except for 16 cases found in a dataset of 8,334 posts. García Negroni and Ramírez Gelbes (2020) stated that forms other than *voseo* were almost no-existent in Argentinian Spanish and this can also be seen here in this work.

In addition, a subsequent analysis demonstrated several lexical features of both Hispanic dialects. The conditional use of *vos* to express contempt was highly associated with Colombian Spanish, while Argentinian Spanish used *vos* with dialectal markers proper of this local variety, such as vocative or derogative *pelotudo* 'dumbass', also used to express contempt. The highly frequent use of *vos* sequences with conditional structures and dialectal markers suggest the incorporation of specific bigrams/trigrams as discursive features of both dialects to signify disagreement and contempt towards others (Schmid et al., 2021). For both varieties, *voseo* posts may express complaints, and derogatory and offensive language towards other specific X users. Likewise, the explicit pronoun displayed the highest proportion of usage. The measurements of lexical sophistication suggest similar values of lexical frequency in both dialects (e.g., 30.87 vs 35.17 lexical frequency per million of words for Colombian and Argentine Spanish, correspondingly).

The status of each 2PS in Colombia and the impolite nature of the overall results of lexical features in both settings warranted an analysis of speech acts and emoticons. It was found a hierarchy of impoliteness in Colombian Spanish, where *ustedeo* had the highest frequency of improper language (0.71) along with specific foul words and phrases. Then, *voseo* took an intermediate spot with 45% of posts with impolite speech, and *tuteo* had the lowest frequency (38%) along with the highest proportion of emoticons use. Following these estimates, I presented a lexical profile of each 2PS that included the most frequent phrases and emoticons. Crucially, *ustedeo* and *voseo* displayed insulting words and emoticons expressing mockery, name-calling, and rude language. In contrast, *tuteo* lacked frequent use of improper language. The case of Argentinian *voseo* used in impolite speech is similar to that of Colombia, except that the lexicon used is composed of colloquial expressions.

In terms of syntactic and grammatical features, there were more similarities and few differences. Posts from Argentina tend to be produced with higher degrees of syntactic complexity. For instance, posts were longer (e.g., mean words per sentence) and contained more embedded constructions (e.g., overall mean of clauses and T-Units per sentence) in *Porteño* Spanish, which shows that Argentine posts are more verbose. For grammatical features, both Hispanic varieties employ similar proportions of nouns, verbs, adverbs, and adjectives and tend to be consistent in the use of present indicative, which accounts for almost 60% of all conjugated verbal forms. This result resonates with previous findings on the River Plate basin (Bland & Morgan, 2020). Other verbal morphology was also used with steady rates in both dialects, which suggests that *voseo* uses consistent verbal constructions despite the geographical distance of both Hispanic dialects. The analysis of grammatical and syntactic features also proves the little effect these indices have on the identification of dialectal differences for these two Hispanic varieties. These findings provide a comprehensive answer to the second research question posed for this work.

Overall results indicate that certain sociolinguistic features are of great value to account for differences across both dialects which, in turn, influence the contextual weights employed by the transformer-based classification model. The sociolinguistic features found in this work include:

1. Alternating use and disparate proportions of other 2PS forms along with their corresponding verbal conjugations;
2. Impolite discourse containing colloquial markers proper of distinct Hispanic dialects; and,
3. Specific lexical-syntactic differences displayed in the production of *voseo* in both settings.

Of equal interest are the other syntactic and grammatical features not considered by the model because they also show the values of no significance for the identification algorithm. In conclusion, the lexical distribution in the sequence of tokens that allows the contextual information needed for the classifier to achieve the identification of dialectal Spanish varieties has the greater effect in the identification system. This is also reflected in the increasing length differences of *voseo* posts and embeddedness used in Argentinian Spanish compared to Colombian Spanish. The results presented here should be considered in future research dealing with sociolinguistic analysis of ML systems.

Confirming previous work in social media, X is a venue of *voseo* for locals of both Argentina and Colombia (Bani, 2023; Cautín-Epifani & Valenzuela, 2018; Bland & Morgan, 2020). Following an NLP methodology for sociolinguistics research (Bland & Morgan, 2020; Restrepo-Ramos, 2021; Roesslein, 2020; Schmid et al., 2021), I extracted X data, pre-processed, trained, and evaluated a ML via specific Python modules and pre-trained models. Particularly, this work was built on current models for language classification, including the LLM of Spanish BERT (Cañete et al., 2020; Devlin et al., 2018). Finally, I used a combination of frequency norms of Spanish (i.e., Subtlex-SP), publicly available modules (e.g., NLTK), treebanks (Recasens & Martí, 2010) and taggers and parsers (Nivre et al., 2016) in customized Python scripts to achieve the automatized analysis of linguistic features from Spanish datasets. Future work on Spanish dialectal research might use this NLP methodology to analyze further linguistic phenomena in large-scale datasets.

Such work would enhance sociolinguistic research by closing the gap between artificial intelligence and language use in an array of variable factors not achievable through previous means (i.e., the advent of large datasets of online language data, limited number of variables that can be analyzed in statistical models, synthetic language created through NLG models, etc.). Moreover, researchers behind NLP and pretrained machine learning models might also take into account the effect of sociolinguistic variables in text production, such as age, gender, education level, dialectal features, etc. The limitations of this study consist of the amount of data and *voseante* varieties analyzed. First, less than 20,000 tweets were obtained for this work. It is believed that the model could have been improved provided more data was included. Likewise, the model was fine-tuned using custom parameters from the prepared configuration file provided by the machine learning module employed (Honnibal et al., 2020). Further work should improve this model with custom parameters for these specific Spanish datasets. Finally, no other South American variety where *voseo* has certain status (e.g., Chile, Uruguay, Ecuador) was examined. By including more *voseo* dialects, this work might have encompassed a wide array of differences, and thus, developed a more robust model of dialectal classification. Such a model should be deployed in future work.

This study has used an innovative NLP approach to produce a model of dialectal variation of South American *voseo*, while digging deeper on the sociolinguistic features of Hispanic dialects in X posts. I hope that future work employs the NLP methods and artificial intelligence approaches proposed here and elsewhere to produce research in Spanish sociolinguistics that enhances our perspectives of language variation across *voseo* dialects.

References

Aaron, J., & Hernández, J. E. (2007). Quantitative evidence for contact-induced accommodation: Shifts n /s/ reduction patterns in Salvadoran Spanish in Houston. In K. Potowski and R. Cameron (Eds.), *Spanish in contact: Policy, social and linguistic inquiries* (pp. 329–343). John Benjamins.

Bani, S. (2023). Ideología (s) lingüística (s): el caso del voseo. *Artifara: Revista de lenguas y literaturas ibéricas y latinoamericanas*, 23(1), 35–51.

Bland, J., & Morgan, T. A. (2020). Geographic variation of voseo on Spanish twitter. In D. Pascual y Cabo & I. Elola (Eds.), *Current Theoretical and Applied Perspectives on Hispanic and Lusophone Linguistics* (pp. 7–38). John Benjamins.

Cañete, J., Chaperon, G., Fuentes, R., Ho, J. H., Kang, H., & Pérez, J. (2020). Spanish pre-trained bert model and evaluation data. *Pml4dc at iclr, 2020*.

Carricaburo, N. (1997). *Las fórmulas de tratamiento en el español actual* (Vol. 48). Arco Libros.

Cautín-Epifani, V., & Valenzuela, M. R. (2018). Variación sociolingüística del voseo verbal chileno en interacciones escritas en la Biografía Facebook. *Onomázein*, 4, 49–69.

Cuetos, F., Glez-Nosti, M., Barbón, A., & Brysbaert, M. (2012). SUBTLEX-ESP: Spanish word frequencies based on film subtitles. *Psicológica*, 33(2), 133–143.

Dant, P. F., Foulds, J. R., & Pan, S. (2022). Polling Latent Opinions: A Method for Computational Sociolinguistics Using Transformer Language Models. *arXiv preprint arXiv:2204.07483*.

Denbaum-Restrepo, N. (2021). Polymorphism of Second Person Singular Forms of Address in Medellin, Colombia: Usage and Language Attitudes [Doctoral dissertation]. Indiana University.

Denbaum-Restrepo, N. (2023). Polymorphism of second person singular forms of address in the Spanish of Medellin, Colombia. *Journal of Pragmatics*, 203, 82–95.

Devlin, J., Chang, M., Lee, K., & Toutanova, K. (2018). BERT: Pre-training of Deep Bidirectional Transformers for Language Understanding. *ArXiv*. /abs/1810.04805

Díaz Collazos, A.M. (2015). *Desarrollo sociolingüístico del voseo en la región andina de Colombia (1555–1976) (Vol. 392)*. Walter de Gruyter GmbH & Co KG.

Española, R.A. (2005). Diccionario panhispánico de dudas [Online]. Retrieved on 5/28/2023. Available on the Web: https://www.rae.es/dpd/voseo#2122b

Flores-Ferrán, N. (2007). A bend in the road: Subject personal pronoun expression in Spanish after 30 years of sociolinguistic research. *Language and Linguistics Compass*, 1(6), 624–652.

Fontanella de Weinberg, M.B. (1979). La oposición «cantes/cantés» en el español de Buenos Aires. *Thesavrvs*, 34(1, 2, & 3), 72–83.

Fontanella de Weinberg, M.B. (1970). La evolución de los pronombres de tratamiento en el español bonaerense. *Thesaurus: Boletín del Instituto Caro y Cuervo*, 25(1), 12–23.

García Negroni, M., & Ramírez Gelbes, S. (2020). Prescriptive and descriptive norms in second person singular forms of address in Argentinean Spanish. *Address in Portuguese and Spanish*, 361.

Hernández, J. (2002). Accommodation in a dialect contact situation. Revista de *Filología y Lingüística de la Universidad de Costa Rica*, 28(2), 93–110.

Honnibal, M., Montani, I., Van Landeghem, S., & Boyd, A. (2020). spaCy: Industrial-strength natural language processing in python.

Hovy, D., & Søgaard, A. (2015, July). Tagging performance correlates with author age. In *Proceedings of the 53rd annual meeting of the Association for Computational Linguistics and the 7th international joint conference on natural language processing (volume 2: Short papers)* (pp. 483–488).

Hovy, D., & Johannsen, A. (2016, May). Exploring language variation across Europe-a web-based tool for computational sociolinguistics. In *Proceedings of the tenth international conference on language resources and evaluation (LREC'16)* (pp. 2986–2989).

Jang, J.S. (2013). Voseo medellinense como expresión de identidad paisa. *Íkala, revista de lenguaje y cultura*, 18(1), 61–81.

Johnson, M. (2016). Epistemicity in voseo and tuteo negative commands in Argentinian Spanish. *Journal of Pragmatics*, 97, 37–54.

Leech, G. (1999). The distribution and function of vocatives in American and British English conversation. *Language and Computers*, 26, 107–120.

Lipski, J.M. (1994). *Latin American Spanish*. Addison-Wesley.

Loper, E., & Bird, S. (2002). Nltk: The natural language toolkit. *arXiv preprint cs/0205028*.

Martínez Barahona, S.Y. (2020). The Usage of Voseo in Social Media: Hondurans and Salvadorans in the United States. *The Macksey Journal*, 1(1), 22.

Michnowicz, J., & Quintana Sarria, V. (2020). A new look at forms of address in the Spanish of Cali, Colombia. *Hispanic Studies Review*, 4(2), 121–139.

Millán, M. (2014). "Vos sos paisa": A study of address forms in Medellín, Colombia. In R. Orozco (Ed.), *New Directions in Hispanic Linguistics* (pp. 92–111). Cambridge Scholars Publishing.

Moyna, M.I., & Rivera-Mills, S. (Eds.). (2016). *Forms of address in the Spanish of the Americas* (Vol. 10). John Benjamins Publishing Company.

Nguyen, D., Doğruöz, A. S., Rosé, C. P., & De Jong, F. (2016). Computational sociolinguistics: A survey. *Computational linguistics*, *42*(3), 537–593.

Nivre, J., De Marneffe, M. C., Ginter, F., Goldberg, Y., Hajic, J., Manning, C. D., ... & Zeman, D. (2016, May). Universal dependencies v1: A multilingual treebank collection. In *Proceedings of the Tenth International Conference on Language Resources and Evaluation (LREC'16)* (pp. 1659–1666).

Pešková, A. (2011). La omisión y la expresión del pronombre sujeto vos en el español porteño. In Á. Di Tulio & R. Kailuweit (Eds.), *El español rioplatense* (pp. 49–76). Iberoamericana Vervuert.

Radford, A., Narasimhan, K., Salimans, T., & Sutskever, I. (2018). Improving language understanding with unsupervised learning. *Open AI*.

Rasmy, L., Xiang, Y., Xie, Z., Tao, C., & Zhi, D. (2021). Med-BERT: pretrained contextualized embeddings on large-scale structured electronic health records for disease prediction. *NPJ digital medicine*, *4*(1), 86.

Recasens, M., & Martí, M. A. (2010). AnCora-CO: Coreferentially annotated corpora for Spanish and Catalan. *Language resources and evaluation*, *44*, 315–345.

Restrepo-Ramos, F., & Denbaum-Restrepo, N. (2022). The Syntactic and Discourse Properties of Second Person Singular Forms of Address in Paisa Spanish. *Studies in Hispanic and Lusophone Linguistics*, *15*(2), 453–482.

Restrepo-Ramos, F. (2021). A changing landscape of voseo in Medellín? In. P. Gubitosi & M. F. Ramos Pellicia (Eds.), *Linguistic landscape in the Spanish-speaking world* (pp. 45–72). John Benjamins.

Restrepo-Ramos, F. (2022). Contrastive language policies: A comparison of two multilingual linguistic landscapes where Spanish coexists with regional minority languages. *International Journal of Multilingualism*, *21*(2), 906–931.

Roesslein, J. (2020). Tweepy: X for Python! URL: https://Github.Com/Tweepy/Tweepy

Schmid, H. J., Würschinger, Q., Fischer, S., & Küchenhoff, H. (2021). That's cool. Computational sociolinguistic methods for investigating individual lexico-grammatical variation. *Frontiers in Artificial Intelligence*, *3*, 547531.

Sinner, C. (2010). «¿Cómo te hablé, de vos o de tú?». Uso y acomodación de las formas de tratamiento por emigrantes y turistas argentinos en España y Alemania. In M. Hummel et al. (Eds.), *Formas y fórmulas de tratamiento en el mundo hispánico*, (pp. 829–856). El Colegio de México.

Sorenson, T. (2016). ¿De dónde sos? Differences between Argentine and Salvadoran *voseo* to *tuteo* accommodation in the United States. In M. I. Moyna & S. Rivera-Mills (Eds.), *Forms of address in the Spanish of the Americas*, (pp. 171–196). John Benjamins.

Stoop, W., & van den Bosch, A. (2014, April). Using idiolects and sociolects to improve word prediction. In *Proceedings of the 14th Conference of the European Chapter of the Association for Computational Linguistics* (pp. 318–327).

Straka, M., & Straková, J. (2017, August). Tokenizing, pos tagging, lemmatizing and parsing ud 2.0 with udpipe. In *Proceedings of the CoNLL 2017 shared task: Multilingual parsing from raw text to universal dependencies* (pp. 88–99).

Sun, H., Wang, R., Chen, K., Utiyama, M., Sumita, E., & Zhao, T. (2019, July). Unsupervised bilingual word embedding agreement for unsupervised neural machine translation. In *Proceedings of the 57th Annual Meeting of the Association for Computational Linguistics* (pp. 1235–1245).

Volkova, S., & Bachrach, Y. (2016, August). Inferring perceived demographics from user emotional tone and user-environment emotional contrast. In *Proceedings of the 54th Annual Meeting of the Association for Computational Linguistics (Volume 1: Long Papers)* (pp. 1567–1578).

Weyers, J. (2016). Medellín cuenta con vos: The changing role of voseo in written communication. *Comunicación, 35*, 67–81.

Weyers, J. (2018). Beer, Hot Dogs and Politics: The Vocative Function of Medellín's voseo. *Bulletin of Hispanic Studies, 95*(5), 475–490.

Postface

Chad Howe
University of Georgia, Athens

Since its inaugural offering in 2002 at the University at Albany, the International Workshop on Spanish Sociolinguistics (WSS) has featured cutting-edge research focused on explaining the varied and complex relationships between language use and social structure. The work of that year's plenary speaker, Dr. Clancy Clements, embodied what was then an atmosphere of methodological exploration and theoretical agnosticism that allowed and in fact encouraged linguists from across the analytical spectrum to ask new questions and to bring new solutions to old questions in language variation and change (LVC). As Sayahi explains in the preface for the current volume, all of this took place in a single-session event in Albany, NY preceding, by almost three years, the paper delivered by Dr. Penelope Eckert at the 2005 Annual Meeting of the Linguistic Society of America that proposed the now widely cited 'wave' model of analytic practice in sociolinguistics (revisited in Eckert, 2012). Eckert notes that these waves "are not strictly ordered historically, and no wave supersedes the previous, rather all three waves are part of a whole" (2005, p. 1), with the third wave being described as "in its infancy" (2012, p. 88). The research constituting this current collection of works presented as part of the 10th iteration of WSS both continues and expands this endeavor as established in 2002 and later defined more broadly by Eckert. As a representation of the 20 years intervening between the First International Workshop on Spanish Sociolinguistics and the 10th, this collection, *Spanish Sociolinguistics in the 21st Century: Current trends and methodologies*, reveals the threads of analytical practice, both in terms of the methods employed and the questions interrogated, that reflect Eckert's wave model and, in tandem, celebrate the many contributions that linguists studying Spanish have made focused on socially linked linguistic variation.

Among the lines of inquiry threaded throughout these chapters are new applications of traditional methods and the continued exploration of topics that, over the last 30 years, have come to serve as 'marquee' variables in the study of Spanish. Perhaps most notably is the study of subject pronoun usage (i.e. SPE variation), a topic whose quantitative analysis was popularized in Cameron (1992, et seq.) and extended in numerous other papers, including the contribution by Franco in this volume who takes a "unified or shared syntax" approach to "pronombrista

https://doi.org/10.1075/ihll.42.10how
© 2025 John Benjamins Publishing Company

studies". Similarly, other well-trodden topics in Spanish linguistics are represented in this collection, including the variable placement of clitics (Viner) and variable mood (Calafate). These papers continue to push the envelope, as it were, by resituating classic issues regarding structural variation across Spanish varieties within modern frameworks and methods. Within this subsample, we can further point to the widespread use of corpus data both as a means of testing previously proposed hypotheses and of offering modern, open science approaches that respond to the challenges faced in linguistics concerning replication of results (Grieve, 2021). This effort is most fully realized in the contribution by Rivas and Brown who, in their exploration of the periphrastic future form *ir a* + INF using an oral corpus of Spanish, argue successfully that the 'meaning-follows-form' argument of grammaticalization should, at the very least, be considered with a more nuanced view. Taken together, these papers illustrate the thread initiated in the Labovian 'first-wave' studies described by Eckert, using quantitative methods to reveal patterns of association between linguistic variables and 'primary' social categories (e.g., social class) and with hints of what would later become the more ethnographic approach characteristic of 'second-wave' sociolinguistic studies.

Where studies in Spanish have accelerated, and indeed out paced, the broader efforts to understand socially situated linguistic variation is in the study of bilingualism and language contact. Further promoting this effort, one that spans first-, second-, and third-wave studies, are the various contributions in this volume that consider Spanish in multilingual contexts and the numerous linguistic (and extralinguistic) outcomes that are observed. Visconte offers an in-depth analysis of code-switching practices among speakers from Puerto Rico, noting the spread of English into the rural community of Loíza. Similarly, Varra's discussion of pauses, fillers, and false starts among Spanish-English bilinguals in New York City demonstrates yet another layer of the complexities that underlie this particularly widespread case of linguistic contact, though providing a novel view through the lens of this particular discourse phenomenon. Bilingualism is also at the center of Sayahi and Bonilla-Conejo's explanation of the variation between [s] and [θ] in the speech of Spanish-Tamazight monolinguals and bilinguals in Melilla, a situation that compels the authors to reconsider the oft-misunderstood manifestation of *ceceo* in the light of more recent approaches that make use of modern quantitative methods (Regan, 2021). Again, these chapters highlight advancements in sociolinguistics that are realized primarily through the scrutiny of the language practices of Spanish bilinguals, further underscoring how closely articulated these studies are to the analytical trends proposed by Eckert.

The take-home lessons proffered in this collection also include new approaches that clearly represent either third-wave sociolinguistic perspectives or more recent methods that have become available only during the last 15 years.

Squarely in the former category, we find Cárcamo's study of language ideologies represented in Catalonia and Spain which explores the use of Catalan in legal contexts as "the language of expression and identity" in trial defenses. For the latter, Restrepo-Ramos revisits a familiar topic in Spanish sociolinguistics, use of the second-person pronoun *vos* (aka. *voseo*), bringing to bear the insights of 'computational sociolinguistics' as articulated by Nguyen et al. (2016). These analyses easily find their place in the present volume as reminders of how the study of variation in Spanish continues to be a driving force for studies in LVC more generally. And, lest an additional reminder be necessary, it is worthwhile to consider the work reviewed in Eckert as underlying the waves of analytical practice. Alongside the widely cited work of scholars such as Labov (1963, et seq.), Wolfram (1969), Rickford (1986), and Bucholtz (2010), among many others, Eckert carefully discusses the work of the late Dr. Jonathan Holmquist, whose 1985 study on phonetic variation among speakers in the Spanish Pyrenees and its relationship to economic and social issues should be considered part of the foundational literature for the ethnographically oriented second wave of sociolinguistic studies. As a reflection of his influence in the field, Holmquist, along with this University at Albany colleague Dr. Lotfi Sayahi, was instrumental in bringing WSS into existence, offering a forum for new generations of scholars to present their work — across all waves of analytical practice — and to participate in advancing and expanding the agenda of sociolinguistic inquiry. This volume showcases Spanish as a locus for innovation, reflecting and in fact pushing the field in new directions, including work on linguistic attitudes (Bugel & Montes-Alcalá, 2020), linguistic landscapes (Gubitosi & Ramos Pellicia, 2021), and more recent literature that explores community-oriented and pedagogical applications (Foulis, et al., 2024). It is in light of these various methodological and theoretical threads that readers should consider the works in this volume as a fully articulated and exemplary representation of the fact that studies of Spanish continue to shape our understanding of language as a social practice.

References

Bucholtz, M. (2010). *White Kids: Language and White Youth Identities*. Cambridge University Press.

Bugel, T., & Montes-Alcalá, C. (Eds.). (2020). *New Approaches to Language Attitudes in the Hispanic and Lusophone World*. John Benjamins.

Cameron, R. (1992). *Pronominal and null subject variation in Spanish: Constraints, dialects, and functional compensation*. Doctoral dissertation, University of Pennsylvania.

Eckert, P. (2005). Variation, convention, and social meaning. Paper presented at the Annual Meeting of the Linguistic Society of America. Oakland CA, vol. 7.

Eckert, P. (2012). Three Waves of Variation Study: The Emergence of Meaning in the Study of Sociolinguistic Variation. *Annual Review of Anthropology*, 41(1), 87–100.

Foulis, E., Alex, S., & Martínez, G. (2024). *Working en Comunidad: Service-Learning and Community Engagement with U.S. Latinas/os/es*. The University of Arizona Press.

Grieve, J. (2021). Observation, experimentation, and replication in linguistics. *Linguistics*, 59(5), 1343–1356.

Gubitosi, P., & Ramos Pellicia, M. F. (Eds.). (2021). *Linguistic Landscape in the Spanish-speaking World*. John Benjamins.

Holmquist, J. (1985). Social correlates of a linguistic variable: a study in a Spanish village. *Language in Society*, 14, 191–203.

Labov, W. (1963). The social motivation of a sound change. *Word*, 18, 1–42.

Nguyen, D., Doğruöz, A. S., Rosé, C. P., & De Jong, F. (2016). Computational sociolinguistics: A survey. *Computational linguistics*, 42(3), 537–593.

Regan, B. (2021). Analyzing Andalusian coronal fricative norms (*ceceo, seseo*, and *distinción*) using a sociophonetic Demerger Index. In Díaz-Campos, M. (Ed.), *The Routledge Handbook of Variationist Approaches to Spanish*, (pp. 137–158). Routledge.

Rickford, J. (1986). The need for new approaches to class analysis in sociolinguistics. *Language Communication*, 6, 215–21.

Wolfram, W. (1969). *A Sociolinguistic Description of Detroit Negro Speech*. Center Applied Linguistics.

Index

Please note that page numbers in italics indicate figures or tables.

A
Acosta-Santiago, J. M. 77–78
Adda-Decker, M. 41
adjective clauses 10
adverbial clauses 10, 212, *221*
affective states 34, 37–38, 51
alternancia (intra-speaker variation) 112, *113*, 115–116
Amazigh (Berber) peoples 111
    Amazigh languages 117
    Amazigh-origin speakers 115–116, 117, 120–121, *121*–126
Andalusia 112, 114
    Andalusian varieties 112, 115
Arabic language 117
Argentinian Spanish 15, 206, 214, 223, 225
    regional dialects 204–5
    voseo as norm 206
Arizona: Spanish speakers 9 *See also* bilingual (Spanish-English) speakers
artificial intelligence (AI) 204
Assemblea Nacional Catalana 167
authenticity
    vs. anonymity dichotomy 172, 173–174, 175
    ideology of 40, 173, 175, 180–181, 183, 184–185
    individual vs. community-based 190, 195–196
auxiliarization 142, *143*

B
Bakhtin, M. M. 170
Bani, S. 207
Barrera-Tobón, C. 153
Barron, A. 3, 73, 73N2
Basque language 118, 174
Bassa, Dolors 167–168

Bell, B. 80
BERT (Bidirectional Encoder Representations from Transformers) 204, 209, 211–212, 225
bilingual (Spanish-English) speakers, 22, 231 *See also* second language acquisition
    and code-switching 70–71, 72, 84, 85–86
    flagging 33–34, 38–41, 43–44, 58–59
    lexical routinization of subjunctive 9, 14–15, 16, 20, *21*, 28–29
    mood selection 8–9
    mood systems 29–30
    New Mexico 20
    and subject pronoun expression (SPE) 151, 153–154
    subjunctive use 26–27
Bland, J. 208
Blommaert, J. 170, 197
Boix-Fuster, E. 174, 197
Bonilla-Conejo, Marina 4, 231
Borràs, Meritxell 168, 185–186, 190, 194
Bosque, I. 10, 11, 12N2
Branchadell, A. 170, 171, 173, 195, 197
Braun, V. 176
Britain, D. 120
Brown, Esther L. 5, 231
Bucholtz, M. 232
Buenos Aires, Argentina 206
Bullock, B. E. 70
Bybee, J. 134

C
Calafate, Isabella 3, 231

Caleño Spanish 151, 203–4, 206
    See also voseo dialects
Callahan, L. 70
Cameron, R. 230
Caminal, M. 171, 195
Candea, M. 41
Cárcamo, Marina 5–6, 232
Castilian Spanish 115, 166
Catalan language 118
    as common language 195, 196
Catalan Statute of Autonomy 167
Catalonia 166–169 *See also El procés* trial
    nationalism and language 175
    normalització lingüística (linguistic normalization) 172
Causa especial 20907/2017 167
    See also El procés trial
ceceo 112, 114, 115
Centre d'Estudis d'Opinió 167
Chafe, W. 35, 41
change of order 35
ChatGPT 209
Chilean Spanish 208
Clark, H. H. 41
Clarke, V. 176
Claudio de Ramón, J. 197
Clements, J. C. x, 230
clitic placement, study of 4, 92–109
    background literature 93–94
    methodology of study 95–98
    national origin 95
    Otheguy-Zentella corpus 94
    overview 92–93
    research questions 93

results of study 98, 98–109, 99–107
Cloze task 209
code-switching See also Loíza, Puerto Rico, code-switching study
  vs. code-mixing 70
  Croatian-English speakers 36
  definitions 69–70
  emblematic switches 85
  intra-sentential vs. intersentential 84
  switch points 39
Colombia
  Cali (Valle del Cauca) 204
  Medellín (Antioquia) 204
  Medellín Spanish 151
  regional dialects 204
Colombian Spanish See also voseo dialects
  vs. Argentinian Spanish 225
  flagging 54
  forms of 203–4
  Philadelphia 150–163
  speaker birthplace, significance of 159, 162, 163
Comín, Toni 167
common language. See *llengua comuna* (common language)
como que (discourse marker) 82–83
complement clauses 10, 17
computational sociolinguistics 6, 208–210 See also voseo dialects
Condicional tense 161
CoNLL formats 212
Consortium for Linguistic Standardization/Normalization (Catalonia) 172
Corpus del Español en el Sur de Arizona (CESA) corpus 8–9, 16–17, 21, 22, 23–24, 24, 25, 27–28
Corpus para el estudio del español oral (ESLORA) 135, 138, 141
Corpus Sociolingüístico de la Ciudad de México (CSCM) corpus 13, 21, 22, 24, 26, 28
Costeño Spanish 162

COVID pandemic x, 161
Crible, L. 35
Croatian-English speakers 36
Cuixart, Jordi 168, 183, 187, 188, 191, 192, 194

D
Dalbor, J. 113
Dant, P. F. 209
Darwich, B. 93
Davies, M. 93, 104
Declerck, M. 153
Deschamps, A. 35
dialects
  and accommodation 152–153
  in Arizona 18, 19–20, 29
  classification models 6, 223–224, 225–226
  Colombian Spanish 151, 152–153, 162, 204–5, 206
  dialect zones in Spain 112
  and machine learning models 213–214
  monolingual vs. bilingual dialects 9
  and social media use 207
discourse markers (DMs) 3–4, 68
  definitions 72
  DMs that trigger code-switching 77–83
discourse particles 72
"disfluency," 33, 34, 43, 58–59 See also flagging
distinción 112–113, 114–115, 120–121 See also interdental fricatives
Duany, J. 72–73
durational shortening following grammaticalization 5, 132–133, 135–136, 139 See also phonological reduction patterns
Dutch language 133

E
Eckert, P. 172, 230, 231, 232
Ecuadorian speakers 54–56, 58
Edwards, M. 40

El catalá, llengua comuna (Plataforma per la Llengua 2008) 171, 187, 195
El procés trial 166–198
  Catalan language: themes and ideologies 179–188
  Catalonia, history and background 166–169
  language choice and usage in trial 191–193
  language ideologies 169–176
  methodology of study 176–179, *177*, *178*
  Spanish language: themes and ideologies 188–191
  trial, relevance and impact 193–198
embedded fluencemes 35
emotions and speech 217–221
  affective states 34, 37–38, 51
English language: phonological reduction 133
Equatorial Guinea 112
Erker, D. 19
European Charter for Regional or Minority Languages 118, 174
European Union 167

F
false starts 35, 39 See also flagging
Ferrara, K. 80
fillers 39 See also flagging
  filler vowels, pitch of 42
  as listener-oriented functions 41
  non-lexicalized 33, 36, 36N1, 37, 46
flagging behavior See also fillers
  bilingual speakers 34
  ethnonationality and flagging 53, 54, 55, 56
  and fluency 37–38
  literature on 37–44
  methodology and results of study 44–58
  in monolingual speech 43
  overview 33–34, 58–61
  and perceived authenticity 56

problematic impressions of 40–41
reaction times to stimuli 38
sociodemographic characteristics of sample 65–67
spontaneous speech/reading texts/translations 38
terminology used to discuss 35–37
words and flags used *51, 52*
fluencemes 35, 36N1
Fontanella de Weinberg, M. B. 206
Forcadell, Carme 167, 168, 183–184, 189–190, 191, 194, 195–196
Forn, Joaquim 167, 181–182, 190
foul language 220, 224
Fox Tree, J. E. 41
Franco, Camila 5, 230–231
French language
 mood selection 12–13
 Ottawa-Hull corpus 21
 subjunctive routinization 29
 subjunctive use 20, 24–25
Fruehwald, J. 42

G
Gal, S. 173, 175
Galicia, Spain
 ESLORA corpus 135, 138, 141
 Galician language 118, 174
García-Amaya, L. J. 114
García Negroni, M. 206, 223
Gardner-Chloros, P. 40, 42N4
Geeraerts, D. 171
Gellner, E. 169
Generalitat de Catalunya 171
generativist methodology 71
Goldman-Eisler, F. 38, 60
Gómez Torrego, G. 136
González-Bueno, M. 114
González Las, C. 115, 124
GPT (Generative Pre-Trained Transformer) models 209
grammaticalization processes 15, 131–133, 141 *See also* phonological reduction patterns

Granada, Spain 113, 114
Gudmestad, A. 93, 103
Guitart, Jorge x
Gutiérrez, M. 93, 98–99, 101, 104, 105–6
Gutiérrez-Rivas, C. 151
Guy, G. x, 19

H
hapax legomena 15, 19, 27–28, *28, 29*
Hartsuiker, R. J. 153
Hebrew language 133
Helasvuo, M. 153
heritage speakers 108, 133, 161
Hernández, J. E. 207
Hernández-Campoy, J. 115
hesitation
 and flagging 35, 40–41
 hesitation and monitoring phenomena (HMP) 36, 36N1
Hlavac, J. 36
Hoff, M. 15, 18–19, 28
Holmquist, Jonathan x, 232
Honduran speakers 207
Hovy, D. 210
Hurtado, L. M. 151–152, 158
hypernyms 36–37

I
identical repetitions 35
identity formation and language 55–56, 59, 77, 152, 169–171, 180, 190, 205
 language-nation-identity 194, 196 *See also* "own language"
Imperfecto tense 161
impolite speech *217*, 217–221, *218, 219, 220*
indicative use 8–9, 10, 11, 18, 19
Intercultural Pragmatics 74
interdental fricatives 111–128
 analysis 119–128, *120–127*
 gender-based differences 120–122, *123*
 methodology 118–119
 overview 111–116, *113*
 overview of Melilla, Spain *116*, 116–118
 research questions 119

International Workshops on Spanish Sociolinguistics (WSS) 1, 230
interpretation, simultaneous vs. consecutive 168 *See also El procés* trial
Irvine, J. 169

J
Jaworski, A. 41
Johannsen, A. 210
Junqueras, Oriol 167, 180–181, 182, 188–189, 190, 191, 195

K
Kasl, S. V. 38
Klee, Carol x

L
Labov, William x, 76–77, 120–121, 127–128, 232
LaCasse, D. 9, 14–15, 17, 18, 20, 21, 25–26, 27, 29–30
Lange, D. 80
language ideologies
 in Catalonia 170–172
 concept of 169
 and linguistic authority 173–176
 and nationalism 169–170
Language Variation and Change (LVC) framework 12, 16, 230
La Plata, Argentina 206
large language models (LLMs) 209, 210
Law of Linguistic Normalization (Catalonia) 172
legal contexts 5, 174, 183, 196, 232
 See also El procés trial
lexical insertion 35
lexical routinization 9, 12–16, 28–29 *See also* subjunctive use
 in Spanish
  pre-modern texts 13–14
  subjunctive use 9, 12–15
lexical sophistication 204, 212, 216, 217, 224
like (discourse marker) 80–81
Limerick, P. 99, 101, 104, 105, 107, 160
Lindqvist, H. 60N13

linguistic authority, ideologies of 169–176
linguistic normalization 186–187
Linguistic Society of America 230
Lipski, John x, 81–82
llengua comuna (common language) 171, 187–188, 195
    Spanish as 188–189
llengua pròpia (proper language/ one's own language) 170–171, 195
Loíza, Puerto Rico, code-switching study 68–86
    analysis 77–86
    background literature 71–73
    discourse markers (DMs) 78, 79, 80
    methodology 73–77, 74–75, 76
    overview 68–71
    research questions and objectives 70–71
López Fernández, S. 116
Lorenzino, Gerardo Augusto x
Lynch, A. 12

M
machine learning (ML) models/ classification 6, 204–5, 213–214, 221, 223, 225–226
Maclay, H. 38, 59
Mahl, G.F. 38
Málaga, Spain 114–115
Maragall, Joan 186
Marchena, Manuel 168
Martinez Barahona, S.Y. 207
matrix clauses 10
Matrix Language Frame theory 71
matrix verbs *14*
May, S. 170, 174, 197
Medellín, Colombia 206
Medellin Spanish 151
Meinecke, Friedrich 169
Melguizo Moreno, E. 114
Melilla, Spain 111
    map *116*
    sociolinguistic profile 116–118
Mexican Spanish 15

flagging 54–56, 58–59
Mexico City 30
Miller, C. 39
Miller, K. 93
minoritized languages
    Catalan as 194–195
    and linguistic authenticity 173
    vs. minority languages 170, 170N4, 183–186
minority languages
    authenticity/anonymity debate 173–174, 195
    Catalonia 170
    vs. minoritized languages 170, 170N4, 183–186
misarticulation 35
modified repetitions 35
monolingual Spanish 19–20
    subjunctive use 26, 29–30
Montero Alonso, M. 117–118
Montes-Alcalá, Cecilia x
mood selection
    for bilingual (Spanish-English) speakers 8, 9
    contact-induced hypothesis 14
    methodology and results 16–29
    mood alternation 10–11
    traditional perspectives 10–12
    variability 12
Morgan, T.A. 208
Morillo-Velarde, R. 114
Morocco 112, 117, 118
morphological substitution 35
mother tongue 179–180, 183, 190
    See also "own language"
Moya Corral, J. 114
Mundó, Carles 168
Muysken, P. 39–40, 70
Myhill, J. 104

N
nationalism
    Catalan 170–172, 196
    and linguistic ideology 169–170
natural language generative (NLG) systems 209

natural language processing (NLP) 204, 209, 225
New Mexico, Spanish speakers 9
New Mexico Spanish-English Bilingual (NMSEB) corpus 14, 21, 22, 24, 25–26
New York City, Spanish-English bilinguals
    clitic placement 92–109
    flagging behaviors 33–61
Nguyen, D. 232
nonce-borrowing 82
normalization 191
    normalització lingüística (linguistic normalization) 170, 172
North Atlantic Treaty Organization 167
nuyorriqueño (Puerto Rican dialect) 72–73

O
"Observer Paradox" (Labov) 77
Òmnium Cultural 167–168
Organization for Economic Cooperation and Development 167
O'Rourke, E. 154
Orozco, R. 151–152, 158, 159, 160
Ortega, R. 174, 197
Osgood, C.E. 38, 59
Otheguy, Ricardo x, 95, 101, 102–3, 152–153, 160
Otheguy-Zentella Corpus (OZC) 44, 94
"own language," 171, 175, 179–180
    See also mother tongue
    Spanish as 189–190

P
Pacte nacional per la immigració (Generalitat de Catalunya, 2008) 171
Paisa Spanish 151–152, 162, 203–4, 206 *See also voseo* dialects
parallel model hypothesis 153
parenthetical insertion 35
pauses 35, 39, 41–42 *See also* flagging
    pausology 35–36, 36N1
Peace, M.M. 93

pedagogical methodology 71
periphrastic future form 132–133, 134, 140, 141–142, 231
Pfaff, C. 39N3
Philadelphia, Pennsylvania
   Colombian communities 160–161
   Colombian Spanish 151–163
   demographics 150–151
Philippines 112
"phonemic slips," 113–114
phonological reduction patterns 131–143
   analysis 138–143, *139*, *140*
   data and methodology *134*, 135–138
   grammaticalization of TAM (tense/aspect/mood) markers 134
   overview 131–135
   post-context speaking rate 138
   preceding pause 137–138
   predictability 138, 140
Placencia, M. E. 74
plurilingualism in Spain 174, 175, 178, 187, 191, 192–193, 197
Pool, J. 170
Poplack, Shana x, 12–13, 17, 23, 39–40, 72, 85
Porteño Spanish 206
Posantí, Clara 167
Potowski, K. 154
Pousada, A. 69
pragmatic markers 72
pragmatic particles 72
"Principle of Tangential Shift" (Labov) 76–77
proclisis vs. enclisis 92–93, 96–98 See also clitic placement
   gendered differences 100N5
productivity measures of subjunctive use in Spanish 13–15, 18–19, 21–22, 25–26
pronombrista studies 151, 153, 158, 161, 162, 230–231
propositional substitution 35
psycholinguistic methodology 71
Puerto Rican speakers *See also* Loíza, Puerto Rico, code-switching study

   bilingualism and code-switching 69–70
   demographics in New York City 95–96
   flagging 54–55, 58–59
   identity formation of migrants 72–73
   nuyorriqueño 72–73
Puerto Rico: history 69, 74N3
Puig, Lluís 167
Puigdemont, Carles 167
Pujol, Jordi 170–171

Q
Quebec French 13

R
Rajoy, Mariano 167
Ramírez Gelbes, S. 206, 223
Raña-Riso, R. 153
rapid visual parallel presentation (RPVP) tests 154–155, 160
Raupauch, M. 59
reading recall tests 155–156, *156*, 158, 160, 163
reduction *See* phonological reduction patterns
Rees, E. L. 172
reformulations 35 *See also* flagging
Regan, B. 115
repairs 35 *See also* flagging
Repede, D. 43N6
Requena, P. E. 93
Requena Santos, F. 114–115
restarts 35 *See also* flagging
Restrepo-Ramos, Falcon 6, 232
Rickford, J. 232
Riera Gil, E. 171, 195
Rivas, Javier 5, 231
Romaine, S. 80
Romance languages *See also* French language
   mood selection 12–13
   subjunctive routinization 19–20
Romeva, Raül 167, 183, 186, 189, 190–191, 193, 195
Rosignoli, A. 42N4
Ruiz Domínguez, M. 115–116
Rull, Josep 167–68, 179–185, 187, 190–191, 194–195

S
Salvadorian speakers 207
Sànchez, Jordi 168, 181–182, 185, 190, 193, 194
Sankoff, D. 39
Sayahi, Lotfi 4, 230, 231, 232
Schieffelin, B. B. 170, 172
Schmid, H. J. 209
Schneider, K. P. 3, 73, 73N2
Schwenter, S. 15, 18–19, 28, 93
second language acquisition 85, 112 *See also* bilingual (Spanish-English) speakers
   flagging and fluency 38–40
second person singular (2PS) address 203–4, 214–215 *See also voseo* dialects
Seliger, H. W. 59
sentence superiority hypothesis 153
Serret, Meritxell 167
seseo 112–114, 115–116, 120–121
   See also interdental fricatives
Seville, Spain 113–114
Shin, N. L. 93, 94, 101, 105, 153
Silva-Corvalán, C. x, 12, 14, 17, 18, 30, 93, 98–99, 104
Sinner, C. 172
so (discourse marker) 81–82
social media use 207–8 *See also* X (formerly Twitter) posts
socioeconomic status (SES) 101, 102–3, 108
sociolinguistic index 34, 42–43, 58
Soler, J. 173
Sonntag, S. K. 170
Sosiński, M. 114
Southwest US Spanish *See* bilingual (Spanish-English) speakers
Spain *See also* Catalonia
   Andalusia 112, 113–114, 115
   dialect zones 112
   Galicia 135
   Málaga 114–115
   Melilla 111, *116*, 116–118
   plurilingualism 174, 175, 177–178, 187, 191, 192–193, 197
   Seville 113–114
Spanish language

Castilian Spanish 112, 115, 166N1
dialect zones 112
heritage speakers 108, 133, 161
and identity formation 69
interdental fricative, emergence of 112
monolingual Spanish 20, 26, 29–30
Paisa Spanish 151–152, 162, 203–4, 206
phonological reduction 133
syntax 10
unified syntax 151–154, 160, 230–231
variation in Spanish-speaking areas 2
Spanish Sociolinguistics International Workshops IX–XI, 1
scope of field 1–2
Staatsnation vs. Kulturnational 169
Statute of Autonomy of Catalonia 170–171, 172
Stenström, A.-B. 35, 41
structuralist methodology 71
subject pronoun expression (SPE) 150–163
analysis 160–163
cognitive predictors 160
gender and subject pronouns 159
linguistic predictors 158
methodology and results 154–160, *155*, *157–158*
overview 150–151
reading recall procedure 155–156, *156*, *158*, 160, 163
sociolinguistic predictors 159–160
SPE variation 5
and unified syntax 151–154
unified syntax and bilingual cognition 153–154
subjunctive use in Spanish 8–30
analysis of study 19–30, *20–28*
lexical routinization 9, 12–16, 28–29

methodology of study 16–19
mood selection 10–12
overview 8–9
subordinate clauses 10, 17
suprasegmental elements of speech 35–36
Süselbeck, K. 170–171, 172
syntactic complexity 204, 212, *221*, 224
synthetic future forms 132–133

T
Tagliamonte, Sali x
Tamazight speakers 116, 117–118
Tannen, D. 41
temporal variables of discourse 35, 36N1
tense/aspect/mood (TAM) markers 134, 204, 223
tenses
present progressive 132
simple present 132
thematic analysis 176–178, *177*, *178*
Toribio, Almeida Jacqueline x, 39, 70
Torres, L. 72
Torres Cacoullos, R. 13–14, 17, 27, 93, 104
transformer-based language models 211–212
translanguaging 70 *See also* code-switching
truncation 35, 135
Turull, Jordi 167–168, 168, 192
tú sabes (discourse marker) 83
Tweets *See voseo* dialects; X (formerly Twitter) posts

U
UDPipe 212, 213
unified syntax 151–154, 160, 162–163, 230–231
United Nations 167
United States *See also* New York City, Spanish-English bilinguals
Arizona, Spanish speakers 9
Philadelphia, Colombian Spanish 150–163

second language instruction in Spanish 112
Universal Dependency Project Treebank 212

V
Vallejos Jiménez, M. 116
Valluno Spanish 162
vamos a variants *See* phonological reduction patterns
Variational Pragmatics 68, 73–76, 73N2
variationist studies 9, 12, 93, 132, 141, 151
Varra, Rachel 3, 231
Vasilescu, I. 41
Via Catalana 166 *See also* Catalonia
Vila, Santi 167, 168
Vilarrubias, M. 197
Villena Ponsoda, J. 114–115
Viner, Kevin Martillo 4, 231
Visconte, Piero 3–4, 231
voseo dialects 203–226
analysis of *214–216*, 223–226
computational approaches 208–210
impolite speech acts *217*, 217–221, *218–220*
machine learning models 213–214
methodology of study 210–213
overview 203–7
social media 207–8
sociolinguistic analysis 214–223
vowels
filler vowels, pitch of 41–42
and preceding sounds 124

W
wave model 230
Westmoreland, Maurice J. x
Westwood, A. 39–40
Wheeler, S. 39–40
Wieland, K. 172
Winford, Donald x
Wolfram, Walt x, 232

Woolard, K. 169, 170, 172, 173, 175, 176, 181, 183, 196
word-borrowing 82
Workshops on Spanish Sociolinguistics (WSS) ix–xi, 1

X
X (formerly Twitter) posts 203–205, 207–8, 210–211, 214, 220, 223, 226 See also *voseo* dialects

Y
Yelp reviews 209

Z
Zentella, Ana Celia x, 95, 101, 102–3, 160